CARBON SOVEREIGNTY

ANDREW CURLEY

CARBON SOVEREIGNTY

Coal, Development, and Energy Transition in the Navajo Nation

THE UNIVERSITY OF ARIZONA PRESS
TUCSON

The University of Arizona Press
www.uapress.arizona.edu

We respectfully acknowledge the University of Arizona is on the land and territories of Indigenous peoples. Today, Arizona is home to twenty-two federally recognized tribes, with Tucson being home to the O'odham and the Yaqui. Committed to diversity and inclusion, the University strives to build sustainable relationships with sovereign Native Nations and Indigenous communities through education offerings, partnerships, and community service.

ISBN-13: 978-0-8165-4866-8 (hardcover)
ISBN-13: 978-0-8165-3960-4 (paperback)
ISBN-13: 978-0-8165-4867-5 (ebook)

Cover design by Leigh McDonald
Cover photo by Cassidy Araiza
Typeset by Leigh McDonald in Adobe Caslon Pro 10/14 and Good Headline Pro (display)

Publication of this book is made possible in part by the proceeds of a permanent endowment created with the assistance of a Challenge Grant from the National Endowment for the Humanities, a federal agency.

Library of Congress Cataloging-in-Publication Data
Names: Curley, Andrew, 1982– author.
Title: Carbon sovereignty : coal, development, and energy transition in the Navajo Nation / Andrew Curley.
Description: Tucson : The University of Arizona Press, 2023. | Includes bibliographical references and index.
Identifiers: LCCN 2022029643 (print) | LCCN 2022029644 (ebook) | ISBN 9780816548668 (hardcover) | ISBN 9780816539604 (paperback) | ISBN 9780816548675 (ebook)
Subjects: LCSH: Navajo Indians—Arizona—Government relations. | Coal mines and mining—Navajo Nation, Arizona, New Mexico & Utah. | Coal mines and mining—Arizona. | Navajo Indians—Arizona—Politics and government. | Energy transition—Navajo Nation, Arizona, New Mexico & Utah. | Energy transition—Arizona.
Classification: LCC E99.N3 C87 2023 (print) | LCC E99.N3 (ebook) | DDC 979.1004/9726—dc23/eng/20220727
LC record available at https://lccn.loc.gov/2022029643
LC ebook record available at https://lccn.loc.gov/2022029644

Printed in the United States of America
♾ This paper meets the requirements of ANSI/NISO Z39.48-1992 (Permanence of Paper).

CONTENTS

ILLUSTRATIONS

FIGURES

MAPS

TABLES

ACKNOWLEDGMENTS

EVERY BOOK ACKNOWLEDGMENT says something profound about the writing process. I don't have anything to say except I'm glad it's done. The work of this book was difficult and remains flawed in ways that are now hard to fix. However, I think I'm telling a story that is important and I want to get out there. So, thank you to everyone who has helped me do this!

This is not *the* truth on Diné experience with coal and development over the past half century but a perspective informed by systematic fieldwork. My greatest fear is the inevitable, that people will disagree with what I write here. Yet this is a healthy response from you, the reader, and I need to welcome and encourage it. Thank you, critics, now and in the future!

It's my name on the book, but a lot of people helped me think through the ideas discussed here. I will miss some important people. Sorry if I didn't include you; it was an oversight from fatigue. This is the last part of the book I'm doing.

First, I couldn't have done any of this without the graciousness and indulgence of the people who let me interview them. I really wish I could have represented your stories better. I thought more was possible during the process of research. I had grand ambitions of writing something definitive or clever, but it turns out the world is full of limitations—many of which I didn't anticipate nearly a decade ago when I did the research.

My fondest memories are waking up in Kayenta, running along the side of the road, or riding my bike on the nice federally funded road that takes you to

Navajo National Monument. It was luxury on the rez. The evening brought stray dogs and incredible sunsets. During the summer months, I experienced some brilliant thunderstorms. Living in that part of the reservation, all too briefly, gave me a greater appreciation for the stories people were telling me. Why it was important to be there. To save the land, culture, and prospects of our people.

I couldn't have found a place in Kayenta without the help of Amber Crotty and Nathaniel Brown, now honorable council delegates. Thanks to our roommate Brandon Begay for sharing space and time for me to develop my research. Thanks to my Flagstaff friends, roommates, and some people I got to know: Natasha Hale, Jordan Hale, Sheena Hale, David Porinchok, and others.

Thank you, Allyson Carter, for seeing this project through, finding reviewers, and talking me through difficult parts of the process. Thank you, reviewers, who gave me helpful criticism *or* motivated me because I hated your comments. Thank you, Wenner-Gren Foundation, for funding the research. This book literally couldn't be this book without this funding.

I want to thank my good friends Alastair Bitsoi and Arlyssa Becenti, the best journalists and my companions during council sessions. Thanks to those working in the tribal government who would let me talk to them or hang out in the chambers when I was obviously taking notes. Thanks to Anthony Peterman for sharing your thoughts on Navajo energy in real time and allowing a degree of transparency during the process. I learned a lot from our conversations. Thanks to Brandon Benallie, Radmilla Cody, Shandiin Yazzie, Dana Eldridge, and the members of the K'é Infoshop for the work you do to hold our government accountable.

Thanks to my friends and mentors over the years, Moroni Benally, Enei Begaye, Tony Skrelunas, Ethel Branch, Wahleah Johns, Janene Yazzie, Wendy Greyeyes, Nick Estes, Melanie Yazzie, Jennifer Denetdale, Lloyd Lee, Dana Powell, Chee Brossy, and Roxanne Dunbar-Ortiz. Thank you, Teresa Montoya and Traci Voyles, for helping me come up with the book title! I need to thank my mentors at Cornell, Angela Gonzales, Paul Nadasdy, Charles Geisler. All of them saw much cruder drafts of these chapters. They did a lot of work. I especially want to thank my advisor, Wendy Wolford.

Thanks to my friends and colleagues from the University of North Carolina at Chapel Hill. First, I need to express gratitude to the Carolina Postdoctoral Program for Faculty Diversity. This program provided the initial time needed to turn this into a book. Thank you, Gaby Valdivia, for helping me during my postdoc. Thank you to my colleagues at the UNC–Chapel Hill Department of

Geography for giving me a chance. I am grateful to all of you who showed confidence in me, and I have fond memories from my time there. I want to thank Banu Gökariksel, Lilly Nguyen, Maya Berry, Danielle Purifoy, and Annette Rodriguez for reading this and other things as part of our writing group, Dangerous Playground.

Thank you, Valerie Lambert, Jean Dennison, and Meagan Ybarra for reading second and third drafts of the book and giving me some of the most important feedback I've received. This new version is largely a result of our workshop and I hope we can celebrate it when it's a tangible thing I can't edit anymore.

Thanks to my colleagues in American Indian studies at UNC–Chapel Hill, a program the university shamefully neglects. These are Daniel Cobb, Keith Richotte, Ben Frey, and Jenny Tone-Pah-Hote. Jenny read early drafts of this and helped me on some critical areas in understanding tribal law and governance. Thank you, Sara Smith, for continued mentorship and friendship. It has been invaluable.

Thank you, University of Arizona geography people. Thank you, Karletta Chief! I look forward to working with you more in the future! Thanks to my wonderful graduate student Majerle Lister and his partner Tatiana Benally. Majerle spent a lot of time listening to us talk about things that would eventually become facets of this book. Thank you, Majerle!

I want to thank my parents, Paula Hale and Lorenzo Curley. They gave me the teachings and discipline needed to complete this. My father worked a lot for our community during the time of this writing and I admire the dedication he's shown to making our nation a better place. My mother was always there to hear out my frustration or give me some valuable insights from her time working on the Navajo Nation. All of this was tremendously helpful.

Thank you to my sisters, Lindsay Curley and Sara Curley, and my nephews, Gabe, Anthony, and Austin. I want to thank the Beck family of Piñon, who have become family to me. Their leadership has moved that community and our nation over the years. I am lucky to know them. I want to thank the Begay family too; they are always there to share a meal and host us. They embody k'é. I am always happy to see them. Thank you, K'éhazbah Beck, Victor Beck Jr., Nathaniel Benzie, my family-in-law, but really my family. Thank you to my core support, my love, Nanibaa Beck—whose contributions to my work and life are immeasurable.

Finally, I want to dedicate this to family we've lost, Albert Hale, Victor Beck Sr., and Eleanor Beck. You gave us wisdom, ceremony, knowledge, and faith.

Albert taught me about government reform and traditional leadership. Victor was there to encourage me, to tell me about his days as a council delegate, and his years growing up in Piñon. Eleanor taught me the most important lesson, dedication to family, a lesson I try to apply every day.

CARBON SOVEREIGNTY

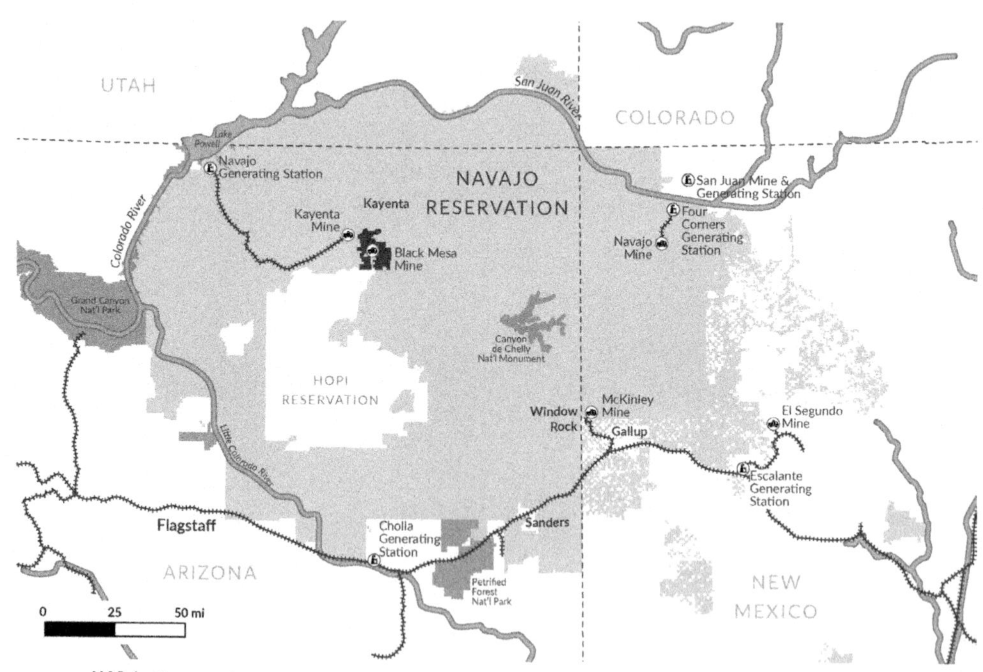

MAP 1. Current Navajo Reservation boundaries.

Legend

Traditional Diné lands

Present-day Hopi reservation boundaries

Present-day Diné reservation boundaries

Diné sacred mountains

Labels indicate additional traditional indigeneous territories.

Source: Native Land Digital and Decolonial Atlas

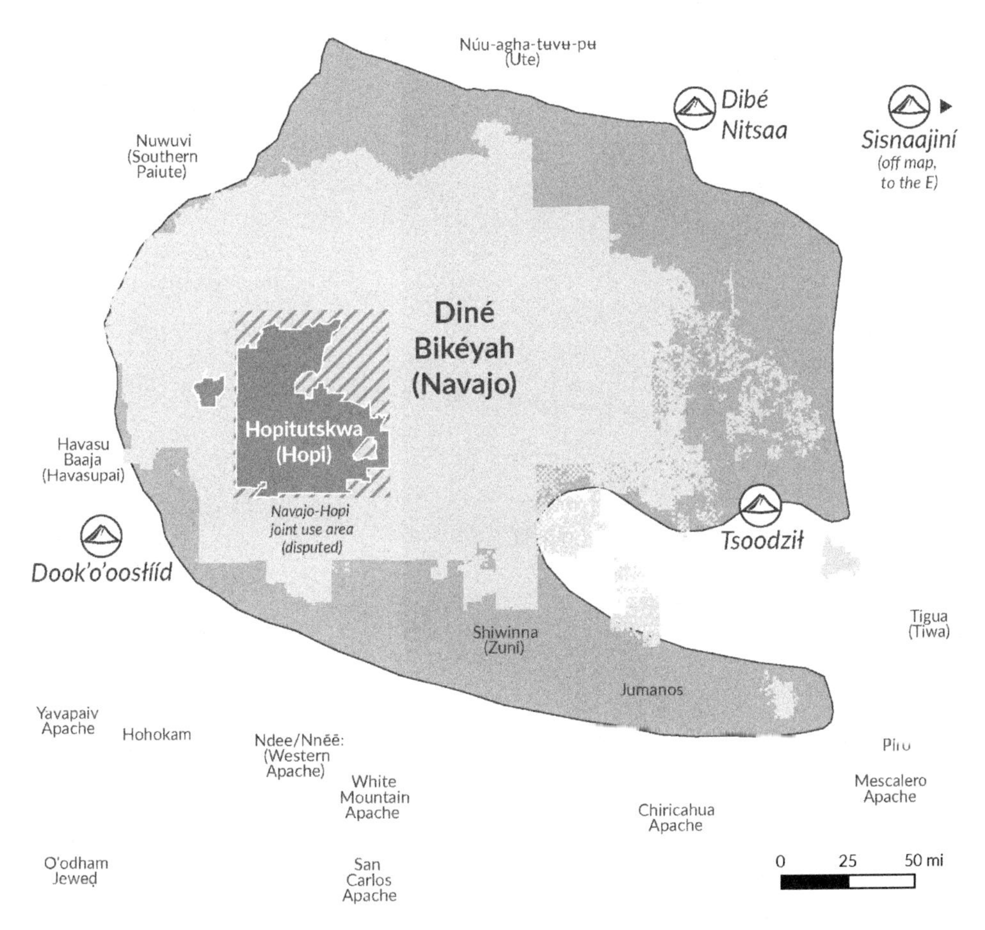

MAP 2. Traditional Diné territory.

INTRODUCTION

ENERGY TRANSITION IS not simply an ideal for the future; it is also empirically a series of past events. Included in energy transition are the marginalization of tribal places, the expansion of unsustainable cities, and the slow violence of toxic spaces. Transition is not just a political rhetoric or rallying point; it is made violent by its implementation on already existing colonial landscapes. While some proposals try to mitigate colonial harm, especially energy proposals that promote green energy technology, the history of energy development on tribal lands is little more than a continuation of colonial violence in new forms. In this book, I document recent events regarding the Navajo Nation's long participation in the coal industry and argue that we've been at the forefront of energy transition for more than fifty years and with dire consequences.[1]

My intent is not to harm the workers or their understandings of prosperity that coal brought to their families and communities. It is to highlight the larger political context of energy development in the Navajo Nation and to show, once again, how the welfare and well-being of Indigenous peoples were the last considerations among colonial lawmakers and industry types who determined the ultimate fate of our participation in energy production. This book focuses on the attempted renewal of a coal lease and power plant, one that supplied energy to critical water infrastructure for Arizona. The plant and mine operated for years, but energy prices shifted against the fortunes of coal, and Arizona's utilities wanted to reduce costs.

Energy transition shut down a coal-fired power plant and coal mine that operated for decades within the Navajo Nation, ending an important source of revenue and jobs for the tribe. Powerful institutions in Arizona that created the coal economy for Diné people blamed "market forces" when they pulled the rug from under the feet of the Navajo Nation.

In this text, I consider how these economic forces were presented to Diné activists, coal workers, and tribal officials. Years after its closure, we can see clearly how price trends, climate discourse, and shifting energy practices create the impression of an inevitability—that the coal plant was destined to close as an artifact of history. But in 2013 this inevitability was far from certain. Diné people with opposite political objectives struggled to make their vision of the future a reality, leading to either the closure and transition of the Navajo coal economy or its continuation for decades more. What Arizona lawmakers presented to the Diné people in 2013 was an opportunity to renew a fifty-year lease between the tribe and the state's most important utility, the Salt River Project (SRP), until 2044. The renewal contained the elements of past colonial arrangements, including the forfeiture of thirty-four thousand acre-feet of Colorado River water for another twenty-five years after the 2019 lease expiration.

During this time, Diné people expressed a sense of carbon sovereignty in their mobilization for or against the renewal of a coal-fired power plant lease. This was a desire for increased control and self-determination over Diné lands, air, and waters conscripted into energy production. Although carbon sovereignty might sound like a corny title to some readers, it does the work of combining scholarship on energy history and tribal sovereignty in a way that I find productive. The concept takes its understanding from Timothy Mitchell's (2009) provocative retort to a resource curse thesis, carbon democracy, arguing effectively that state building in the Gulf was built on carbon resources. Oil in the gulf made modern state building possible.

Carbon stands in as reference for fossil fuels. It's not literal carbon but literal carbon is part of it. It's about both the conversion of things like oil and coal into energy but more importantly the social and political relations that emerge and are shaped by these processes. For "energy rich" tribes, carbon has been a source of nation building, of assertions of sovereignty, of moving out of the paternal control of the Bureau of Indian Affairs and controlling fate of nations. Carbon as nation building for tribes, in the form of oil, coal, natural gas, and other fossil fuels, is of critical importance. You can't fully understand modern Indigenous life in North America without accounting for carbon sovereignty. This text begins in 2013 but explores the brief history of a mine, a power plant, and how these infrastructures and networks of energy production shaped sovereignty in the Navajo Nation for more than fifty years.

A 2013 COAL RENEWAL, AS IT HAPPENED

In the early morning hours of April 29, 2013, a chartered bus pulled into a largely empty Bashas' parking lot in Kayenta and loaded between twenty and thirty Diné workers who worked at the nearby Kayenta Mine—a 44,073-acre coal mine located on the edge of nearby Black Mesa.

Kayenta is on the northern boundary of the Navajo Reservation—near the picturesque Monument Valley, which has served as the backdrop for many Hollywood movies. The Diné mine workers were members of a union, affiliated with the United Mine Workers, and it was their union that paid for the bus. They got in the bus to travel to the tribe's capital, Window Rock, 133 miles to the southeast.

On their way to Window Rock, the workers trekked across a two-lane road in some of the most remote parts of the continent. Diné families have lived here since before Europeans even knew about this side of the world. Anasazi, the ancestors of Diné and Pueblo peoples, built complicated and elaborate cliffside communities not too far from Kayenta and the mine site.

Six hundred years ago, the people who lived in a slot canyon had luxuries Europeans could only imagine: regular food, clean water, fresh air, and beautiful country. They were free from most viruses and diseases that would later plague generations of Indigenous peoples. They didn't live in fear of neighboring kingdoms or as people without rights and bound to someone else's land like the ancestors of today's white people, whose families escaped to our country from the oppressiveness of European feudalism.

In April 2013, the workers were en route to a Navajo Nation Council session (figure 1). The council was considering legislation that would renew a lease between the tribe and one of Arizona's most important utilities, the SRP, over the Navajo Generating Station (NGS)—a 2,250-megawatt (MW) coal-fired power plant that consumed Kayenta's coal.

Although the mine had operated for decades in the heart of the Navajo Nation, on Black Mesa, the lease between the power plant and tribe was set to

FIGURE 1. Diné coal workers gathering outside the Navajo Nation Council chambers in support of the NGS lease, April 29, 2013. Photograph by Andrew Curley.

expire in 2019. If it was not renewed, the mine would also close, and the workers at both the mine and the power plant would be out of a job.

The lease was first signed in 1969 for a fifty-year term. The Salt River Project, one of the most important and powerful utilities in Arizona, was the operating manager of the plant and its second-largest shareholder—the Bureau of Reclamation being the first. For SRP, in its crude colonial calculation, coal was cheaper than other energy sources. Committing to the plant and mine for another twenty-five years made the most fiscal sense. But to do this, the utility needed the Navajo council's endorsement.

Although 2019 was six years away, SRP figured it would take time for the Department of the Interior and other federal regulators to sign off on the lease. Getting the Navajo Nation's endorsement early would ensure the process was complete by 2019.

Much had changed since the original lease was signed in 1969. In the 1960s, climate change was not well understood. Coal was the environmentally friendlier alternative to large hydroelectric dams. At the time, conservation groups advocated for coal over dams. This is something hard for modern environmentalists to imagine.

But by 2013, we were aware of greenhouse gases and coal's contribution to climate change. This book asks, "How would this new political landscape impact existing approaches to tribal sovereignty? What would be the fate of the coal workers who spent decades in the mines generating wealth for the tribe while sustaining a good living for them and their families?"

I had been in the field for nearly a year by this point. I had returned to the Navajo Nation the previous spring to study the political and cultural questions of coal in the reservation and identify what I presumed were underappreciated social consequences of the industry on our people. I was looking for Diné coal workers' understandings of coal and how it might help us appreciate the industry's long-term presence on our lands.

What I found were the raw experiences that contributed to the broader social phenomena we call colonialism and capitalism. It isn't enough to use these words to describe what I witnessed or the experiences of people on the ground. What this renewal entailed was contested meaning and high political stakes. The renewal was about continued work for people at the mine and plant. It was about substantial revenues for the tribe and the future of life on the planet.

Four years earlier, in 2009, I witnessed the same Navajo Nation Council pass "green jobs" legislation that was meant to start the transition from coal to alternative energy investment in the reservation. The tribe was aware of climate change and its threat to the planet. But more fundamental to tribal lawmakers was the fate of workers and revenues.

The original leases were signed during a time of profound social change among Diné people, during the 1960s. Coal spurred some of these changes. It helped move a subsistence workforce into industrialized labor. The coal mines provided wage-labor jobs in a place defined by what you could grow and graze on the land. For those who participated in the industry, coal ushered in a capitalist work week. Coal mining cut families from their homesites, displaced residents, and made life in some sections of the reservation hard to sustain. Since coal leases were signed and the first shovel plowed into Black Mesa, community members in and around the mine sites have resisted the coal industry. This resistance has taken many forms over the years. It regularly shows itself in quiet disapproval, a petition of grievances with elected leaders, or outright agitation.

What I learned during this fieldwork was that time, land, and life were under constant negotiation in the reservation—between settler designs and Indigenous needs. At the time of the lease renewal, the State of Arizona was also asking the Diné people to relinquish our claims to the Colorado River and its tributaries—forever—in exchange for limited "rights" to waters that reach the reservation.

Language going backward and forward in time, from *forever* and to *time immemorial*, are the temporal markers of treaties and water settlements. The lease for the Navajo Generating Station was for fifty years and set to expire in 2019. If renewed, the lease would continue coal in the Navajo Nation until 2044. This was a temporal binding, connecting the energy economy of 1969 with 2044. Time in the form of treaties and contracts sets the terms of colonization.

At the same time, environmental activists called for dramatic carbon reductions in near future dates, such as cutting greenhouse gas emissions in half by 2030. When I asked an environmental organizer about their work against coal, they said, "Strategically if you want to stop global warming you have to reduce the amount of carbon in the atmosphere and the quickest way to do that is to move beyond coal—to stop using coal." The time frame used by environmental activists, the time frame that contained a threat to humanity in the not-too-distant future, motivated immediate action against existing sources of greenhouse gasses such as coal-fired power plants. Extending the coal economy into 2044 was anathema to the politics of climate change.

The Kayenta Mine and the Navajo Generating Station, in combination, also constituted an important economic pillar for the Navajo Nation. The workers who mobilized outside the council worked to preserve not only their incomes but also their ways of life—their moral economy. They had worked in the coal industry for decades, many starting out shortly after high school. Some workers I interviewed integrated traditional Diné ethics of work and livelihood into regimes of industrial labor. They did not want to stand by and watch their source of livelihood close. The power plant and mine employed at its peak eight hundred workers.[2] Coal leasing and mining contributed $30 million to $50 million annually to the tribe's budget—25 percent of nonfederal revenues.[3] The stakes for Diné people were high.

During the lease renewal, tribal officials fully supported the continuation of the coal mine and power plant. The reasons were clear: jobs and revenue. Many elected leaders and community members were aware of the costs and risks of coal to the community and natural environment. They knew the sordid legacies of extraction on the land, especially in the case of uranium mining (Brugge, Benally, and Yazzie-Lewis 2006; Eichstaedt 1994; S. L. Smith and Frehner 2010; Voyles 2015). Despite this knowledge, Diné lawmakers tried to renew the lease and continue the industry. It was just too important, and the tribe was too dependent on the mine and plant to close them down. This part of the story is well known. I wanted to find out what it was about coal that left it so politically entrenched in the Navajo Nation. It wasn't that lawmakers and coal workers referred to this structuring condition—in fact they rarely mentioned them. In ideology and practice, they believed in coal. It was a livelihood upon which sovereignty, self-determination, and even the continuation of culture rested. These features of coal and extractive industries were less understood.

This paradox was forefront in my mind while I formed my research questions. In a failed National Science Foundation proposal, a reviewer asked me, "Why would this be any different than in West Virginia?" Why would we describe the Navajo Nation as different from West Virginia? What were the underlying assumptions in the reviewer's response? I hadn't even mentioned West Virginia in my proposal, yet it was immediately compared with the Navajo Nation. This is not uncommon. We often insist on this comparison ourselves. But when we think about it more deeply, the social, political, cultural, and historical circumstances that went into forming modern West Virginia are the opposite of those that formed the Navajo Nation. In some ways, the only thing Diné people have in common with people in Appalachia *is* coal. And even this comparability breaks down after superficial inspection. The kind of coal produced in these regions is very different. Yet social scientists were asking for this comparison, in a quixotic quest for something generalizable. This forced me to think about how we are thinking about energy and energy transition on national and international scales, often abstracted from particular social and political contexts. It was this deeper history and aspiration toward sovereignty that better explain why people believe the things they do about coal in the Navajo Nation.

What my proposal reviewer wanted was a universal claim about the experience of coal work, something I could thread through West Virginia, the Navajo Nation, and other coal-reliant communities while ignoring or downplaying the messy details about the place in order to arrive at some generalizable sociological facts. This was the basis for a false start, for a project that would lose history, context, and specificity. To treat Indigenous peoples and spaces as anything but a captured racial minority in the colonial claims of the United States, one had to depart from what C. Wright Mills ([1959] 2000, 50) calls "abstracted empiricism," which says nothing to either theory or experience, and to reach out for the "promise of sociology," where "history and biography" (structure and agency) meet.

This book historizes the Diné coal experience. It cannot account for every angle, every facet, every personal narrative in the making of the Navajo coal economy and its eventual decline. However, this book tries to put many of these experiences into context, to make unique what is often assumed to be universal, and to make historical what is assumed to be a contemporary problem. First, I make a historical-spatial argument using secondary sources about the history of Diné people to argue that Diné lands were *made* into extractive spaces, designed to fit within the racial logics and colonial practices of U.S. capitalism. The limitations of Indigenous sovereignty are defined within what the Lumbee law professor Robert A. Williams Jr. (2005) calls the racial dictatorship of the U.S. Congress. This is the colonial process at work. It is a process not simply of settlement but also of enclosure, forced federalism, and a particular legal-political configuration of "tribe" that is defined in notions of race, capitalistic notions of territory and land, and exploitative ontologies of resources. In combination, these material and symbolic changes create the conditions for colonial capitalism in and around the Navajo Nation. In other words, the Navajo Nation, as a legal-political creature of federal Indian law, works consistently with capitalist understandings of space and time. These are necessary to make resource extraction possible.

Second, this book examines the history of colonial capitalism in the Navajo Nation and tribal responses (at times, resistance) to it. What emerges are an understanding and practice of tribal sovereignty that are built from resource extraction—*carbon sovereignty*. The material conditions of this form of sovereignty include the revenues coal brought into the tribal government and the jobs created and maintained with the expansion of coal mines and power plants. Finally, this book looks at the grounded impacts of coal itself. These are the costs to the local environment, air, water, and land. Coal provided jobs and revenues, but it also displaced families from their traditional lands and permanently contaminated land that Diné families used for subsistence for generations. Although the story of coal in the Navajo Nation is understood often in colonial terms, it is also a deeply personal experience for many people. This was a story of intimate geopolitics, of bodies, community, territory, and plans for the future (S. Smith 2020) as well as one of structural conditioning created by and through coal.

To empirically account for carbon sovereignty, I draw on fieldwork conducted in the Navajo Nation between 2012 and 2014 and follow-up interviews in 2017. These two years of ethnography helped me reestablish my research questions. Namely, it became clear that I needed to connect coal's material and ideological practices in the Navajo Nation to the networks of energy and water infrastructures serving regional (colonial) places such as Phoenix and Tucson.

I interviewed tribal officials, coal workers, and environmental activists. I lived in Flagstaff, Kayenta, and Sanders during this time. I briefly worked at the *Navajo Times* and covered community events and arts and culture instead of tribal politics because my father was on the tribal council and the paper wanted to avoid the appearance of bias. In 2017 I returned to the Navajo Nation and reinterviewed several people about the recent change in coal's fortunes. I also witnessed several events related to the social and political reproduction of coal in the Navajo Nation. Key among these events was the passage of a lease renewal in 2013 before the industry shutdown at the end of 2019.

To understand coal's fate in the Navajo Nation (epitomized in the closure of the Navajo Generating Station in 2019), I focus on the history of energy and water infrastructures in Arizona that necessitated the building of the Navajo Generating Station and the Kayenta Mine in the first place. Although these projects are not the entire story of coal in the reservation, they are important bedrocks of the coal industry in the nation that until now have been underexamined. When I started this project in 2012, I went to the Navajo Nation thinking that water, as in water from the N-Aquifer just below Black Mesa and the Kayenta Mine, served the coal industry, which in turn profited the Peabody Coal Company. This was the standard narrative about coal on Black Mesa (Nies 2014). My research, focused on the terms of renewal, found that water served coal but also coal served water—a different kind of water and one consequential for the State of Arizona. The coal-energy-water nexus was built to incorporate Diné bodies and resources for the movement of Colorado River water to Phoenix and Tucson—what I call "colonial beachheads" (Curley 2021a). Finally, I consider the lasting impacts of the closure of the mines and power plant for the Diné people. I contemplate what was gained and lost.

Ultimately, I suggest we must think about Indigenous futures in the twenty-first century as a commitment to a politics of decolonization. All of this is to say that the Diné people were brought into the fold of colonial capitalism through complicated and overlaying structures and events over time. The history of coal mining within the Navajo Nation demonstrates this. Settler colonialism has become a useful way to think about the impacts of colonization on tribes, but it has limitations. Although using history, in effect the theorization can be ahistorical. It often does not allow for history to fundamentally change the conditions of human existence and experience. To run the thread of continued and ongoing land dispossession through a cache of historical experiences—and to remind us colonialism is a structure and not an event—analytically, the settler and "the Native" must remain in an unchanged, dichotomous relationship over five hundred years. As a result of the settler-colonial framework, Indigenous peoples in 2020 are treated the same as Indigenous peoples in 1492, and colonial mechanisms are left unchanged—like a machine marching across the continent. There is obvious allure to the settler-colonial framework. It gives us a sense of the power of history and a clear picture of the monster that is colonization. However, the dispossession of Indigenous peoples from their lands (one of the key elements of settler-colonial theory) changes shape and practice over time. Colonialism is a shape-shifter. The colonial state is not a discrete unit, representing a unified actor with a set of clear discernable interests, but is instead a mess of issues spilling onto Indigenous lands, incorporating enslaved Black people, sucking up and pushing out immigrants, polluting while destroying and then conserving resources. "Domination" can be messy business, and sometimes we lose track of the actors involved in reproducing and remaking colonial regimes in the twenty-first century.

Colonialism is a series of events that structures the possibilities and limitations of Indigenous life and lifeways. There are some long-standing tendencies within the framework worth pointing out, such as dispossession, racialization, and notions of white supremacy. But these things need to be put into historical motion and allowed to change meaning over time, and thus we will better understand how they creep in, over, and through tribal communities.

Capitalism can serve as a blunt explanatory device. When we see inequality, racism, and clear examples of greed, corruption, and violence among ruling elites, we reach for our folder labeled "capitalism" and file these instances into it. But what *is* capitalism, really? And how does it work and play out across Indigenous communities? Capitalism might suffer from *over*explanation because it has different meanings for different peoples. It is not just a reference to economic practices but a key term in ideological discourse over the past century. So much is written about capitalism that it cannot be summarized in any useful way. So, for our purposes, what do Indigenous activists *mean* when they refer to capitalism? What do tribal leaders mean when they use the word? Or Diné coal workers? While my ethnography falls short of comprehensively explaining each actor's unique understanding of capitalism or references to it, I work to explain what I mean by capitalism and how I think capitalistic practices impact each of these actors differently. Capitalism is a form, practice, and understanding of economy that combines with colonial forces to create a unique configuration of powers, incentives, and invisible social and political limitations on tribal peoples and institutions. This configuration, unique to place and time, produces and reproduces the unequal relationship between the tribe, state, and federal government over water and energy. This is what I call in this book colonial capitalism.

The founding of the Navajo coal economy was part of a new kind of energy economy—a technologically distinct network of power lines, power plants, and political power that was the development of the Southwest. Diné coal was conscripted into a unique energy system that included power plants in California, Arizona, Nevada, and New Mexico, while selling power in all four states. Diné coal was part of a history, which included the damming of western rivers, of providing cheap energy to the expanding Sunbelt. This geographic history further distinguished Navajo coal extraction from the history of extraction in Appalachia. A key focus of my research was moving beyond direct comparisons between entrenched coal economies. Instead, I asked: How did the coal industry enter the reservation in the first place? What were the social and political circumstances that gave rise to this specific form of energy economy? What did coal contracts in the 1960s seek to accomplish? And what *did* coal accomplish? The legacy of coal turned out far different from what was promised. By studying what was promised in the past and comparing that with what actually happened, we dispel the intoxicating myth of development and progress. The coal economy, like many promises before, fell far short of early expectations.

The early literature on extractive industries in Indian Country addressed some of these questions. Building on the sociological frameworks of "world systems" and "dependency theory," researchers and polemicists alike pointed to the structuring forces that created the possibilities for extraction in the first place. These new ways of understanding centered on the tragic social and environmental repercussions of extraction in Indian Country (Ambler 1990; Churchill and LaDuke 1986; Nies 2014). Although these structuralist explanations accounted for coal's persistence as a basis for extractive capitalism, they did not address social and political forces working inside reservation communities. These earlier analyses did not account for the internal push for coal among Diné people in the Navajo Nation. The literature did not explain the social meaning coal produces among key actors and people within the Navajo Nation.

Critics suggest it was the Navajo Nation's reliance on coal for jobs and revenue that explains the industry's persistence. Noticeably absent from this story (especially apparent to Diné people and those who live in the Navajo Nation) are the perspectives of coal workers and tribal officials who saw coal as a source of jobs, livelihood, and a means to cultural survival. In 2013 the renewal of the

Navajo Generating Station coal lease exposed some of these social forces at work: the unseen forces that structure, maintain, and reproduce coal as a mode of development, economy, and way of life within the reservation. These workers pressured the Navajo Nation to stay in the coal business because of new social understandings about the resource.

More recent scholarship on the Navajo Nation, particularly by Western historians, finds that the neo-Marxist structural arguments used to explain the exploitation of Indigenous peoples and the environment are too totalizing. For example, the labor historian Colleen O'Neill (2005), whose rich archival work is used throughout this book, wrote that dependency theory does not account for the agency of tribal actors. This was the problem that informed the paradox that sparked my early interest on this topic—except I was coming at the question from a different angle. For my work, dependency theory didn't talk enough about how enthusiastic Diné coal workers were to see their livelihoods renewed, to keep the supposed dependency going. Nor did it mention the eagerness of tribal officials as they imagined the future economic windfall of renewed coal contracts. The tribal officials and Diné coal workers didn't enter with trepidation into a Faustian bargain—where jobs were gained at the expense of the environment—but made a full embrace of the coal work and industry. This coal-committed ideology needed acknowledging as well as explaining.

However, we do not need to abandon structural insights to account for agency. We can put the two into conversation. The job of social science is to identify the unseen forces shaping the limits and possibilities of agency. In the case of coal mining in the Navajo Nation, we see the limitations of agency in legal language (that of land leases, coal contracts), what dependency theorists call "the uneven terms of trade." Ultimately, despite the will of the Navajo Nation, major parts of the coal industry were shut down and there was little the tribe could do beyond mitigation.

Another critique of dependency theory comes from the Lumbee political scientist David Wilkins, whose work on Indigenous political systems is used extensively throughout this book. In a 1993 critique, at the height of dependency theory's popularity, Wilkins wrote that dependency theory and other underdevelopment theses could not account for positive economic outcomes in Indian Country. One outcome he was referring to was the booming casino development that was generating vast new revenues for tribes whose lands were close to urban centers like Los Angeles, Phoenix, or Boston. In dependency theory and other neocolonial accounts, the failure of tribal economies results from the colonial theft of Indigenous lands and resources for the benefit of the core economy. Wilkins (1993) argues that this understanding predicts economic failure for tribes.

When translating the insights of Mexican and other Latin American economists, the critical economist Andre Gundar Frank (1967) coined the phrase *the development of underdevelopment*. He and economists based in Latin America were referring to how global capitalists in colonizing nations exploited developing economies for their own benefit. This meant that places dependent were also underdeveloped, but the meaning of underdeveloped is vague and subsequent critiques point out that dependency and underdevelopment theories are still operating with an implied modernity in the background (Escobar 1995). Yet, as James Ferguson (2006) points out, when we say all things are modern or nothing is modern, we lose the ability to highlight the effects of globalized capitalism on places like Africa, a continent lost in globalization discourse but at the center of development work. A more generous reading of dependency theory can move beyond the meaning of underdeveloped and think through what remains useful in the framework.

Building on these critiques, but not disregarding the usefulness of dependency theory to explain natural resource development in the Navajo Nation, I return to the historical sociologist Philip Abrams's (1982) understanding of "the event" to account for both the structuring forces and the agency of people. There are real limitations within colonial capitalism that impact Diné people's attitudes and actions on the topic of coal (Curley 2019b). In fact, federal Indian law is premised on the idea of "dependency," referring to Indigenous people as "domestic-dependent" nations. But the notion of "dependent" as it is treated in dependency theory is often applied too broadly and vaguely to account for complex social and cultural attitudes on the ground. We can read critiques of coal, water, and energy in scholarship and still not recognize the Diné people who participate in these industries. It is to capture these complex and at times contradictory attitudes toward the environment, development, and tribal sovereignty where this book intervenes.

To put structure and agency in productive relation, this book treats political mobilizations around coal as *events* with no predetermined or predestined outcome. In historical sociology, events serve as objects of analysis in search of sociological conclusions, perhaps "laws" and not simply a chronology of happenings or narratives as is sometimes found in history. This book draws upon historical sociological debates about temporality when interpreting social actions at a particular place and time. Philip Abrams (1982) argues that events are structuring—they produce and reproduce social, legal, and political limitations—yet their outcomes are never certain. Events such as the Navajo renewal of coal in 2013 reveal both the possibilities and limitations of Diné actions during this time of revolutionary change across the energy landscape. These feelings or immediate reactions to the question "Why did the Navajo Nation and many Diné people support the renewal of these leases in 2013?" point us in the direction of an "eventful temporality," where we are attentive to "the transformation of structures by events" (Sewell 2005, 100). Events such as the signing of the NGS lease in 2013 account for the reproduction of structural and structuring forces as they pertain to energy, development, and climate change in the Navajo Nation.

CARBON SOVEREIGNTY

The term *tribal sovereignty* is defined and used in different ways. It contains deep understandings of home, livelihood, and cultural belonging. Tribal sovereignty is also a practical day-to-day concept used in official documents and discussions and vocalized in meetings within the upper echelons of tribal authority. In its governmental application, tribal sovereignty loses much of its emotional resonance and becomes a mix of confusing and sometimes contradictory practices. These practices reinforce hierarchal spaces of colonization and control between the federal government, state governments, and tribal nations. Sovereignty is informed by structural incentives, favoring efforts to modernize and develop along capitalist lines within tribal lands. In this book, I refer to this political-governmental practice of sovereignty as "carbon sovereignty," a sovereignty that in practice responds to and works within the structural constraints of colonial law. In the Navajo Nation, acts of modernization and development (part of a day-to-day governmental sovereignty) favor continued coal mining, large-scale water projects, and even the ownership of power plants. These "modernizing" actions significantly affect how tribal peoples see and understand their lands and resources.

Using *carbon sovereignty* as a concept, we can examine how energy transition and climate change affect Indigenous peoples. Through an exploration of resources, we can learn the central mechanisms of colonialism in the twenty-first century, perhaps as a final enclosure on Indigenous spaces. Carbon sovereignty also accounts for capitalistic expansion, primitive accumulation, proletarianization, and economic displacement of Indigenous peoples while lands, waters, and air security are tussled from the control of Indigenous nations. These twin processes, colonialism and capitalism, are not always the same thing, but they impact Indigenous peoples simultaneously.

What is sometimes problematic about the language of tribal sovereignty is its connection with the power of modern states. Within critical Indigenous studies, "sovereignty" is under increased scrutiny, seen as a language that is both "colonial" and an important discourse for tribal self-determination (Barker 2005; Biolsi 2005). My research builds on understandings of sovereignty grounded in Indigenous ethnographies of "the state" (Dennison 2012, 2017; Lambert 2007; Nadasdy 2017) with critical scholarship on development and historical materialism. I show how competing and contested moral economies produce categories like work and livelihood, sovereignty, and "sustainable development" as ideological constructs maintained in the political economy of coal in the Navajo Nation (Curley 2019b). They are interpreted through ideas and practices of power, authority, and representation within tribal institutions, communities, and places of work. Tribal sovereignty shapes how Indigenous actors respond to the contested political terrain of energy and transition, sustainability and development, and climate change.

Much of the cited literature on sovereignty articulates the limitations of political rights for Indigenous nations under federal and state laws. It is often a legalistic discourse. What "carbon sovereignty" advances here is the metabolic connection of raw resources and consumption within abstract notions of political economy that influence what tribal actors do with their sovereignty and what is made possible. This builds on Timothy Mitchell's (2009) provocation about carbon democracies in the Gulf states. Mitchell argues against resource curse literature. He says it wasn't that oil prevented development in these places but that it actually made state making possible—funding infrastructure, social services, militaries, and government positions. This is a powerful insight that should be used to understand both the meaning and the practice of Indigenous sovereignty in the twentieth and twenty-first centuries.

Among "energy rich tribes," extractives like coal, uranium, oil, and gas have flooded tribal coffers. The revenues derived from land leases, water leases, and royalty rates associated with these industries funded college scholarships, stipends for meetings, roads, water projects, tribal government jobs, and so on. These are the everyday performances of sovereignty that aren't discussed in theoretical and legalistic debates. Sovereignty is not just about rights and self-determination, about territory and progress; it is also about living, building, and sustaining work on the land. This was the biggest difference I observed between "sovereignty" and all its paradoxes debated about in academic scholarship and the ways in which it was understood and practiced on the ground.

Although coal tells us something about Diné tribal sovereignty, it also tells us something about the people. The Diné coal workers I spoke with defined the resources as a source of livelihood. In important ways, their sovereignty was community and kinship focused. Diné life and survivability were found not in the maintenance of tribal institutions but in the ability of Diné people to live from the land. In ironic terms, the destruction of the land in search of coal allowed for this. The replacement of sustainable livelihoods for wage-labor jobs was a colonial violence, and Diné workers at the mines and power plants responded by finding work within the reservation, often near their ancestral homes. Understanding tribal sovereignty as rooted in real political and economic anxieties allows us to appreciate it as an ideal constructed in response to social and economic change happening *to* people and not necessarily with their assistance. While Diné coal workers, officials, and environmental activists maintain agency (they still shape the course of their lives), they are unable to change the larger, more powerful forces that are transitioning the U.S. energy landscape.

CAPITAL INCORPORATION

For centuries, colonial powers claimed Diné lands but didn't control it. When New Spain proclaimed Diné Bikéyah as Spanish territory in the sixteenth century, Diné lands became part of New Spain—at least in the minds of Spanish colonizers. Similarly, Diné lands (nominally) became part of Mexico when Mexico liberated itself from Spain in 1820. But Mexico was not so defined a geography at the time. Contestation for power placed the frontier lands, including Diné Bikéyah, far into the recesses of political concern for the struggling Mexican-Spanish-U.S. factions (Alonso et al. 1994).

Diné people resisted colonial control. Neither Spain nor Mexico had any real claim over Diné lands. Diné lands were incorporated vaguely and abstractly into colonial maps. There was no Spain or Mexico in these parts. Diné people were free from the worst aspects of colonial control well into the nineteenth century. It was only after 1848, when an imperial United States seized half of

Mexico, that Anglophone colonization crept into Diné territory. The U.S. war with Mexico was initiated by a southern, proslavery Democratic administration that envisioned the expansion of slavery into newly conquered "territories" west of Texas. In 1849, a year after revolutionary agitation in Europe and Karl Marx's publication of *The Communist Manifesto*, all future interactions with the continent's Indigenous peoples were transferred from the U.S. Department of War to the Department of the Interior as a move to consolidate Indigenous lands into an expanding U.S. empire (R. Dunbar-Ortiz 2014).

Race became an important idea in the social and political construction of new U.S. territories. Indigenous peoples and their lands were incorporated into an expanding United States and racialized at the bottom of its "civilizing" narrative. In the United States, white supremacy became the racial order (Olson 2004). Indigenous peoples, who generally (but not always) had phenotypes distinct from their colonizers, were marked by this difference. Race, religion, cultural beliefs, language, and even governing practices were made social markers of difference during nineteenth-century U.S. state formation. On the front lines of this imperialism and administering the racialization of Indigenous peoples were recent immigrants to the United States—peoples who had only recently become white, such as Irish and Italian immigrants (Ignatiev 2009). Enumeration and quantification of Indigenous racial identities were administered inconsistently, haphazardly, and through crude surveys between the 1830s and 1930s. These surveys assumed that physical differences set Native peoples apart from other Americans. To this day, these surveys (often called *rolls*) serve as the basis of "tribal" membership for federally recognized "tribes." Today, this form of membership creates serious problems in determining who is or is not Indigenous. It was cruel, it divided families, and it was based on biological racism and not kinship practices existent in Indigenous communities.

Spatially, the United States created "reservations" out of territories it claimed but neither controlled nor understood. The U.S. military attacked Indigenous civilians not at war with settlers. The U.S. Army torched homes, destroyed crops, and killed sheep, making survivability for a people who relied directly on the land perilous. It was not military defeat but the threat of starvation that forced thousands of Diné people to surrender to the army between 1862 and 1868. For decades, historians have prioritized the perspectives of aggressors, quick to rationalize murder and theft while dismissing the stories of the victims who remember in graphic detail the brutality of these pogroms (Denetdale 2009). Most histories of the Diné identify "livestock reduction," nearly seventy years later, when Diné subsistence economies were destroyed and the Diné people were made "dependent" on capitalism for survival (White 1983). However, following Marx's own approach to "primitive accumulation," we should caution against clear and definitive dates for when Diné subsistence economies were clearly undermined. It was a decades-long process and in many ways is still ongoing.

The history of American capitalism followed a different trajectory than that of Europe. The United States emerged not as a site of industrialization from feudal lands but as a commercial slave power from stolen Indigenous lands. Indigenous peoples developed maize, tomatoes, cocoa, and other crops that would become commodities in the making of "the world system." They also grew tobacco. This, along with imported crops like sugar cane, became a financier of colonization as European appetites for American goods exploded (Mintz 1986). Colonizers appropriated the wealth of Indigenous peoples and circulated it into European economies during a transition from feudalism to capitalism. Colonization of the Americas helped shift the balance of power away from feudal lords, whose dominion was limited to Europe (Wallerstein 1974). The wealth that Europeans violently expropriated from Indigenous peoples was integrated into the world system of colonization, trade, and consumption that was dominated by the empires of Spain, England, and France. Over time, European kingdoms divided into nation-states and incorporated colonies as territories with exclusive markets to their home countries, ensuring the dependency and underdevelopment of the colonized. By the 1840s when the United States entered Diné lands, the state was rapidly expanding its borders westward and threatening to extend slavery into new territories. In the United States, capitalism matured with racial and class differences expanding, creating an economy of "racial capitalism," a process that consumed black and brown land and labor for the benefit of a white racial order (Robinson 1983).

TEMPORAL BENDING

The way Diné people deploy time scales in climate debates points to a politics at work. To tell stories about the future, Diné coal workers, environmental activists, and tribal officials relate their past in ways that implement different temporal and spatial scales. The use of time in service of political positions is a form of temporal bending—a distortion of time to lengthen or shorten perceptions about the passage of time built from competing ideologies. In a carnival funhouse, mirrors are bent to distort one's reflection. The subject can be made to look longer by bending the mirror outward. The subject can be made to appear shorter by bending the mirror inward. In the case of the Navajo Nation, coal workers understand coal in terms of their lifetimes but also in the sense of time immemorial. The mirror is bent backward, then forward again. Diné environmentalists understand coal at a scale of the Anthropocene—billions of years in the making (mirror bent out)—but also in terms of the past fifty years as coal was developed in the reservation (mirror bent in). Diné tribal officials think of coal in scales of decades or centuries, in fifty-year contracts but also in year-to-year annual income as a basis of projected tribal revenues. Sometimes the *longue durée* is important; sometimes it is the anxiety produced in crisis that matters.

This intersection of time, place, and social structure tells us something about the Diné people's incorporation into larger processes of capitalist expansion and colonization. Both proponents and opponents of coal maintained their own ideas of what was in the best interest of the Navajo Nation and the Diné people. Each set of actors was earnest in its professed beliefs, although propagandizing occurred on all sides. They maintained different interpretations of the past and visions of the future. Although this is a book focused on Navajo coal, the ideological formations at work during the 2013 debate were connected to both U.S. and international politics on climate change. Global connectedness was imagined in competing ways. "Diné-ness," as it were, was no longer confined to the Four Sacred Mountains. A *global* imaginary was at work. The Diné actors were responding to a global Indigenous phenomenon, whether it was part of a U.S. subjectivity or a pan-indigeneity.

OVERVIEW OF THE BOOK

In chapter 1, "Shape-Shifting Colonialism and the Origin of Carbon Sovereignty," I provide a historical accounting of Diné lands. In this chapter, I argue that the history of federal Indian policy, the creation of the Navajo Tribal Council in the 1930s, and the move toward natural resource development in the 1950s rendered Diné Bikéyah an extractive space for coal development. The paternal federal government drove these political and social changes. Colonial policy entered the region with New Deal policies designed to modernize the "Navaho" people and assimilate them into an "American" (white Anglo-Saxon

Christian) core. U.S. colonial actors bent time forward and erased the past, replacing it with their own characterizations of the present and future. These colonial actors paved over Diné stories of survival and overcoming hardship, of slaying monsters and tricking Tricksters with stories of Mayflowers, Thanksgiving, and benevolent colonialism. This new narrative was depicted in mural form on the very walls of the Navajo Tribal Council chambers. The mural surrounds tribal lawmakers to this day. It portrays civilization and progress as an American invitation to Diné people. This narrative opens the land for extraction. It ushers in capitalistic relations with Diné land and people, and builds a regional economy that ultimately benefits Phoenix, Tucson, Los Angeles, and Las Vegas.

In chapter 2, "Carbon Sovereignty," I account for a particular rendering of tribal sovereignty, one bound to the extraction and exploitation of resources in Diné lands. The sense of power, real and figurative, in resource development was not simply a perpetuation of colonial relationships; it also ushered in a new confidence in decolonization and "self-determination." The decolonial paradox results from the continued economic inequalities that remain after a colonized country earns independence. In the case of the African nations, Kwame Nkrumah (1965) referred to this continued relationship as "neo-colonialism," as part of a larger project of imperialism. Indigenous commentators have described the kind of colonialism experienced by tribes as "internal colonies" (Snipp 1986) and "radioactive colonialism" (Churchill and LaDuke 1986) among other framings before settling on settler colonialism (Wolfe 2006). In this chapter, the themes of anxiety and shape-shifting continue. My research finds that the 1960s served as an important moment of transformation in Diné national aspirations, and in Diné political and economic development. Research (mine as well as that of others) shows that the Navajo Nation was rendered into a resource colony during this time. More recent work highlights how the resource colony was built on Navajo aspirations for self-determination—what historians refers to as "Navajo nationalism" (Needham 2014, 213) or "sovereignty for survival" (Allison 2015). In the end, I recharacterize these relationships as "carbon sovereignty" or a sovereignty built on the expansion of energy resources.

In this chapter, I review the transcripts of the Navajo Tribal Council in the 1960s while delegates deliberated new coal leases. Tribal lawmakers did not concede to coal development simply because they didn't anticipate or understand the true costs of coal on the land and the people (although there is some truth in this narrative). Rather, I suggest that tribal lawmakers brought coal into the reservation as a pragmatic concession to colonial interests and pressures during the federal era of "termination," when tribes were eliminated from federal recognition or placed under the control of state governments. The State of Arizona threatened to develop energy infrastructure on tribal lands without permission of the Navajo Nation. Navajo Nation chairman Peter MacDonald and Arizona senator Barry Goldwater became notorious rivals over Navajo–Hopi land partitions, which intersected with coal land leases. I argue that by taking steps to develop its coal resources and to fight the expulsion of Diné communities on contested Navajo–Hopi lands, the Navajo tribal government exercised decolonial nationalism and sovereignty. "Carbon sovereignty" refers to a practice of sovereignty that is shaped by colonial limitations and entanglements. Carbon sovereignty bends time backward and forward, replacing the foundational narrative of Euro-American colonialists with origin stories based in Diné oral history.

In chapter 3, "Carbon Treatymaking," I analyze the coal and climate question at a time of uncertainty in the industry. In 2013 the entire Navajo coal economy could have shut down forever. Leases were coming up for renewal while utilities and mining companies alike showed only lukewarm interest in continuing coal work in the nation. Coal workers and tribal officials grew anxious. If the tribe's two coal mines and two power plants closed, the results would be catastrophic. And although the mines and plants remained open for a time, the workers' and officials' fears were not unfounded—six years later, one mine and one plant *did* close. At the same time, Diné environmental groups sought to bend the sovereignty time scale back further, extending it to billions of years of history and connecting it to geologic time and the current Anthropocene. In this chapter, I argue that the Navajo Nation Council's 2013 renewal of the Navajo Generating Station lease was a modern example of carbon sovereignty at work—with the lease renewal, the tribe once again conceded water rights to the colonizing government. The 2013 lease was a near exact replication of the 1969 one that forfeited Navajo claims to the Colorado River for fifty years. The 2013 lease extended this concession for another twenty-five years. "Sovereign" time and the time scale of the Anthropocene came into direct conflict. Tribal lawmakers debated the water concession in particular. During the council sessions when the lease was considered, future Navajo Nation president Russell Begaye said it was unjust. Other delegates felt that water was drying faster than ever before. Water would be the resource of greater importance in the coming years due to climate change. For a moment (whether intentional or not), these claims connected the lawmakers to the Diné environmental groups. During the debate on renewing the coal lease, tribal lawmakers reinterpreted these tropes into the framework of tribal sovereignty, grafting the anxiety of a changing climate into the political project of Navajo national self-determination. In this way, the Navajo Nation Council worked to preserve Diné control over its resources while trying to expand rights, sovereignty, and governing prerogatives into new areas. Yet these efforts failed, and the resolutions eventually passed the council unaltered. The colonial conditions of 1969 were copied and pasted into the 2013 agreement. The actions of two very different tribal councils nearly fifty years apart reveal the ways in which carbon sovereignty encourages energy development projects in reservation lands and limits what can be done about them.

In chapter 4, "Workers' Perspectives on Coal," I examine how Diné coal workers incorporated mining into their identity and politics. This chapter relies on ethnographic research and in-depth interviews with coal workers, family members, and community members that I conducted in Kayenta and Window Rock between 2013 and 2014. I lived in Kayenta in 2013 when the lease for the Navajo Generating Station was discussed and renewed in Window Rock. At that time, the political issue of coal was sensitive and divisive. By the time the lease was renewed, coal could no longer be seen simply as money on the ledger books. It was both a political and a social issue. It was also an embedded economy, a source of livelihood and meaning for Diné coal workers. For those who supported the renewal, the Diné idea of "t'áá hwó' ají t'éego," or "you are responsible for your own well-being," captured their feelings about coal. It also bent time forward and backward in ways that served the politics of coal extraction.

The phrase *t'áá hwó' ají t'éego* is rooted in a particular sense of sustainability. It refers to a time when Diné life was derived from living on the land. Importantly, this reference does not engage colonial questions directly. The colonizer is absent when framing Diné life during the time of t'áá hwó' ají t'éego. For my coal miner interviewees, it was not a precolonial time that mattered but a precapitalist one. This speaks to the larger phenomenon operating in the background—the anxiety about cultural loss. Within the problem of cultural loss, the most immediate challenge was language loss. Many younger Diné people do not know how to speak Diné bizaad, or the Navajo language. The loss of Navajo language increased dramatically for children born after 1980 (T. S. Lee 2007). The workers I spoke with started labor at the mine in the 1970s, at least a generation older than the children of the 1980s. Most workers were proficient in Diné bizaad. They believed their work kept them on the land to maintain cultural practices and knowledge. The idea of traditional Diné culture was intertwined with the work of the mine. Their work in the coal mines empowered the workers to stay at home (instead of leaving their homelands for work), practice Diné culture, and impart their teachings to their children and families. Coal work was a response to the anxiety of cultural loss. It bent the temporal significance of coal backward again into the time of traditional Diné teachings. Coal work was not simply the beginning of modernization and development of the Navajo Nation (as it was originally conceptualized in the 1960s). For these workers, coal had become the basis for cultural survival.

In this chapter, I argue that coal workers used the idea of t'áá hwó' ají t'éego to form a "moral economy" of coal mining that demanded the perpetuation of a political system that ensured their class survivability for the foreseeable future. Through new forms of socialization, such as the coal workers union, this moral economy took shape and life to become an operating rationale for lease renewal by 2013. In this chapter, I argue that t'áá hwó' ají t'éego was a subsistence ethic rooted in presence on the land. For coal workers, the mine fulfilled this ethic. However, t'áá hwó' ají t'éego spoke not only for continued coal mining but to a self-determination set against colonial constraints. The term is also used in a political discourse that is deployed for decolonization, independence, and liberation. At the time of this writing, some Diné groups use this term to advocate for transition away from coal. This is culture at work, responding to the conditions of change imposed on a people and preparing them for practices of survivability.

In chapter 5, "Toward Energy Transition," I extend the insight of t'áá hwó' ají t'éego as a Diné concept to consider the language of "transition" used by environmental organizers and Diné people concerned about climate change. Since the closure of the Black Mesa Mine in 2006, the Navajo Nation has considered the future of coal as a permanent feature on the Diné economy. While Diné coal workers worked for the industry's preservation, Diné environmental organizers, activists, and those critical of the coal economy openly talk about "transition" away from coal. This transition discussion is based on an understanding of Diné relationships with the earth. To exemplify this nonlinear understanding of history, I highlight a mural produced during this crisis. The *Water Is Life* mural (part of the series *Water Writes*) on a youth theater wall in Phoenix depicts the uneven history of coal mining and environmental exploitation in the Navajo Nation. Ironically, the mural was commissioned in Phoenix while the Navajo Nation decided on the renewal of fifty-year-old coal leases. The mural centers the Diné spiritual figure Changing Woman (Mother Earth), who gave birth to the Warrior Twins. In the mural, the Warrior Twins are the antidote to monsters plaguing the people. Their presence is timeless. Conceptually, the mural is about balance and not linear stages of time.

Transition implies epochs. There is considerable debate about what form transition should take, from neoliberal developmentalist approaches to anticapitalist ones. Each ideological understanding maintains different relationships with science and technology. Since 2006, the discursive terrain of "transition" has changed as the result of Indigenous activism and new forms of decolonial thinking. This chapter focuses on the clean energy campaign of Diné environmental actors in 2013. In their work—centered on land, sustainability, and an alternative vision of survivance of the people—these critics of coal redefine t'áá hwó' ají t'éego as an idea grounded in Diné Fundamental Law. Their definition centers Diné lifeways (instead of extractive industries) as the pathways toward sustainable development.

Finally, in "Conclusion: All That Is Solid Melts into Air," I consider the legacy of coal for the Navajo Nation. Its fifty-year promise comes to an end. What was gained? What was lost? In this chapter, I argue that coal created the modern Navajo Nation in response to development pressures from the State of Arizona and regional utilities. In the end, these colonial partners abandoned the Diné people. Here, the analysis will do the temporal bending, bridging coal's fifty-year story in the Navajo Nation with a five-hundred-year story of colonial occupation. The Diné economy was broken not by coal but by free-market capitalism. The political economy of Navajo coal was that of a "resource frontier" (Tsing 2005, 28), places of renewed transnational investment (and ecological destruction) because of "discovered" or renewed interest in the known raw commodities important to shifting global capitalism that is contained within. As Anna Tsing writes, "Frontiers aren't just discorvered at the edge, they are projects in making geographic and temporal experience" (2005, 28–29). The chapter subtitle comes from Marx, whose phrase *all that was solid has melted into air* captures the current mood of social change.

The Navajo Nation was made underdeveloped by its participation in colonial capitalism. By focusing on the Navajo coal economy, this book demonstrates the mechanism of capitalism through colonialism over the fifty-year period of 1969 to 2019. Colonialism was not a juggernaut. It was not Christopher Columbus, Kit Carson, Barry Goldwater, or Jon Kyl. Colonialism is a shape-shifter. It was an evil spirit that first killed and exiled Diné people from their lands, Hwéeldi, then moved Diné families once again to open up new lands for mining and ranching and give revenues to the Hopi Tribe (Navajo–Hopi land dispute). Colonialism then became (through water settlements and infrastructures tied to coal leases) the structural abandonment of Diné people. In sum, these chapters speak to the construction of carbon sovereignty, in both the Navajo Nation's embrace and its rejection of a coal economy—some doubling down on coal while others advocated for energy transition. These political struggles ultimately shaped how we should understand coal, capitalism, and climate change as issues of nuance and complexity where history and the contemporary intermingle, with lasting consequences, in everyday life.

FIGURE 2. Mother Earth and Father Sky depicting the way the world is understood in Diné traditional stories. Illustration from the Navajo Nation Code, Title 1, "The Foundational Laws of the Diné," 2002.

CHAPTER 1

SHAPE-SHIFTING COLONIALISM AND THE ORIGIN OF CARBON SOVEREIGNTY

MOVEMENT WAS FUNDAMENTAL to Diné history. It defines the people. Figure 2 represents the boundaries of the Diné people as is understood in Diné cosmology. According to Diné oral history, the Diné people emerged into the modern, "glittering" world after traveling through four previous worlds. The Diné word for human, *bíla' ashdla'ii*, refers to "the five-fingered earth-surface-people" who walk horizontally across the earth. In the production of Diné space, there was both horizontal and vertical movement. The vertical movement happened when Diné people moved from one epoch to the next. When moving between worlds, Diné ancestors climbed to the surface of the earth from worlds below.

For Diné people, the images shown here represent two competing conceptualizations of space. They are found or defined within the Navajo Nation Code, the governing laws of the tribe. Today, both images are official representations of Diné space. Yet the story of each image implies a different ideology of governance at work, with contrasting senses of time, place, and purpose. Figure 3 is an illustration in the code found within the section called "The Foundational Laws of the Diné," a 2002 addition to the Navajo Nation Code. This section of the code attempts to decolonize the tribe's government, tacitly acknowledging that many of the code's original laws were colonial in origin (more on this later).

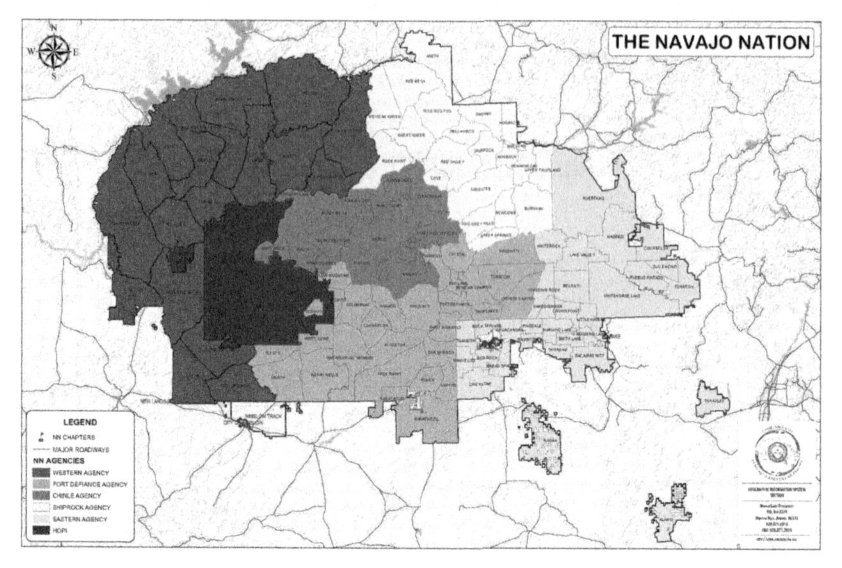

FIGURE 3. Navajo Nation chapter house boundaries. Map by Navajo Nation Land Department.

In this chapter, I account for the construction of the Diné nation as an extractive space in anticipation of carbon sovereignty. This is a new phase in the history of the people, one in which things that came from within the earth defined life on it. This world was not "natural" in any familiar sense of the word. It was built. It was a world constructed to fit within colonial law and notions of progress and development. Colonial pressures defined internal and external practices, hardening borders between "reservation" and settlement. It is important to emphasize that this construction was largely accomplished through violence. After the U.S. Army hunted and killed Diné men, women, and children in the 1860s, the military interned survivors at a place called Hwéeldi for five years. Many of us refer to Hwéeldi as a place shaped by a series of events in the near distant past. But the original violence of Hwéeldi never ended. In this way, it is an event that structures Diné political possibility. This is a sociological use of the term *Hwéeldi*, to think about it as the basis of colonial "legitimacy" and control.

We will proceed to understand the spatial construction of Hwéeldi first by defining the traditional boundaries of Diné Bikéyah through the mountains that surround the Navajo Nation while accounting for the violence used to enforce these boundaries.

Border towns engender relationships between captured nations and parasitic communities. Border towns are white settlements built on the edges of reservations that both punish and prey upon Indigenous people, lands, and resources. These settlements, which have now become urban centers, act as leeches on Diné life. They are the nodes of a predatory network of capital accumulation that consumes the people and wealth of Diné Bikéyah. Once border towns were established, the internal drive to develop and expand extractive industries emerged. The BIA paternalistically partnered with outside industries on the tribe's behalf to bring gendered versions of wage work onto the reservation. The construction of extractive spaces in the Navajo Nation started as violent border making and displacement between reservation and settlement spaces but later moved toward the incorporation of these spaces into regional economies. For colonial officials, this move was premised on the anticommunist ideology of "development" as coined and implemented after 1947, when modernity began.

FIRST FOUR WORLDS

In the first four worlds of the Diné origin story, Diné people encountered many difficult challenges and dangers such as malicious insects and supernatural monsters. Diné people moved vertically through a small opening in each of these worlds on a ladder, and they had to keep moving upward to escape the dangers from the world below. In these stores, Diné people understand place as both horizontal and vertical. Often traditional Diné prayers ends with the refrain "May it be beautiful and peaceful above me, below me, in front of me, behind me, all around me. May I walk in beauty and peace this way." It is this prayer that sets both the space and ideological understanding of Diné place making, as containing both vertical and horizontal movement, projecting hózhó into the future and the past.

Diné people emerged into the current world, the Glittering World, more recently. This became the fifth world. In this world, the Holy People instructed the Diné on how to live within the geophysical boundaries known as Diné Bikéyah, boundaries defined by the Four Sacred Mountains (figure 3) on the edges of the sphere. The fifth mountain, in the center, represents Navajo Mountain and Black Mesa, two of the remotest regions of the Navajo Nation that are also sites of spiritual and historical significance. Black Mesa is also the center of the Navajo coal economy.

The western boundary of Diné Bikéyah is the Sacred Mountain Dook'o'oosłííd.[1] The mountain is represented by abalone shell, which comes from the California coast. Abalone is an important material for Diné jewelers and is part of Diné origin stories. The presence of abalone in Diné cosmology demonstrates long-standing networks of international trade prior to Euro-American colonization. The hundreds of nations living on the continent traded with each other from one end to the next. Another globalization is not only possible but already existed between Indigenous nations in the Americas before European contact. As Roxanne Dunbar-Ortiz (2014) writes, corn moved from central Mexico all the way to the subarctic. However, for Euro-American colonialists today, the mountains of Dook'o'oosłííd are called the "San Francisco Peaks." At the base of this mountain is Flagstaff, Arizona. It was founded as a railroad depot in the 1880s and immediately became the center of a logging industry in northern Arizona. Euro-American settlers arrived to the region and looked for resources to exploit. The rich, lush northern Arizona pine became feed for logging mills.

The southern boundary of Diné Bikéyah according to Diné philosophy and teachings is the mountain Tsoodził. Tsoodził is a larger mountain than Dook'o'oosłííd. It was once a huge volcano that erupted millions of years ago. The charred, black rocks at the base of the mountain are remnants of this explosion. These rocks reach as far as Albuquerque, New Mexico—nearly seventy miles to the east. For Diné people, the mountain is represented by turquoise, another important stone. It is said that the Holy People cannot see Diné people unless they wear turquoise. Today, silver and turquoise define the aesthetic of southwestern jewelry. At the base of Tsoodził is Grants, New Mexico. Grants was also a rail depot, named after land speculators, the first white Americans to claim the area. The permeance of rather recent names like "Grants" and "Flagstaff" and the erasure of older, Indigenous place-names is part of the contemporary colonial experience. Grants was also once the center of the uranium boom in the 1950s and 1960s (Voyles 2015).

Forming the eastern boundary for Diné people is the mountain Sisnaajíní. Sisnaajíní is represented by white shell. The mountain is in southern Colorado and is today closer to two Ute reservations than the eastern edges of the Navajo Reservation. The northern boundary of Diné Bikéyah is Dibé Nitsaa. The black jet stone represents Dibé Nitsaa to Diné people. Dibé Nitsaa, in what is today southwest Colorado, is located between the border towns of Cortez and Durango.

Sisnaajíní and Dibé Nitsaa represent the traditional boundaries of the Diné people, yet the Navajo Nation has no reservation lands in Colorado. Colorado denied Diné people reservation lands in the state, even though two of the Diné people's sacred mountains are in Colorado and form the northern and eastern boundaries for the nation. The mountain towns of Durango, Cortez, and Alamosa are all in the region. Not only do these communities benefit from the violent theft of Indigenous lands, but much of this region is dedicated to industrial-scale agriculture and ranching. White farmers and ranchers use water from the Colorado River and its tributaries to flood their fields, waters denied to the Navajo Nation.

CONSTRUCTING A CAPITAL CITY: MODERNIZATION, DEVELOPMENT, AND COLONIAL TIME

Shape-shifting colonialism is a contingent way to think about the settler-colonial process, to understand and amplify the trickery and obfuscation used in signing leases, settling water claims, or agreeing to resource contracts—modern forms of resource dispossession. It refers to the legal-judicial challenges to tribal sovereignty that try to reduce, contain, and weaken the inherent rights of Indigenous nations. The mural shown in figure 4 surrounds the interior of the Navajo Nation Council chambers and epitomizes the construction of a modernist and development-oriented ideology in the Navajo Nation. Painted by famed Diné artist Gerald Nailor Sr. over a period of fifteen months in 1942 and 1943, *The History and Progress of the Navajo People* was part of the federal government's New Deal initiative (McLerran 2012). The Navajo Nation council chambers in Window Rock was built to reflect white notions of modernity. The entire tribal headquarters was also constructed during this time and became the central site of governance for the largest Indigenous nation in the United States.

It was the only attempt by the Bureau of Indian Affairs to build a capital city within an "Indian" reservation (Leibowitz 2008). Relics of the New Deal, such as the mural, are found throughout Window Rock. They symbolize an ideology under formation. This ideology was characterized by federal policies: the Indian Reorganization Act of 1934, the Indian Mineral Leasing Act of 1938, the Indian Self-Determination and Educational Assistance Act of 1975, the Indian Mineral Development Act of 1982, and the Indian Energy Development and Self-Determination Act of 2015. This ideology is the shape-shifting colonizing

FIGURE 4. Gerald Nailor Sr., *The History and Progress of the Navajo People*, mural in Navajo Nation Council chambers, Window Rock, Arizona, 1943.

ethos. It is *shape-shifting colonialism*. Colonialism no longer took the form of blue-coated soldiers but of legal documents and courtroom motions.

The mural in the council chambers highlights central features of the modernist narrative operating in the Navajo Reservation at the time. The mural depicts time working in a linear direction. It begins with Diné people precontact near the entrance of the chambers. Then it depicts phases of colonization, from the Spanish to Mexican to American periods. The signing of the Treaty of 1868 is featured prominently. In the chronology of the mural, Diné people are featured going to school, building infrastructure for livestock, and working monoculture fields of corn. The mural established notions of the past and projections about the future. The children in the center of the mural wear modern clothes and represent the end point of a colonial-civilizing telos. Yet they are already past, looking like schoolchildren of the 1930s and not children today.

Colonialism started at the intimate level, that is, the nuclear family. Modernity was built on the attempted destruction of Indigenous social, cultural, and political institutions. Children were removed from homes, forced to forget the

Diné language and beliefs. Instead, in boarding schools Diné children were compelled to learn and recite "the pledge of allegiance" in English. The mural depicts a mythology of progress. At the end point of the civilizing process is education—the liberal, democratic ideal in a modernist narrative that becomes the justification for violently suppressing traditional institutions.

The anxiety created by state violence is supposedly resolved through assimilation and forced education by the end of the mural. This is a civilizing narrative, one that says white settlers brought Diné people gifts of modernization. It says white settlers brought the railroad, modern animal husbandry, monoculture, agriculture, gendered division of labor, and education. Coal mining in the Navajo Nation represents a part of this larger modernizing project in the Navajo Nation. Coal mining demonstrates the form and shape of this manifestation of colonialism.

BORDER TOWNS AND CAPITAL INCORPORATION

The racial regime of the United States arrived in Diné country via the expansion of railroads (Karuka 2019). The railroads fundamentally changed Diné life forever. Although the Spanish and Mexicans were genocidal, they never managed to fully control Diné people or lands (Curley 2014). It was U.S. colonization that became the origin of modernization in the Navajo Nation. U.S. colonialism was the beginning of a new timeline, a particular epoch in Diné history. It was the beginning of another world. The Hwéeldi moment initiates the modernization and development project in the Navajo Nation. It was the starting point for the timeline represented in the mural shown in part in figure 4.

Hwéeldi is the Diné word for the place of forced removal of Diné people from homelands to Fort Sumner. Temporally, it refers to violence from roughly 1864 to 1868. Our ancestors were allowed to return to Diné homelands following the Treaty of 1868. During those four years preceding the treaty, groups of mercenaries under the direction of U.S. general Kit Carson terrorized Diné people. These warlike bands of white colonists torched homes and fields, and killed Diné people who resisted. U.S. historians casually referred to this violence as "the Navajo roundup," as if Diné people were cattle on a range (Denetdale 2009; Kelly 1970). It is important to recognize that dehumanization of a people is a necessary element for a colonizer to carry out ethnic cleansing and genocide.

American capitalism followed a different trajectory from that of Europe. Capitalism in the United States did not emerge out of the social and political institutions of feudalism. It was built on chattel slavery and Indigenous land dispossession, requiring racialization of stolen Africans and the continent's Indigenous nations. Cedric Robinson calls this version of capitalism "racial capitalism"—a practice and process of exploitation (fundamental to Marx's argument) that consume brown and Black bodies and places for the benefit of a white majority. His phrasing helps us understand how racism was necessary for colonial exploitation and land theft (Robinson 1983). Much like how the "bloody legislation" of England's Parliament targeted rural peasants while enclosing "the commons," in the United States white supremacy targeted peoples seen as nonwhite and forced them into the lowest rungs of wage labor.

When the United States entered the Indigenous Southwest and replaced Mexico's colonialism, the U.S. Army branded Diné and Apache peoples as unconquered and ungoverned peoples, and therefore targets for colonial violence and conquest. Between 1848 and 1864, the troops garrisoned in the area made casual forays into Diné lands. Following the brief conflict between Confederate and Union soldiers in New Mexico (1862–63), however, Union victors turned their attention toward Diné and Apache peoples. The war machine was in motion. As some historians are writing today, the so-called Indian Wars and the Civil War were entwined (Kelman 2013; Nelson 2020). In New Mexico territory, the expulsion of the Confederates and the violence directed toward Indigenous groups were part of the same constellation of actions. Between 1864 and 1868, the U.S. Army sacked Diné peoples' homes, burned fields of corn and squash, killed sheep, and murdered men and women. Each violent campaign into Diné land brought more prisoners. The U.S. Army forced more than eight thousand Diné men, women, and children to walk more than three hundred miles, from their homes to a small dusty compound in eastern New Mexico called Bosque Redondo.

At Bosque Redondo, the military tried to force Diné people into sedentary agriculture. The military provided seeds, bags of flour, and other rations and expected Diné people to grow their own food in alkaline soil and with second-rate rations. Private contractors overcharged the military for shoddy provisions (Iverson 2002). In 1868 U.S. general William Sherman visited Bosque Redondo and said the camp was a waste of money—never mind genocide. He wanted it closed. Sherman recommended to President Ulysses S. Grant that Diné people should be moved to "Indian Territory," now Oklahoma. Diné leaders pleaded to return to their original homelands in Diné Bikéyah. Sherman agreed, and today he is a celebrated figure in Diné history. One can find a depiction of Sherman negotiating with Diné headmen in the mural Gerald Nailor Sr. painted in the council chambers. It is the beginning of the modernization timeline.

In order to return home, however, Diné leaders were forced to sign a treaty with the United States. The politics of this leadership were not well understood. Diné people did not choose leaders like "chiefs"—a common political stereotype given to Indigenous peoples. Naat'áaniis, or "leaders" (lit. "the one who orates/makes a speech"), were people selected to advise the direction of the people during a particular crisis (Wilkins 2013). These were organic speakers with no real power to force their will on the people and without a clear, marked constituency—very different from today's political systems. The Diné headmen who signed the Treaty of 1868 were selected by the U.S. Army. As far as we know, Diné people did not select these men to sign final peace terms between the people and the United States. All the signers of the Treaty of 1868 were men, despite the long tradition of woman and gender nonconforming leaders in Diné history (Denetdale 2007; Thomas 1997). The U.S. Army, conducting the negotiation, only recognized male leadership. The patriarchal tone of the treaty, including the immediate disenfranchisement of Diné women, is evidence that the document was a peace accord and attempted social engineering. Although the social engineering would take decades to accomplish, it articulated a blueprint for what was to come. As the Ojibwe scholar Scott Richard Lyons writes, "treaties compelled Indians to change how they lived" (2010, 2). Treaties between "tribes" and the federal government were always unequal and served colonial interests (Prucha 1994).

The original 1868 reservation boundaries differed considerably from the imagined homelands of Diné cosmology. The space the U.S. Army made into a reservation was absolute, with hard borders. This reservation did not match Diné understandings of space or place. It did not include any of the Diné sacred landmarks. On a map, the reservation was an oddly placed rectangle on the edges of what was then the Arizona and New Mexico territories. The lands were also tied to a centralized political authority, the headman system that the U.S. government worked hard to legitimize. These changes were outlined in the treaty's articles. This was the first form of territorialization of Diné lands that was made consistent with white notions of territory. As Stuart Elden (2013) writes, "territory" is a concept linked not simply to land and terrain but to techniques of governance, including notions of jurisdiction. The Treaty of 1868 was both a state formation and a boundary making that replaced aboriginal jurisdiction over the land. Shiri Pasternak (2017) describes a similar process for the

First Nations communities in Ontario, Canada. In Pasternak's study, the idea of "jurisdiction" is central to political contestation between the two nations. It is a question of land and especially the jurisdictions over these lands. Territory was and is a Western imposition on Indigenous spatial practices. After Diné leaders signed the treaty in 1868, Congress quickly ratified it and created the "Navaho Indian Reservation." Diné scholar Melanie K. Yazzie (2018) argues that colonialism and notions of progress were built on "biopolitical death drives" toward development, one defined by a colonial shape-shifter and Wiindigo economy (LaDuke and Cowen 2020).

Techniques of exclusion that are today essential to modern statecraft had little to no documentation in Indigenous oral histories. The right of the state to exclude others as a function of territorialization is a historically recent experience for Indigenous peoples. Diné people, even when retaining aboriginal jurisdiction, enjoyed overlapping control of space. This is not to suggest all nations lived harmoniously with each other. Diné people had neighbors who might attack, steal, or kill. There are locations in the reservation such as the community of "Steamboat," with the place-name "hoyéé," meaning "place of fear." In a casual conversation I had with a chapter manager in 2008, that person gave me this translation and said it referred to water springs that Ute warriors would hide near and ambush Diné. This was deep in the heart of what is now the Navajo Nation and is indicative of overlapping movements of people and nations.

Ute, Diné, Pueblo, Piute, Apache, Hopi, and Zuni all had interlocking and overlapping land practices in Diné Bikéyah (see map 2). Modern tribal governance blends old and new understandings of space and governance into new institutions. In some instances, exclusionary politics are exercised, but in practice tribal governments maintain little right to exclude outsiders. There are no hard boundaries at reservation lines, and even non-Indigenous criminal offenders are largely excepted from tribal jurisdiction. Today, Piute people live in the Navajo Nation on the western end of the reservation and use Diné tribal services. Diné and Hopi people share roads. Ute and Diné people maintain overlapping sacred sites. What is more, there are intermarriages between tribal nations that blend Indigenous national identities and combine and expand one's kinship spaces. Someone might be half Diné and half Lakota and have land relationships with both places in different ways. These intermarriages defy colonial and anthropological categories of "tribe" and "race" and hint to very different understandings of space.

It was after the Treaty of 1868 that Euro-American concepts of race became an important factor in reservation life. The Treaty of 1868 was a spatial and political imposition on the Diné people. Yet federal Indian policy transformed the language of the treaty into a biopolitical meaning. Treaty "rights" delineated political systems based on geography. The treaty mentioned nothing about tribal membership, just places of tribal authority. In other words, the treaty specified *where* Navajo could happen but not *who* was Navajo. There was an implied geopolitical definition of Diné political authority. The members of the tribe who lived within the reservation were subject to the terms of the treaty. Diné people living outside the reservation were bound by *U.S.* law. A membership criterion was absent from the treaty document. During the reservation period, Diné people pushed against these boundaries. They returned to their former homesites—wrecked by the U.S. Army—that were no longer recognized as Diné territory. Yet the state governments did not consider Indigenous peoples as U.S. citizens. Citizenship was reserved for white people. Indigenous peoples were defined externally as noncitizens by territorial governments before internal definitions of membership were practiced and institutionalized by tribal governments.

Indigenous peoples and their lands, incorporated into an expanding United States, became subject to brutal policies that placed tribes at the bottom of a racial hierarchy. The entwining of biological notions of heritage, race, and tribal identity became a cornerstone of federal Indian policy. The Navajo Nation lawyer Paul Spruhan (2006) argues that "blood," "as a metaphor" for Indigenousness, draws on traditions of inheritance long practiced within English common law. It was not until the passage of the Indian Reorganization Act of 1934 that blood quantum as a means of tribal membership was concretized for many Indigenous nations (Spruhan 2006). At the same time, the United States long used biological notions of race as a form of citizen making. As America was an empire built on Indigenous land dispossession and slavery (Goldstein 2014), race became a powerful operating concept when employed for wealth accumulation and westward expansion. As the historian Nancy Shoemaker (2006, 129) documents, it was during the eighteenth century that race became a governing logic based on perceptions of physical difference within the English colonies. Indigenous peoples were marked by their perceived difference in physical appearance, cultural beliefs, and language (Perdue 2005). Racialization was important for the expansion of slavery. Even among white people, notions of "good breeding," "stock," and other livestock metaphors were common to distinguish between classes. Social Darwinism, racism, classism, and patriarchy were the central ingredients for white supremacy ideology that served as a basis for U.S. state formation from the eighteenth to the twentieth century (Isenberg 2017). However, the front lines of racialization were not the intellectual architects of it but often the people who had only recently become white, such as the Irish and the Italians (Ignatiev 2009). Alongside the Chinese, new white people worked the railroads crossing the continent.

In an effort to fulfill treaty agreements, the federal government hired "Indian agents" to staff regional bureaus around reservations. On July 4, 1884, Congress passed appropriations for tribes that required Indian agents to record the number of adult males over eighteen, girls over fourteen years of age, the number of schoolchildren between six and sixteen, and the number of schoolhouses on reservations. Although the intent was to enforce schooling and assimilation, these Indian agent reports were foundational for the creation of tribal memberships based on "degrees of Indian blood." Afterward, the U.S. government created instruments for taking censuses across reservation communities, to document who was or was not "Indian," and assign them a blood quantum. The Dawes Commission, established in 1898 to divide Indian land among tribal members and sell what was deemed "surplus" to non-Indians, is perhaps the first U.S. entity to systematically racialize Indigenous peoples (Debo 1973).

The increased use of census rolls and notions of "blood" and inheritance to define Indigenousness transformed the U.S. relationship with the continent's Indigenous peoples. Expulsion and displacement (spatial forms of repression) formed the backbone of U.S. imperial expansion and ethnic cleansing campaigns during the nineteenth century. The federal government established the reservation system under the War Department in 1847 to move Indigenous nations such as the Cherokee away from white settlement. The goal was to maintain distance between the settler population and the settled. Until 1871, the United States signed treaty agreements with Indigenous nations that carved out competing jurisdictional domains. It was implied that the governing laws of the Indigenous nations would apply within reservation lands. The laws of the territories, states, and the United States would operate outside the reservation boundaries. As mentioned previously, this was a territorialization of Indigenous spaces.

In 1867, while some in the Grant administration openly discussed ethnic cleansing and genocide of Indigenous peoples, the administration ultimately pursued a "civilization" and Christianization approach among remaining tribes. Congress created the Indian Peace Commission to enter into treaty agreements with many western tribes directly in the pathway of railroad expansion (Oman 2002). Grant appointed General Sherman, who signed the Treaty of 1868 with the Navajo people at Bosque Redondo. The Indian Peace Commission created boilerplate treaties that it used in negotiation with the Kiowa, Comanche, Kiowa-Apache, Northern and Southern Cheyenne and Arapaho, Crow, Diné, Eastern Shoshone and Bannock, and the Brulé, Oglala, Miniconjou, Yanktonai, Hunkpapa, Blackfeet, Cuthead, Two Kettle, Sans Arc, and Santee bands of Lakota Sioux (Oman 2002, 35). Many of these treaties included a "Bad Man" provision that ultimately resulted in competing spatial jurisdictions over criminal offenses. The "Bad Man" clause is indicative of spatial understandings of Dinéness at the time. It required Diné leadership to turn over to U.S. or state officials any "bad man" who had committed an offense outside the reservation. The same was true in the other direction. If the Diné found evidence of a wrongdoing against them, they could present evidence to law enforcement and extradite the offending party to the reservation for judicial process. Soon, as the result of powerful federal policies, this spatial understanding would be transformed into a biopolitical one, in which jurisdiction was tied to notions of race, not territory.

The 1884 requirement to start counting reservation populations, the 1885 Major Crimes Act, the 1887 Dawes Allotment Act and subsequent Dawes Commission, and the 1934 Indian Reorganization Act all transformed "Indianness" into an inherited, biopolitical identity. The Nazis would use similar techniques in their own campaigns of ethnic cleansing and genocide with the passage of race laws in the 1930s (Neumann 2009). Raul Hilberg's study on the Holocaust demonstrates the bureaucratic muckiness and sometimes arbitrariness of Nazi antisemitic laws and policies. Being Jewish under Nazi occupation was eventually linked to enrollment records (such as seized membership lists from a synagogue) and one's relation, both near and distant, to someone on that list (Hilberg 2003). Nazi racial law used broad strokes to classify Jewish people and sometimes came dangerously close to implicating core Nazi leadership as lacking sufficient Aryan heritage.

With U.S. colonization, the Southwest changed. Following the conclusion of the Mexican-American War in 1848, settlers from the United States moved into the region and transformed its landscape, governance, and economic practices to conform with Anglo-American norms, including land tenure laws, notions of water rights, and industrial exploitation of natural resources. To this day, the original streets of Albuquerque, where many white settlers moved, bear the names "Gold," "Lead," "Coal," and "Silver," after the resources they hoped to find in the region. Most Diné people lived in what was called "New Mexico Territory," which included the current states of New Mexico and Arizona. In the mid-nineteenth century, rail was a lucrative and corrupt industry. It was not long after the conclusion of the Mexican-American War that railroad companies started laying tracks from St. Louis to California. Today, the Burlington Northern Santa Fe (BNSF) Railway, part of the largest network of railroads in the country, runs along the southern boundary of the Navajo Nation. The U.S. Congress originally chartered the railway in 1859, nine years before Sherman outlined it in the 1868 treaty with its first clause dealing with the rights of railroads (Grant 2022; Montoya, forthcoming).

The Treaty of 1868 introduced the settler-colonial power difference. The United States practiced (and continues to practice) absolutism over Indigenous spaces. These early reservation years (1868–1922) were profoundly transformative. They established the social conditions from which reservation spatial practices would later emerge (Curley 2014). The centralization of land and leadership, against the backdrop of violence and removal, ushered in unshakeable senses of anxiety. The Office of Indian Affairs opened agency bureaus around the Navajo Reservation. Eastern missionaries were encouraged to Christianize Diné people, starting with children in boarding schools (King 2016; Woolford 2015). The trauma of the reservation was the U.S. alternative to genocide. White settlers could only tolerate Indigenous peoples as a benighted Native in need of "saving." Independent nations with long-standing political and cultural traditions threatened white hegemony over the continent. Especially in the early reservation years, the federal government surveilled and interfered with social and political life in the reservation. This sixty-year period from 1868 to 1938 was fraught with increasing poverty, racial harassment, and the displacement and murder of Indigenous peoples at the hands of white cowboys (Kelley and Francis 2019).

After Bosque Redondo, Diné people returned to their homelands, where they rebuilt animal herds and planted fields (Denetdale 2009). As Diné sheep and horse herds expanded, so too did the reservation boundaries. Over the next sixty years, subsequent U.S. presidents added more and more lands to the original reservation boundaries through the legal mechanism of "executive order." That expansion was arrested, however, in 1934 when Congress failed to pass legislation that would have consolidated "checkerboard lands" on the eastern half of the Navajo Reservation into contiguous reservation land. In the 1930s, John Collier, President Franklin D. Roosevelt's Commissioner of Indian Affairs, pushed hard to consolidate Diné reservation lands on the eastern end of the reservation. Had the effort succeeded, the Navajo Nation would have had one consolidated land base. But New Mexico politicians blocked this. The failure of this effort was due to New Mexico's strong opposition to Diné people in the state. New Mexico's white political elite did not want Diné people to gain territorial claims within the state. The state lobbied against land consolidation in Congress and won. To this day, the eastern half of the reservation remains fragmented, a shatter zone of colonial policies. This area is still referred to as the "checkerboard" because of the patchwork pattern of private and Indian trust lands as it appears on a map (Grant 2022).

In 1934 the Indian Reorganization Act (IRA) institutionalized blood quantum as a basis for tribal membership for many Indigenous nations. The act accomplished this by requiring tribes to adopt "constitutions" in which membership was defined by degree of lineal descent from an Indian on a census roll (Ellinghaus 2017; TallBear 2013). The Navajo Tribe rejected the IRA constitution in 1934 and did not ratify a constitution. Membership for the tribe wasn't formalized until 1953 when the Gallup Indian Agent and the tribe's white attorney persuaded tribal lawmakers to pass a council resolution recognizing one-quarter lineal decent from a 1940 base census roll as the only criterion for tribal membership (Spruhan 2007).

When the Navajo Nation Council debated tribal membership in 1953, many council delegates were confused about what membership was. Some delegates believed that membership was a spatial definition, not a racial one. They believed tribal membership was contingent on living within the reservation as was spelled out in the Treaty of 1868. This spatial understanding of membership was consistent with notions of citizenship in the modern, "territorial" United States. In a letter to the Commissioner of Indian Affairs, however, the regional Indian agent recommended against spatial definitions for membership (Spruhan 2007).

The commissioner observed that many Diné lived outside the reservation for employment reasons. It might not be the best idea for the Navajo Nation to disenroll these members because they had to find work outside the reservation. Council Delegate Manuelito Begaye asked the council to consider a kinship basis for membership (Spruhan 2007, 7). Familial relationships are still the basis of Diné identity throughout Diné Bikéyah and even in the Navajo Diaspora. In public as well as private settings, many Diné people still introduce themselves with the clans to which they belong, thereby invoking an identity that supersedes notions of "blood quantum" in Diné political and cultural life.

The consequence of this racialization is still felt. Tribal membership remains tied to notions of blood, race, and heritage. All tribal people today must prove direct lineage to people who appeared on a government survey, such as the Dawes Rolls that were used from the eighteenth century until 1934. Criteria such as one-half or one-quarter lineal descent were required to be considered Indigenous in the United States. These policies were inherently divisive and still cause problems today.

Most histories of the Navajo point to the federal policy of livestock reduction, nearly seventy years after Bosque Redondo, as the point when Navajo subsistence economies were destroyed and Navajo people were made “dependent” on capitalism for survival. In Marx’s understanding of primitive accumulation, the process of socioeconomic transformation is not so neat and clean that it can be pegged to one specific range of dates or set of policies like livestock reduction. Rather, it is a culmination of policies, enforced by colonial laws, that over time works to make subsistence life impossible and forces the region’s Indigenous peoples into capitalist relations and participation—at which point the maintenance of Indigenous life becomes difficult. In the next section, I discuss the origin of carbon sovereignty, the beginning of a fossil fuel regime in the Navajo Reservation that moved efforts toward modernization and development in a specific direction. The federal government in concert with tribal officials established the legal and political infrastructure needed to extract subterranean wealth and put it into capitalist circulation.

OIL AND THE ORIGIN OF CARBON SOVEREIGNTY

For the first half of the twentieth century, the United States was at the center of the world’s most lucrative resource. Much of the oil boom happened in the western states, particularly Texas and Oklahoma, what had only recently been “Indian Territory.” The Osage in Oklahoma were the first tribe to fall victim to the cruelty of oil entrepreneurs (Fixico 2012). The federal government built the refugee Osage Nation on an identity based on census rolls, land allotments, and mineral rights. This was a biological, political, and material sense of being. Oil found within Osage land was bound to the bodies of Osage people (Dennison 2012). What happened next was a vicious cycle of murder and subterfuge and increased policing throughout Indigenous lands as white settlers sought to steal Osage land and resources (Strickland 1995).

Popular books like *Killers of the Flower Moon* by David Grann (2017) have sensationalized the murders and highlighted that the killings served as an important impetus for the creation of the Federal Bureau of Investigation. Grann leaves us with the impression that the federal government solved the problem of the murders and created a national institution that benefits the United States. For many Indigenous peoples, the creation of the FBI was not an extension of justice but another form of corrosive control and intrusion into tribal sovereignty. Oil initiated the violence, but the FBI did not solve it. Today, Indigenous women bear much of this violence (Anderson, Campbell, and Belcourt 2018). Poor, vulnerable, or exploited women are channeled into "man camps" burgeoning around oil drills, and many do not return. The status of these women remains uncertain. Prairie and Plains Indigenous communities are particularly impacted, but the problem follows oil rigs and construction crews (Dorries et al. 2019) across the country. In the Navajo Nation, oil, gas, and fracking are old industries that ushered in cultural political change and gender violence (Denetdale 2006; McPherson and Wolff 1997).

Oil was found near the Diné community of Shiprock in 1922 (Chamberlain 2000). Prospecting for oil became a lucrative business. President Warren G. Harding appointed New Mexico senator Albert Fall as secretary of the interior. Fall was corrupt and took bribes from oil companies. He worked to open the Navajo Reservation for oil prospecting. The Treaty of 1868 required that three-fourths of the male population had to consent to any land leasing by outside interests. This was a provision that Grant's peace commission almost always included. This vague, patriarchal form of democracy was not workable for oil contracting. The Office of Indian Affairs and local Indian Agency offices worked to grant title to Diné people living in New Mexico on so-called public domain land but beyond the 1868 treaty boundaries. Federal policy at the time favored assimilation. The General Allotment Act of 1887, the Major Crimes Act of 1885, the Dawes Commission of 1895, and the Mineral Leasing Act of 1920 were all policies bent on the assimilation of Indigenous peoples into a mainstream American society. Key to this goal was the alienation of Indigenous lands from their collective holding by Indigenous nations (Kelly 1963).

Initially, Secretary Fall treated parts of the Navajo Reservation that were not originally defined in the 1868 treaty as "public domain" lands that fell outside of the provisions of the 1868 treaty. But Fall resigned when news of the Teapot Dome scandal loomed. He was caught receiving kickbacks from oil speculators for no-bid contracts on public lands. After Fall resigned, the Office of Indian

Affairs treated executive order lands and treaty lands legally and politically as the same thing. The tribal jurisdiction over mineral leasing that now extended over all reservation lands revealed the need for a governing body for the Diné people. The Department of the Interior organized the tribe's first "business council" in 1922 for the purpose of agreeing to lease contracts between the Navajo Tribe and outside companies and corporations (Kelly 1968).

Often, those who interpret the tribal government as an instrument of colonialism conflate the 1920s and 1930s councils. The early council was a product of oil boom in the region and the corruption that went into Teapot Dome scandal. Questions of governance weren't important for the federal officials setting up this government. They simply wanted any kind of political body that could sign leases on behalf of the entire tribe. But after 1927, oil prices collapsed and bids on oil in the reservation declined. It was not until the 1950s that oil really took off across the reservation. Between the early 1920s and 1950s, a reworking of American capitalism and U.S.–Indian relations required questions of governance and development to reflect the New Deal and the early welfare state.

The origin of modern tribal economies in Native North America is arguably found in the 1928 Merriam Report commissioned by the Department of the Interior. The report, by the Brookings Institution, confirmed what many already knew at the time about reservations. The authors and researchers found that U.S. assimilationist efforts had failed and had only further impoverished tribes (Deloria 1985). With the fall of the U.S. economy in 1929 and the Democratic Party's strong win during the 1932 election, the federal government changed its approach toward public spending and relief efforts. New Deal policies guaranteed work and galvanized investment in rural infrastructure development. This change in the political landscape also impacted federal Indian policy. Roosevelt appointed New Deal Democrat Harold L. Ickes as secretary of the interior. Ickes believed in the reform of Indian policy. The Merriam Report provided the impetus for a dramatic overhaul of federal–Indian relations by the time of the New Deal in the early 1930s (Kelly 1968, 138).

Ickes brought in reformer John Collier for the important role of Commissioner of Indian Affairs. Collier worked to reverse decades of assimilation policies rooted in the General Allotment Act of 1887. He believed it was important for Indigenous nations to maintain the collective space of the reservation for modernization and development. Through Collier's efforts, Congress passed the most important federal Indian reform of its time, the Indian Reorganization Act of 1934 (Deloria 1985). The cornerstone for notions of the Navajo

Reservation, the Navajo Tribe, and the Navajo Nation is the Indian Reorganization Act.

Importantly, the Rural Electrification Act of 1935 largely bypassed reservations, leaving the project of infrastructure development to the underfunded Office of Indian Affairs. In the Navajo Nation, Collier focused on creating industrial centers, cities and towns, where Diné people could work. Window Rock was one such industrial center with permanent buildings and even a small power-generating station located at the capital (Glaser 2002).

The Indian Reorganization Act of 1934 changed the nature of tribal governance. It was probably the greatest advancement for Indigenous people in realizing anything that looked like "sovereignty." The IRA was the first and most significant exception to a century's worth of debilitating and controlling legislations and Supreme Court rulings. As the legal writer Stephen L. Pevar (2012, 10) writes, the act was meant "to rehabilitate the Indian's economic life and to give him a chance to develop the initiative destroyed by a century of oppression and paternalism."

An ideology of progress and development was an inherent part of these reforms. On one end of colonial law, assimilationists believed Indigenous peoples were premodern and needed to learn Western liberal values of democratic rule and capitalist industriousness, and also to adopt nuclear family structures. On the other end, cultural preservationists like Collier wanted modernization and preservation at the same time. They exoticized, essentialized, and misread social change among Indigenous peoples. They considered "culture" to mean "difference," which rendered Indigenous practices inconsistent with Euromerican beliefs.

This was also a time of profound racism in the United States. During the 1930s, fascist parties across the globe took over governments with weak institutions and failing economies. These parties broadcast racist agendas and implemented genocidal policies, some of which were inspired by U.S. "Indian Wars" and the reservation system. With the passage of the Indian Reorganization Act in 1934, tribes like the Navajo Nation were encouraged to participate in wage-labor regimes, first through the Civilian Corps, then through military participation in World War II, and finally through the construction of railroads and highways up to and through Indigenous lands (Hosmer, O'Neill, and Fixico 2004). For U.S. colonialists, the solution to the "Indian Problem" was to transform reservation spaces into sites of work, development, and modernization. Extreme poverty was already a trope in the lexicon of federal Indian discourse.

It was used as a tool to justify unjust interventions. But it also placed tribes in a linear narrative of progress.

The tribal government was the legal infrastructure within Diné territory necessary for the expansion of Western capitalism into the region beyond just mineral leases. In 1922 oil developers realized that there was a lack of applicable laws in the Navajo Reservation for oil leasing. Developers needed something to legitimize and protect their property and investments. The greater meaning of the tribal government was not how it facilitated access to minerals but how the government consolidated jurisdictions and governance under a *single political infrastructure*. The Indian Reorganization Act reflected Collier's social reform agenda. It changed the federal government's relationship with Indigenous nations across the United States. The IRA empowered modern "councils" as the governing organization of reservations, and by so doing ignored individual treaties between the U.S. federal government and Indigenous nations.

During the 1930s and 1940s, government soil scientists blamed the Diné and their abundant livestock for desertification and erosion in the Colorado Plateau. The anthropologist Clyde Kluckhohn, who wrote the definitive work *The Navaho* in the 1940s with Dorothea Leighton, using an anglicized *h* instead of the conventional *j*, was also a strong proponent of livestock reduction and government programs designed to change Diné life. In the preface to a 1951 book of photographs by Leonard McCombe, Kluckhohn and the anthropologist Evon Z. Vogt jointly wrote: "It is perhaps true that the difficulties of adjustment to the White man's world are overemphasized at the expense of satisfactions remaining from the aboriginal culture and the genuine rewards brought to the Navaho from our modern world. Nevertheless, the drama of the story at the moment is mainly that of clash, maladjustment, and this is what the pictures appropriately reflect" (McCombe, Vogt, and Kluckholm 1951, n.p.). In this assessment, Kluckhohn and Vogt refer to a preexisting "aboriginal culture" that is defined separately against "the White man's world" and implies one is gradually replaced by the other. This was a teleology foundational to early anthropology. It is also one of the reasons why the Navajo Nation Council specified that "Navajo" should be spelled with a *j* and not *h* in the Navajo Nation Code.

By placing blame squarely on the Navajos, the government ignored the cattle industry that surrounded the reservation and pushed Diné people into concentrated areas of grazing (Weisiger 2011). To "improve" the soil (a colonial motif), the federal government stole and murdered Diné sheep, often on site, compensating Diné people with money that did little good in the 1930s reservation economy. Agricultural specialists also developed a new breed of sheep at nearby Fort Wingate. The government intended to replace the Churro sheep (descended from sheep introduced by the Spanish colonialists) with sheep engineered at Fort Wingate that were designed to eat less grass and produce lighter wool. These new sheep served as biopolitical intrusions on Diné lifeways. Throughout the reservation, people protested this program, euphemistically called the Navajo Livestock Reduction. For Diné people impacted by it, livestock reduction was a violent assault on their lives and ways of life. The colonial destruction of Diné sheep herds was a traumatic assault on Diné people.

Some Diné people say, "Dibé éí iiná," or "Sheep is life." Today, there is a regular conference dedicated to the cultural maintenance of Diné sheepherding. Sheep remain central to Diné life, from familial relations to spiritual well-being. The killing of Diné sheep was immediately compared with the trauma of Hwéeldi. It was a continuation of the same violence, just in a different form. Each kind of violence was an attack on Diné ways of life. Hwéeldi simultaneously took Diné people away from the land and transformed them into agricultural homesteaders. The colonizer's aim was to make settlers out of the colonized. Hwéeldi did not end with the signing of the Treaty of 1868 but changed form and location. Diné people moved back to traditional homelands but under colonial conditions. In this way, the spatial overlap hides more than it reveals. Because Diné people returned to life between the Four Sacred Mountains, many believe that colonization was thwarted. Diné people were not exiled to Indian Territory like so many eastern Indigenous nations. The Diné people did return to their homeland. But Diné people still had to live within reservation boundaries and subject their children to colonial schooling. At the same time, the tribe had to give way to the railroad and cattle industry. Immediately after Hwéeldi, the needs of colonial expansion and capital accumulation defined and circumscribed the future of Dinéness.

Livestock reduction and the centralization of political power in Window Rock were related events. The Indian Reorganization Act that Congress passed required Collier to secure a majority vote from tribes. A referendum had to be held to support the creation of tribal councils as the governing authority within reservation spaces (G. Taylor 1980). Today, the Harvard Project on American Indian Economic Development refers to the resulting tribal constitutions as "boiler plate" constitutions. They were dreamed up in Washington, D.C., and did not reflect the particular values of the nations that adopted them (Jorgensen

2007). Many who voted in these referendums did not fully understand what they were endorsing. Regardless, Congress considered simple majority votes sufficient to permanently change the nature of political leadership in Indigenous nations. The Navajo Reservation was Collier's main prize. It was the largest reservation in size and population. He worked hard to secure the Navajo Nation's endorsement of the IRA. Diné people, however, recognized that policies of livestock reduction were directly tied to IRA reforms. In a referendum vote in 1934, Diné people rejected the law, thwarting Collier's goal.

Yet the rejection of IRA did not mean that Diné people would return to traditional forms of leadership. Federal policy needed centralized governments in reservation spaces. IRA acceptance or rejection impacted the details of the structure of governance, but it did not change the context of law. Even though Diné people rejected the IRA, they received an IRA government nonetheless. Collier had to organize something legible for the Department of the Interior to remain consistent with U.S. law, now defined by the IRA. To reconcile this need for a central government, Bureau of Indian Affairs officials identified seventy "traditional leaders" from throughout the reservation to create an alternative central government (Wilkins 2013). What they proposed is unknown, but Secretary of the Interior Ickes rejected it. Instead, he told Collier to organize these leaders into a tribal council, but one not based on a constitution, as was the case in IRA governments. These constitutional delegates simply became the new tribal council. It was this government and not the one created in 1922 that is the antecedent to the government currently in Window Rock (Curley 2014; Wilkins 2013). It was with this council that the secretary of the interior invested the tribe's "governing authority" under colonial law.

The historian Lawrence Kelly is arguably the most responsible for our interpretation of the Navajo Nation Council as a 1923 creation. In his 1963 article, "The Navaho Indians: Land and Oil," Kelly writes, "An important by-product of the discovery of oil was the creation of the Navaho Tribal Council" (16). Since then, historians and other scholars have built on Kelly's analysis. There is an obvious truth in the association between oil and government. However, there is much missed in this statement. The evolutionary dynamics of Diné society and governance over the forty years after 1923 are lost with a simple reading of "oil and government." In an indication of the limited scope of the "oil" reading, Kelly himself was careful to downplay the influence of oil on the Navajo Nation, arguing at the end of his article that the oil economy did not really take off in the reservation until the 1950s.

The creation of the Navajo Tribal Council ushered in a way of thinking that is today the way Diné people understand their government and political decision-making in the reservation. This governing system includes such features as democratic elections, a capitalistic economy, and an appeal to the rule of law. For oil developers, a governing authority was a requisite for development in the reservation. It is also one that has rendered tribal economies dependent on extractive industries (R. Dunbar-Ortiz 1979; Nies 2014; Reno 1981; Snipp 1988). The 1937 Navajo Nation Council confirmed an ontology of governance and resource management within reservation spaces. New governing powers vested in the tribal council incentivized a relationship with extractive industries that came to define the nature of Diné sovereignty. This was the birth of a notion of *carbon sovereignty*—a sovereignty defined by colonial violence and an enforced patriarchal governance.

PARTITION, TERMINATION, AND DEVELOPMENT

On the front page of the November 30, 1947, issue of the *Arizona Republic*, the banner headline read, "Palestine Partition Voted." The accompanying story described a United Nations resolution that passed 33–13 the previous day in support of a Soviet–American partition plan to break up Palestine and establish a Jewish country in the "Holy Land." The 1947 vote established the conditions of the Nakba (Arabic for "catastrophe") the following year—the violent creation of Israel in 1948. On that same front page of the *Arizona Republic*, the third headline down read, "State Group to Aid Navajo." The story described Arizonans organizing relief for the Navajo Reservation. The winter of 1947 was particularly harsh for the Diné people. Reports from white officials visiting the reservation described near-starvation conditions, although reports were widely exaggerated and full of racist stereotyping. Citizen relief groups organized pilots to airlift food supplies and winter clothing for starving Natives. The Diné airlift anticipated the Berlin airlift by nearly six months. Throughout November and December 1947, readers of the *Arizona Republic* were told of the desperate situation for Diné people in Window Rock, Monument Valley, and elsewhere in the Navajo and Hopi Reservations.

Although the partition of Palestine and relief efforts to the Navajo Reservation are treated as unrelated happenings, these events are linked in history. Both were foundational for the legal-political direction of U.S. foreign and

Indian policy during the Cold War era. The headlines and stories informed the American public about what was possible for European Jewish refugees, emerging Arab states, and Diné people at the time. The winter crisis of 1947 created the political conditions in the United States to make consequential reforms to federal Indian law and policy. In the fall of 1949, Congress passed the Navajo-Hopi Rehabilitation Act, ushering in millions of federal dollars for road development, water infrastructure, housing, and the relocation of Diné families from the Navajo Reservation into cities throughout the West.

At the same time, Congress terminated the federal government's relationship with more than one hundred tribes. The reordering of the world after World War II included partition, termination, and development across the globe. India and Palestine are the most well-known examples of partition, development, and colonizers retreating (Åsbrink 2017). On the Colorado Plateau, Diné lands were formally partitioned from Hopi places, creating unresolved divisions between the two peoples, which have been explained as an "ancient feud." This explanation created powerful myths about an intrinsic discord and dispute between the tribes, but it is important to understand that the modern arguments between the Hopi and Navajo peoples are contemporary and political.

This section of chapter 1 is called "Partition, Termination, and Development" because termination was the federal government's response to reservations. As the United States expanded its commitments abroad to "fight the spread of communism," Congress worked to extinguish tribes (a policy called "termination") under a similar justification. Colonial overseers conflated notions of primitivism, underdevelopment, and communism. While the implementation of termination was inconsistent, the federal government did set the tone for a heavily assimilationist era for tribes. Over the 1950s, the Bureau of Indian Affairs (BIA) implemented a "relocation" program, which was designed as a volunteer initiative but was actually a form of racist anti-Indian assimilation. U.S. president Harry S. Truman appointed Dillon S. Myer (who oversaw the war relocation program that targeted Japanese Americans) to lead the BIA. Myer created a program tantamount to cultural genocide, moving thousands of Indigenous families from their home communities to cities under the naïve assumption this would accelerate assimilation (Fixico 1986).

The postwar era introduced ideas of modernization and development for formerly colonized places throughout the world (McMichael 2011). During the Bretton Woods Conference in 1944, held on the unceded lands of the Abenaki people, capitalist countries of "the West" mapped a new international order that was designed to challenge "communist" countries following the defeat of Nazi Germany. Architects of this new international order felt it necessary to create the World Bank and International Monetary Fund. Publicly, these institutions were meant to challenge communism in the Third World through development aid. Kwame Nkrumah, the first president of Ghana (the first decolonized nation in Africa), described these organizations as an extension of monopoly capitalism and a form of neocolonialism (Nkrumah 1965).

Within global studies, the postwar modernization drive is understood today as the beginning of the idea of "international development." The development studies scholar Gilbert Rist (2002) writes that Truman used the term *development* for the first time in its conventional understanding in an inauguration speech in 1948. He was referring to the diffusion of aid, technology, and skills to underdeveloped places in order to ensure their participation in free markets and avoid the influence of communism. What is often missed in development studies is that much of the U.S. postwar approach to "the darker nations" was learned in Indian Country. Colonialists built reservations as sites for social interventions (Hosmer, O'Neill, and Fixico 2004). Two years later, upon signing one of the largest funding packages for Indigenous nations in the United States, Truman expressed much of the same "civilizing" narrative he used to describe developing countries. The historian Brian Hosmer points out that popular press biographies of Truman exclude any reference to federal Indian policy. Hosmer (2010, xiii) writes that this could be a result of the dominant international issues that have come to define the Truman legacy, such as the Marshall Plan, civil rights, and the recognition of Israel. However, this chronology of postwar events forgets centuries of colonization built on foreign intervention. This section intends to link the history of postwar federal Indian policy with U.S. foreign policy. The United States continued its imperial expansion and eventual global hegemony by employing the lessons it learned from expelling Indigenous nations from their homelands and confining them to reservations. The state used "hard" and "soft" power as forms of violence and intimidation and employed development aid and propaganda. Even the colonial terminology of frontier violence, like "Indian Country," continued to be used by the U.S. military (R. Dunbar-Ortiz 2014).

Truman's notion of progress in the Third World mirrors his sentiment toward Indigenous nations at the time. Both kinds of places (the Third World and reservations) were understood as in need of Western aid and assistance. This link between Third World spaces and Indian reservations, however, is rarely recognized. Scholars in development studies take U.S. Cold War proclamations at face value and do little to interrogate long-standing development practices in reservations. Arguably, U.S. development ideology and practice begin in 1868 rather than 1948 and are linked to the civilizing mission of the Grant administration.

It is important to understand global developments happening alongside reservation history. Reservations were not only places of military recruitment (as is often cited, especially in relation to the high numbers of Native people who enlisted in the U.S. military in World War II), but they were also sites of social activism. Indigenous social movements often made connections with international decolonial and liberation movements (Cobb 2008; Estes 2019). These global connections directly informed the practice and rhetoric of post-war tribal sovereignty. We cannot understand the creation of the Council of Energy Resource Tribes (CERT) in the 1970s without acknowledging the global impacts of Israel's invasion of the Sinai in Egypt in 1973, the subsequent embargo of the Organization of the Petroleum Exporting Countries (OPEC), and a consumer oil crisis. Indigenous leaders worked to link their struggle with global developments. At this point in history, we must understand the reservation as a global place.

It was during this time of renewed colonial violence that many Indigenous nations initiated large-scale contracts with mining companies to develop mineral resources. The Navajo Tribe was one of the first to embark on coal. This became the origin point of carbon sovereignty in Indian Country and mirrored the carbon democracy in the Gulf states, organized around oil, happening at about the same time (Mitchell 2009).

National leaders in the colonies of Africa, Asia, and parts of North America organized movements of self-determination to decolonize the empires of Europe. They had to confront their own "national questions" in decolonial spaces. These places became the Third World—neither First nor Second World nations (Prashad 2008). Frantz Fanon joined Algerians in petitioning for independence from Greater France, writing his influential text *Black Skin, White Masks* (1991) on the nature of colonialism and coloniality on subjected peoples. Kwame Nkrumah returned from obtaining an education in the United States and the United Kingdom to throw in with existing independence movements in the British colony of Gold Coast in West Africa. What sometimes emerged from these movements were national movements that excluded parts of the former colonial population in various ways, creating tribal, religious, or linguistic conflicts. Nationalism had destroyed much of Europe and was now unleashed onto the rest of the world. Nearly forty years after independence, the African historian Basil Davidson, who also lived during World War II, reflected on the similarities of both places. Davidson (1992) believed that nationalism had brought war onto Europe and was doing the same in Africa. He referred to this as "the curse of the nation-state."

By the second half of the twentieth century, the empires of the United Kingdom and France could not financially or physically maintain these colonized places across the globe. Nazi Germany had crushed their militaries and economies. The United States emerged as the world hegemon and was interested in opening the world to its own influence. Yet it was not possible to consider colonization and decolonization without considering the settler-colonial nations—the United States, Canada, Australia, New Zealand, South Africa, and others. Indigenous peoples in these countries were not new to international forums. At the end of World War I, Akwesasne leaders had traveled to Geneva, Switzerland, to petition the League of Nations for rights to self-determination. These leaders were ignored. U.S. and Canadian colonialism were left unexamined in international forums while the globe divided itself into capitalist and communist spheres. The Anishinaabe scholar Sheryl Lightfoot (2016, 7–8) writes that United Nations declarations on decolonization had to turn to a "salt water thesis" of colonization—colonization only happens across large oceans—to allow for countries in Africa, Asia, and parts of North America (such as the Caribbean) to gain independence from the UK and France while denying Indigenous nations in the United States, Canada, Australia, and New Zealand the right to self-determination.

The winter of 1947 was used as a justification for the U.S. Congress to pass the 1950 Navajo-Hopi Rehabilitation Act. The act was one of the most important federal interventions in the making of the modern Navajo Nation. It remains the cornerstone of Navajo modernization. To paraphrase Swedish writer Elisabeth Åsbrink (2017), it was "when now begins" for the Diné people. As the preamble of the act reads, it was intended to "promote the rehabilitation of the Navajo and Hopi Tribes of Indians and a better utilization of the resources of the Navajo and Hopi Indian Reservations." The act appropriated millions of dollars toward development in two isolated reservations, unprecedented at the time: $20 million was set aside for the construction of roads and trails throughout the reservation, $25 million was put toward the building of new schools, and another $3.5 million was reserved for "off reservation employment and resettlement." Importantly, the act set aside $500,000 to survey the reservations for timber, coal, and other mineral projects. With the Navajo-Hopi Rehabilitation Act, progress and mineral development were intertwined.

The historian Peter Iverson (2002, 181) says that it was during the 1950s that "the Navajo 'tribe' started to become the Navajo Nation." The 1950s did not so much bring about a change in this direction as this period was an enhancement of it. Following World War II, anticommunist paranoia among white elites targeted communities of color who had long pooled community resources to survive centuries of repression, including genocide and slavery. In the minds of U.S. lawmakers, these collaborative practices were hotbeds for communism and had to be stamped out. We know the sordid history of the FBI's paramilitary activities against the Black community. For tribes, the caprice of lawmakers made it possible to eliminate the federal government's recognition of tribes. Whole nations were denied recognition by the United States, and although they did not stop being Indigenous, they were limited legally and politically in how they could protect their lands and identity. The "elimination of the Native," as Patrick Wolfe (2006) puts it, was accomplished through legislative fiat.

CONCLUSION

Since 1868, Diné people have lived in a new world and one not entirely of their own making. This is a colonial world, dominated by a capitalist economy. This world was oriented toward new industries, new understandings of nature and gender, and new places. It is a world where Diné lands are resources for other places, and not for Diné use exclusively or primarily. In the remaking of capitalism, capitalist countries abandoned uninhibited free markets for strong state interventions. In the United States and England, this took the form of Keynesian welfare policies. Investment in public work projects to stave off unemployment increased. Such changes accompanied political revolutions. This period in Native American history is linked to reforms in federal Indian law such as the 1934 Indian Reorganization Act. The IRA centralized political leadership into elected "councils" that could then make decisions on behalf of the tribe with outside interests. In 1947 the Navajo Tribe became a nation, in a time after development was the catalyst for social change and the solution to the long effects of colonialism, displacement, and racism on a people and land. This development would take shape in carbon sovereignty, an expression of self-determination through the expansion of mining, drilling, and extraction.

For the Navajo Tribe of Indians, the governing political apparatus expanded its engagement in resource extraction. In an environment of anticommunism, termination, boarding schools, and Christian missionary practices, Diné people became more incorporated into capitalist processes and resource extraction. During the 1950s, the political institutions and governing practices of the Navajo Tribe solidified. The council-chairman system reflected anticommunist, procapitalist welfare governing ideologies. It was in 1950 that the trajectory of what would become the Navajo Nation was set into place. The Navajo-Hopi Rehabilitation Act of 1950 provided millions of dollars for the construction of roads, water wells, schools, and health facilities among other things within the two reservations (Iverson 2002, 190). It was consistent with Congress's interest in both terminating and developing tribes, when "the focus of acquisitive interest in Indian resources had shifted from land to water and energy reserves" (Reno 1981, 4).

Following the cementation of the Diné resource regime, as an anticommunist form of tribal development, border towns swelled in economic importance. Without colonial restrictions, white and Hispanic entrepreneurs took advantage of the swell of cash afforded to a new proletarian labor force. Diné men, conscripted into gendered forms of wage labor, spent their money in new stores located just outside the reservation. The racial regime that worked to dispossess Indigenous nations of their lands also stripped them of their humanity. Pawn shops, auto dealerships, bars, and restaurants preyed on the limited wealth of tribal members. Sales tax went to the state, debt to Diné community members. This was how racism and capitalism worked together as structural forces of dispossession.

Modernization and development told a different story. The narrative of post-1947 global capitalism was one of unrealized prosperity. It wasn't colonization but a lack of development that explained precarity, poverty, and other effects of colonial control. The post-1947 world created the conditions for both carbon democracies and carbon sovereignty—a world order built around oil, consumerism, and a global division of labor. In this global shift, after the end of welfarism and neoliberal hegemony, Diné space is cheapened. Land—for pastoralism and small-scale agriculture, and far from highways, rail lines, and airports—becomes less valued. Settler colonialism explains the utility of land theft but not land devaluation. The currents of modern capitalism made reservations into spaces of poverty redeemable through development in the form of extraction, or carbon sovereignty.

CHAPTER 2

CARBON SOVEREIGNTY

FOSSIL FUELS WOULD come to define a particular brand, practice, and understanding of tribal sovereignty, which was under threat and flux by changes in federal policy. Many Diné social commentators and scholars date the establishment of the first Navajo council in 1923 as the origin of a political regime built on fossil fuel exploitation. However, several important features of today's sovereign practices were decades away from fulfillment. In fact, Indigenous peoples were not even citizens of the United States when the first tribal council was created in the interest of simply agreeing to contracts between Diné people and Standard Oil. To read that council and the politics of the time into the large-scale development projects today would be inaccurate. The more significant social and political transformations related to the use and understandings of fossil fuels and carbon occurred during the 1960s.

This chapter articulates the transformative power of the coal leases signed between the Navajo Nation, utilities, and energy companies during the 1960s—leases that made coal extraction on Black Mesa and elsewhere possible. There were other leases and mining in the reservation before coal. There was oil leasing and uranium extraction. But coal as an energy source would emerge at a unique conjuncture of Diné history, a point of rising nationalism, growing confidence in modernization and development, and the wedding of tribal political authority with resource economies. This blend of social forces was the basis for carbon sovereignty.

RESOURCES TO SOVEREIGNTY

The idea of resources is a colonial concept. The land, sky, water, air, and the other nonhuman persons that inhabit our world are not objectives for development, statecraft, or employment. They are not meant to be transformed into commodities. They are entities and places with stories, histories, and relationships to the people. Yet colonial authorities worked to stamp out these ways of thinking. They confined Indigenous nations onto reservations, and killed off caribou, whales, bison, sheep, and salmon. In the United States and Canada, colonial authorities introduced cattle, cotton, and other cash commodities across the western half of the continent. The transformation of the landscape from Indigenous to colonial ensured that Indigenous peoples couldn't maintain traditional ways of life unaffected by new uses of rivers, land, and animals. What was under the surface of the earth was no longer a mystery, or a place where people didn't go. Resources became sources of wealth within a capitalist system. In chapter 1, I showed how colonial policies made extraction within the Navajo Nation possible. In this chapter, I suggest that Diné people, working through and against tribal institutions, redefined fossil fuels in the language of sovereignty, self-determination, and sustainability—carbon sovereignty.

Following a wave of national independence movements after 1947, nations throughout Africa, Latin America, and the Middle East used fossil fuels as sources of revenues for expanding state apparatuses and infrastructure development. Often these industries were already existing and local leaders simply continued colonial economies. Resource development was a strategy for greater independence. Import substitution and the nationalization of key sectors of the economy were pathways out of underdevelopment. This was influential thinking for how political leaders in developing nations tried to move out of the colonial nature of global capitalism. Leaders and political parties redefined resources in the language of national independence. They aspired to recirculate wealth among the people. Many were socialist and worked with the Soviet Union to nationalize key sectors of their economy. The United States and the West violently attacked these efforts. The United States joined forces with former colonial powers to finance right-wing military coup d'états over the nationalization of economies critical to the postwar capitalist economy. The violent assault on nationalization throughout the world was part of the reason resources failed to deliver on promises of development.

Relying on colonial industries for independence inevitably preserved key elements of colonial economies. Newly independent nations found themselves reliant on foreign markets, which were dominated by capitalists and increasingly hostile to independence projects. Starting in the late 1970s, capitalist interests throughout the world organized the global dismantlement of national economies and welfare states. Through lending institutions such as the International Monetary Fund and World Bank, capitalists in Western nations persuaded countries throughout Africa, Latin America, Asia, and elsewhere to abolish key protectionist institutions and markets that shielded small farmers and new industries from larger, more profitable industries in already developed nations. At the same time, capitalists in the West and policy makers organized new treaties between nations to obligate "free trade" of goods (not people) and prevent nations from regulating foreign business operating within their territorial claims (Chomsky 1999). Many political and economic geographers have worked to define this system of trade, development, finance, and influence (Dicken 1998; Harvey 2001; Klein 2000; Peck and Tickell 2002). This reorganization of the global economy around disaggregate production and increased profit is called neoliberalism. Whereas capitalists increasingly worked to make industry flexible, extractive industries were immovable.

After decades of resource exploitation with little to show for it, some economists challenged modernization narratives and said resources acted more as a "curse" than a source of wealth. Fossil fuels not only dominated national economies; they became their prime focus. Economies were structured and captured by resources. Resource economists sometimes argue that once a nation embarks on resource development, it becomes too difficult for it to change course. Post-war civil sectors (where technocrats work within a state bureaucracy) and workers themselves make economies path dependent. Colonial powers exert tremendous pressure to keep captured nations within a global economy that benefits that nation's elites. These economists referred to overreliance on resources as a "resource curse" or "Dutch disease." When examining the economies of newly independent African nations, resource curse analyses highlight the paradox of pernicious underdevelopment in places with a bounty of natural resources (Murshed 2018). Their critique was that newly independent nations invest too much time, money, and state planning into resource sector(s), ignoring other potential industries.

As useful as the resource curse thesis was for challenging market-oriented orthodoxies among development economists, it still operated within the framework of economics, which lacks context and history to a fault. The resource curse thesis often fails to address the historic conditions that produced resource dependency in the first place. For Indigenous nations in North America, rendering the natural world into "resources" was part of the state-formation experience. In applying dependency theory to the Navajo Nation, the historian Richard White (1983) claims that livestock reduction and the development of resources like oil, coal, and uranium became the origins of Diné underdevelopment. More recently, the legal scholar Ezra Rosser (2021) highlights some of the corrupting influences of resources on tribal lawmakers and how these impact development decisions. These explanations are all part of the dependency and resource curse frameworks.

Inverting the resource curse thesis, the political anthropologist Timothy Mitchell (2009) argues that resources were not the cause of underdevelopment but made modern statecraft achievable. In places like Saudi Arabia, revenues from oil paid for roads, schools, government employees, military personnel and equipment, and all other things we associate with modern state making. Mitchell writes that carbon democracy describes governing practices that resources "made possible" through extraction, exploitation, and combustion. More recently, the environmental historian Victor Seow (2022) has written about carbon technocracy in East Asia, showing how we live in a world carbon made possible. Seow goes on to say that the tendency to think about coal and carbon resources as both the basis of modernity and in abundance "has often fostered an imagined inexhaustibility and a carelessness that comes with believing that to be true" (14). Or as Navajo Nation Council speaker LoRenzo Bates told me in 2018, "I recognize the fact that the industry is under a lot of strain, . . . given that, we have one hundred years of a resource, one hundred years in the ground . . . and if you research the coal industry and you look at it beyond just burning it to create electricity . . . but coming down the path is technology that allows for coal to be used for other purposes. . . . That technology is not here today. Nonetheless, eventually it will get there. There's not enough money to get back into it, because you'll be starting all over."

Here I expand on this idea to think about what is increasingly made possible and not possible with changing global understandings of carbon, especially in Indigenous reservations against the spatial order of disaggregate production that is part of global neoliberalism.

When looking at reservation economies, shaped and limited by colonial forces, we find that carbon becomes a pathway toward development and self-determination. Fossil fuels were foundational to the Indigenous experience in the twentieth century. Transnational corporations partnered with tribal governments to open lands for extraction. At the same time, national movements for self-determination used coal, oil, and uranium as a basis for modernization.

Responding to shifting energy structures in the United States, extractive industries emerged as the basis of sovereignty for many Native nations. This is the nature of carbon sovereignty—a sovereignty made around changing understandings of carbon. The Indigenous experience in the twentieth and twenty-first centuries is a record of assaults from all forms of resource development—from land dispossession to water damming and diversion, the building of dams all throughout the West's most vital water sources, and the history of Cold War uranium extraction and nuclear testing alongside coal, oil, and natural gas development.

Carbon sovereignty refers to ideological understandings, pronouncements, and governing practices of tribal nations that are conditioned by rapidly changing understandings of climate change. In the Navajo Nation, coal was made possible by waning support for damming but became an outdated energy technology forty years later when solar, wind, and natural gas were preferred. Coal mines were opened as a promise of development and prosperity but closed because they were seen as too polluting, too expensive, and outdated technology. The future becomes the past in the timescale of a lease, contract, and business cycle.

CARBON BEFORE SOVEREIGNTY

An understanding of the world as composed of resources must be learned, shaped, and disciplined. The formation of colonial governance over and through Diné people—with conquering institutions (Office of Indian Affairs) and institutions designed to represent an abstract "will of the people" (tribal governments)—created the conditions from which the idea of "resources" arose.

Over the twentieth century, Indigenous nations recovered much of their social standing, political rights, and material land bases. This was won through decades of toil, activism, and changing cultural attitudes in the United States and Canada. The number of Indigenous peoples in census counts doubled (Thornton 1990). As discussed in chapter 1, in 1934 Congress passed the Indian Reorganization Act, which established constitutions and councils for tribes with existing relationships with the federal government. This act remains the cornerstone of tribal self-rule in U.S. colonial jurisdictions. It granted councils the ability to establish membership criteria, pass laws, or sign mineral leases. It did not grant full independence to tribes. For many of these decisions, the tribe still required colonial review. As Melanie Yazzie (Diné) (2018) writes, Indigenous decolonization can't follow the same path as decolonial movements in other parts of the world because of the nature of settler colonialism, a permanent displacement of Indigenous peoples and colonial land appropriation. The Bureau of Indian Affairs stationed agents near or on reservations to ensure that its policies were carried out. This was not the context of an independent nation but of captured tribes. Only four years later, Congress also passed the Indian Mineral Leasing Development Act, which granted tribes the ability to sign leasing contracts. The act followed the logic of the 1872 Mining Law, which encouraged the establishment or expansion of extractive industries on federal lands.

For more than sixty years, the search for cheap or strategic energy turned Indigenous lands into sites of extraction, waste, and toxicity. For the Navajo Nation, carbon sovereignty manifested in the development of oil, uranium, coal, and even wind and solar energy. Other Indigenous nations developed coal, oil, uranium, and natural gas. These industries accomplish vital development goals; they provide jobs and revenues. This is perhaps the most important (and studied) feature of resource economies. Yet there are other dimensions to a community's relationship with resources that are underexamined. What many scholars, researchers, and commentators on energy and resource extraction in Indian Country often fail to appreciate is the way resources shape attitudes, political opinion, mobilization, and ideology in the establishment, protection, and expansion of these industries within tribal communities. The formation of action and ideology in favor of extractive industries is particularly true for development projects that build on a people's collective yearning for national self-determination and decolonization—politics that took on new meaning and importance across the globe from the 1940s to the 1970s during waves of national independent movements in Africa, Asia, and the Caribbean.

Coal and oil were already important sectors in the Navajo tribal economy before Indigenous activists mobilized to challenge the colonial authority of the Bureau of Indian Affairs at events such as Alcatraz in 1969, the Trail of Broken Treaties in 1970, and Second Wounded Knee in 1973. Some of the demands of activists were to challenge federal authority over tribes and call for national independence. Responding to these criticisms and larger calls for racial justice, Congress convened sessions on the status of Indian economic development.

For political lawmakers in the mainstream of U.S. policy making, the lack of development was the source of the problem. The political inequality between tribes and colonial institutions wasn't addressed. The narrative was that these places were neglected. In 1975 Congress passed the American Indian Educational Assistance and Self-Determination Act. The law is sometimes referred to as Public Law 638 (PL-638). The law didn't create new authorities or expand funding. The kinds of institutions tribes now run through PL-638 are police stations, hospitals, and court systems. These institutions, some of which were the most punitive and intrusive in everyday Indigenous people's lives, are now under the control of many tribal governments.

As the coal sector expanded in the Navajo Nation, coal work became foundational for jobs and revenues for the tribal government and for the communities near the sites of extraction. For those who worked at the mine in the early years, it also introduced industrial temporal regimes. Days and nights became work shifts. Peabody Coal distributed paychecks every two weeks. Weekends turned into trips to border towns such as Flagstaff, Gallup, or Farmington. Coal created the conditions for a profound social transformation in this part of the reservation. After years of working in the coal industry, workers and their families identified with it. They worked to preserve the industry, to keep it essential to Diné development and life. At the same time, the federal government worked to expand the authority of tribes to make decisions on contracts, resource use, and development projects across reservations.

THE DEVELOPMENT DECADE

From the late 1950s until the early 1970s, four coal mines opened in the Navajo Reservation. The surveys funded through the Navajo-Hopi Rehabilitation Act found substantial coal deposits on Black Mesa in the center of the reservation. Suddenly, the Navajo and Hopi Reservations had energy reserves. Regional utilities like Arizona Power Service (APS) of the Salt River Project could put this coal toward energy projects. It was during the 1960s that utilities from Arizona, California, Nevada, and New Mexico partnered with mining companies like Peabody Coal to convert the high desert lands of Diné Bikeyah into coal fields (Needham 2014). During this period, state making for Arizona and the Navajo Nation saw tribal reservations as opportunities, not obstacles in resource exploration.

In 1962 the Pittsburgh Mining Company opened a smaller coal mine between Window Rock and Gallup, New Mexico. This was the McKinley Mine, perhaps named for the county in which it was also located. Construction on the Four Corners Generating Station (FCGS) started in 1960 on the northeastern corner of the Navajo Nation, near the border town of Farmington, New Mexico. The Navajo Coal Mine was expanded south of the plant shortly thereafter. When APS opened the Four Corners Generating Station in 1963, it was suddenly one of the most modern and large-scale coal-producing power plants in the world. FCGS concretized carbon ambitions. It expanded mining at the Navajo Coal Mine in the northeastern part of the reservation. As Needham (2014, 156) writes, the mine used the largest dragline in the world at the time.

It was during this era of termination and relocation that younger educated Diné with lived experience outside the reservation returned to the reservation to assume positions within a burgeoning tribal government. Many Diné men (in a gendered military) fought for the United States in World War II and the Korean War and had been changed by their experiences. They had traveled around the world and back. They returned with Western educations and military discipline. They understood, too, the double standards of the federal government toward tribes. Diné veterans returned to the Navajo Nation dealing with trauma from boarding schools or war. They returned to Window Rock to replace white Bureau of Indian Affairs employees who treated tribal leaders like children. The new kinds of tribal leaders to assume positions within the tribal government during the 1960s and 1970s believed strongly in possibilities of renewal, resurgence, and self-determination by taking over the functions of colonial administration.

In 1962 the Diné people elected Raymond Nakai as chairman of the Navajo Tribe. The late historian Peter Iverson (2002, 228) described Nakai as the "first modern Navajo political leader" in the Navajo Nation. Whereas the previous generation of leaders tied their hair in tsiiyéél (traditional buns) and wore ranching clothes, Nakai and fellow Diné politicians dressed in business suits. They cut their hair short and wore trim suits and skinny ties. They resembled the BIA officials they wanted to replace (figure 5).

Nakai used media purposefully and strategically, emulating the evolving political landscape of the 1960s (Iverson 2002, 228). His campaign practices reflected changes happening in the United States. Two years earlier, John F. Kennedy was elected president, narrowly defeating Vice President Richard Nixon. Kennedy was the youngest president at the time and brandished (some felt arrogantly) a new crop of planners and technocrats. These were (employing

FIGURE 5. Raymond Nakai reelection campaign poster, *Navajo Times*, November 1970.

a colonial trope) the "New Frontiersmen."[1] Kennedy was ambitious and a modernist. One of Kennedy's key advisors was W. W. Rostow, who wrote *The Stages of Economic Growth* ([1960] 1991), a text that reflected U.S. postwar development narratives and that shaped the political mood of the early 1960s. The climate within the Navajo Tribe reflected the overly optimistic sense of possibility in the United States at the time.

Nakai also wanted to modernize the Navajo Nation. During his administration, the tribe built new courtrooms complete with jury boxes (although federal law limited tribal jurisdiction to noncriminal issues). Nakai worked to update the capital city, Window Rock. The Window Rock Community Center, constructed in the 1950s, hosted plays, concerts, and other events. Musicians such as Louis Armstrong and Johnny Cash played at the center. Banks, restaurants, and other businesses were opened in the capital city (figure 6).

One of Nakai's first acts was to codify previous council resolutions into a governing law for the tribe, what would become the Navajo Tribal Code. The code would become the basis for law in the Navajo Nation (Wilkins 2013). Nakai was not the only one bringing outside civic practices into Diné lands. In 1959

FIGURE 6. Navajo families celebrating Christmas at the Civic Center in Window Rock, AZ, December 22, 1959, Navajo Nation Public Relations, NNM.L-0789B2. Navajo Nation Museum. SCA Item Number: 131370.

the Diné journalist Marshall Tome took over the BIA newsletter and formed the *Navajo Times*. He worked to improve it from a BIA status report on the five agencies the BIA administred within the reservation to a news and opinion newspaper that covered stories and events all across the reservation. Today, it is one of the most respected newspapers in Indian Country and one of the few papers with its own printer. The ideas of "freedom of speech" presented in the *Navajo Times* reflected an emerging civil sector that accompanied the growth of goverance and sovereign ambition in Window Rock.

Finally, the agricultural fairs that the BIA also sponsored moved from white practices of stock competitions and beauty contests to exhibitions of jewelry and textiles. The fairs now featured rodeos, powwows, traditional song-and-dance, and a Miss Traditional Navajo contest, where the contestants were judged on their language skills and cultural acumen and not Eurocentric notions of beauty (Denetdale 2006).

In Window Rock today, one can see the remnants of this development era. Throughout the capital, buildings are aging and roads are full of potholes. But in the early 1960s, everything was new and built in the styles of the time. The Navajo Nation created a forestry company in 1964 and opened a sawmill just north of Window Rock in the community that became Navajo Pine. The tribe helped construct houses around the sawmill as a place where workers could settle and live. Just down the road in Fort Defiance, Arizona, the Navajo Nation established an official "national" cemetery for Diné military veterans and other national figures. This mimicked Arlington National Cemetery in Washington, D.C. The place looked new and full of possibilities.

The 1960s were also when resource sectors expanded across Indigenous communities in the western states. It was at this time that coal increased in scope, scale, and practice within the Navajo Nation, Northern Cheyenne, and Crow Reservations (Allison 2015). As historians of this era demonstrate, colonial lawmakers and businesspeople looked at reservations as potential sites for energy development. The postwar West needed energy, and energy was found on reservations.

Importantly, the Navajo coal economy also emerged during a time of nascent nationalism. Between these two mines, hundreds of Diné men entered longstanding regimes of wage-labor work. It was gendered labor, and some of these men had already worked in uranium mines. Others came from other infrequent forms of employment outside the reservation, such as seasonal labor on large farms in central or southern Arizona. For many, coal work was a first form of wage labor. But before the decade was through, hundreds of Diné men were dying in Vietnam or returning home with missing legs. They were drafted into an expanding, unpopular, and polarizing war.

The coal leases were signed, and power plants built at the end of the 1960s were more water intensive, more earth changing than what started on the eastern end of the reservation. To save money on transportation costs, the California private utility Southern California Edison insisted on a water slurry over the conventional practice of rail. Bechtel designed the slurry and Peabody Coal operated it, but it was the utility that asked for it. This would create one of the most damaging environmental problems on the Colorado Plateau to this day, the depletion of drinkable aquifer water for energy production—which served consumers outside the reservation. The next major intrusion was the construction of the Navajo Generating Station and the Central Arizona Project (CAP), the most important infrastructure in Arizona. CAP moves water from the Colorado River west of Phoenix into the Salt River Valley. It assuages the natural limitations to Phoenix's growth. The undoing of the Colorado River for Phoenix required the removing, transporting, and burning of coal from the Navajo Nation. It was the reason for the power plant and mine. To understand Navajo coal in the second half of the 1960s, we also have to understand the colonization of the Colorado River.

COLONIAL BEACHHEADS AND THE COLORADO RIVER

The Colorado River is not a thing but an idea. The waters that flow through the Grand Canyon and empty into the Gulf of California travel through high plateaus to low-lying desert. These are all very different kinds of places brought together under the concept of the river. The Colorado River is one of the most important and disputed water sources in North America. What we normally think of as a "river" is much vaster and broader than what colonial delimitations allow. The river, as a thing in reference and public imagination, is a constantly flowing body of water that snakes through lowlands of terrain, eventually draining into oceans and even larger rivers.

The Hohokam, ancestors of six Arizona tribes, lived along the Salt River, Gila River, and other tributaries of the Colorado River. They built sedentary communities in these low valleys, diverting water to flood fields for corn, squash, beans, and other Native crops. When the Spanish colonists came, they stole Indigenous crops, moved into their communities, and appropriated their knowledge of water ecology to feed their own crops. They also introduced livestock such as sheep and cattle to the region. In northern New Mexico, a culture around the maintenance of these waterways (or "acequias") became a core cultural practice of Hispanic communities. The Hispanics were colonial, and their land grants were land grabs. Yet they did not dramatically reshape the ecology of Arizona and the Southwest as the white settlers from the United States would later do (Snedden 2015; Worster 1985). It was the American colonizers who moved into the region at the end of the nineteenth century who did the most to disrupt desert ecologies.

The Colorado River is a colonial abstraction. It is physically defining. It defines Arizona's western border, creating real political barriers between California and Nevada. Within colonial law, rivers are much more than rivers; they are the forecasted annual flows, the bases for rights of diversion, which in turn are the foundations for past, present, and future economies. Geographers and others define rivers sometimes in expansive areas called "basins," which include tributaries that eventually flow into larger river systems. This comprehensive appreciation for rivers is different from understanding the environment according to local ecologies or sustainable economies built on centuries of limited, minute, and often bounded environmental observations. In the past, Indigenous environmental sciences did not limit rivers to basins or categorize them within systems. As with observations of the land, traditional knowledge was based on a different episteme, one inclusive of land and animals. Although these are also topics of environmental sciences, our academic division of labor and emphasis on specialization cause us to focus on narrow questions at the expense of holistic social, cultural, and political considerations.

The river as a social and political construct became a site of continued colonial dispossession. *Aqua nullius* was made onto the continent's water sources. Water became an unfolding legal and political resource grab. Federal legal transformations of land and water into simple and abstract commodities made colonialism increasingly possible. Rail, cattle, eastern meat markets, boom and bust mining towns, and dams were colonial beachheads. These places and infrastructure made future dispossession more achievable.

To understand carbon sovereignty in the Navajo Nation, we must also expand our understanding of the political economy of water in the Southwest. It was for the making of a national water infrastructure that coal became central. It was part of state making in Arizona and made urban growth (gentrification, displacement, and expanding carbon emissions) possible. Where land is seemingly abundant, water is scarce. While the colonization of the western half of North America was indeed a land grab, it was also a colonial enclosure on the limited *water* sources in the West. Whereas white settlers moved into the western plains in the late nineteenth century, the Southwest experienced much of this enclosure and settlement during the early twentieth century, when the United States funded and built massive dams.

The Colorado Compact divided the river among the states. Arizona and New Mexico had only been states for ten years when the compact concretized complete control over the Colorado River and Rio Grande River despite centuries of Indigenous governance. Modern practices of tribal sovereignty are informed by much longer histories of colonial violence and dispossession. Indigenous sovereignty is a response against colonial aggression. It is perhaps only a rhetorical challenge against the United States or Canada. Maybe it is a set of limited institutional practices designed to empower tribal communities. Yet it is a real force of politics. It is both ideology and everyday governance.

The legal and political divisions of the Colorado River within Western water law transformed the river for settler communities and tribal nations alike. To state governments, water planners, and agriculturalists, the river consists of fifteen million acre-feet of usury rights for commercial and industrial activities. It is the basis for economic growth in the state and in the region. Indigenous water rights were deferred. They were set apart from state interests, a problem for the federal government to resolve. Indian water interests were only mentioned to say they were not part of the compact.

The compact builds on white settlers' desire to transform the environment of Arizona. The Roosevelt Dam, built at the turn of the twentieth century and named after President Theodore Roosevelt, who helped spearhead the project, was the first significant dam in the Arizona region (Hansen 2008). The Arizona Water Resource Center describes dams as reflective of the moment in history in which they are made.

The Roosevelt Dam initiated a phase of water and energy infrastructure expansion that created the modern Arizona political and economic system. The Salt River Valley Users' Association was founded in 1903 to ensure that landowners downstream of the dam benefited from the project. The Salt River Valley Users' Association eventually became the overseer of the Salt River Project.[2] The organization was one of the most active advocates for the Central Arizona Project during the 1960s.

The Central Arizona Project, it should be noted, was much more ambitious than most other water engineering initiatives to that point in time. It dwarfed other reclamation projects in Arizona in size, scale, and costs. The CAP was transformative of the economy and the environment. It was against this political backdrop in the mid-1960s that the Navajo Nation committed itself to the coal industry as a source of jobs and revenues. The tribe hesitantly agreed to its role in the coal-energy-water nexus to protect tribal sovereignty against the State of Arizona's brazen threat to dam Colorado River water along the Navajo Reservation regardless of tribal consent. Navajo sovereignty was built on fossil fuels and turned into a form of political power against the colonizing state and federal government. This was *carbon sovereignty.*

ENERGY FOR WATER

In 1961 the Arizona Power Authority (APA) applied to the Federal Power Commission to build and operate two dams along the Colorado River near the Grand Canyon and on the western end of the Navajo Reservation. These were the first steps by a utility to develop energy along the Colorado River for the purpose of supplying power to a major canal project that would take water from the river to Phoenix. It was not the first time that settlers in central Arizona worked to change the direction of waters and ecology of the region. But it was a time when political officials inside and outside Arizona believed they had the political power and force to realize the water project. Arizona's senior senator, Carl Hayden, was the majority leader. Stewart Udall, from St. Johns, was the secretary of the interior. The U.S. Supreme Court ruled in favor of Arizona over California for rights to the Colorado River. For Arizona's political class and the managers of the state's power utilities, the early 1960s was the time when the state should press its case for an expensive water project that would bring Colorado River water into Phoenix.

APA proposed two dam projects. The names of the dams would become notorious. The Marble Canyon Dam and the Bridge Canyon Dam would hold back water into the Grand Canyon, one of the most iconic landscapes in the world. For the political elite in Arizona, the dams were necessary for progress, for modernization, and for survivability. The dams weren't simply a question of development but reproduced colonial understandings of the environment. The Arizona Power Authority struck a nationalistic tone, demanding the Colorado River for Arizona's benefit. It took on aggressive posturing toward both tribes and other state governments.

The prospect of damming and diverting the Colorado River took on dimensions of sovereignty—both national and international. Not only was there a question about what the United States owed Mexico in annual flow of water, but also the Colorado Compact ensured that the seven states that claimed some interest in the river got a sizeable portion of its annual flow. Tribes were on the bottom of a long list of interests. To this day, many tribes, including the Navajo Tribe, still lack any kind of rights to the waters of the Colorado River.

According to the tribe's white then-attorney, Norman Little, APA told the Federal Power Commission that the Navajo Tribe had no right or interest in the projects during a public hearing in Washington, D.C., in May 1961. The Navajo attorney delayed further hearings on APA's application and objected to it outright. The Department of the Interior, for its part, insisted that water rights between California and Arizona be resolved before any new dams were considered along the Colorado River. With Little's prodding, the Navajo Tribal Council passed a resolution in late May 1961 opposing the Marble Canyon Dam. In so doing, Little drafted the language to respond to the legal-political questions along the river, appealing to arguments over jurisdiction. In the resolution, about a page in length, the Navajo Tribal Council resolved that the chairman of the tribe (a) publicly oppose APA's application before the Federal Power Commission, (b) work with the Bureau of Reclamation on plans for a dam, (c) get Congress to fund and build the dam and consider the Navajo Tribe a beneficiary of the dam, and (d) make sure the Navajo Tribe had the right to buy power generated at the dam.

All these points were in reference and in refute of APA's project. In this resolution, the Navajo Tribal Council (figure 7) didn't object to damming or power generation on the Colorado River; it simply opposed who was doing it and at what cost to the Navajo people. According to Little, APA was insisting it had complete control over the project, regardless of the Navajo Tribe. It had no duty to consult, work with, or provide power to the Navajo people. Its interest was in generating power for settler communities. Little worked hard to make the situation better for the Navajo Tribe. By drafting the resolution, the tribe openly challenged APA's plan while endorsing the role of the federal government.[3]

At this point, it is useful to distinguish between social analysis and historiography. A historian would continue the chronology of events and tell you what happened with APA's proposal. Spoiler—it became NGS, which we will get to. But here I want to take some time to focus on something that gets less attention than the history of energy development in the region—the tribe's evolving understanding of these issues. What is unique to this book is a consideration of the transcripts of council delegates. We see the tribe's "official" position in the resolution that Little helped draft. But Diné understanding of these questions was far different than the text reveals.

If we read this as the will of the council, we are missing important contextual considerations in the making of the resolution. On the one hand, the council was under considerable influence by the dictates of white people with power,

FIGURE 7. Navajo Council delegates in session at the Navajo Council Chamber in Window Rock, AZ, May 1960, Navajo Nation Public Relations, NNM.L-1084G. Navajo Nation Museum. SCA Item Number: 131552.

arrogance, and command of the English language, which was the official language of legal and political debate. The delegates, on the other hand, experienced punitive boarding schools and racist border towns, and spoke English as a second language. They were more cautious, circumspect, and at times cunning in thinking through the trapdoors of colonial jurisprudence.

What I analyze here is simply the recorded English testimony of delegates who opposed APA's project. We don't have the behind-the-scenes conversation in Diné bizaad that might reveal more of people's attitudes at this time. Still, the recorded English text is revealing. During the council debate on the resolutions supporting the dams, Navajo council delegates recorded their own reasons for supporting the legislation that were different from Little's framing about state and federal authorities. For example, the official resolution accompanying support for the Marble Canyon Dam emphasized the fact that

> the existence of a state-controlled dam at Marble Canyon in between the Federal Reclamation Project at Glen Canyon, Davis, Hoover and the Parker Dams on the Colorado River, would create a conflict of authority between the State and Federal Governments.

How was the integrity of federal authority in the area a concern of the Navajo Tribal Council? It was only a concern in how tribal rights were impacted by the difference between federal and state authority. This difference was made palatable in the early history of white settlement in the West and Southwest. Settlers on the frontier were shock troops of expansion. They were prone to genocidal violence. The federal government sometimes intervened in outright killing. With water rights, the federal government protected its interest in rights to water and, by extension, it guaranteed some rights to water for tribes.

The resolution supporting the Marble Canyon and Glen Canyon Dam projects appealed to the interests of the federal government and suggested that preventing competing authority over the project (i.e., between the federal government and the state governments) would reduce the costs of these public projects. This was the framing that Little gave. However, in recorded testimony during deliberation, Diné delegates emphasized the callous disregard of Navajo interests, demonstrated by Arizona trying to develop this project without consulting the tribe and its council. For tribal officials, this was a question of tribal sovereignty. Council Delegate Howard Gorman from Ganado said:

> The Arizona Power Authority only wants to produce power for the Salt River Valley and sell primarily to water users in Arizona, leaving the Navajos out, ignoring their rights entirely. . . . Therefore, we want to endorse the Bureau of Reclamation to build the Marble Canyon Dam because the Bureau of Reclamation recognizes the rights of the Navajos. . . . I am quite sure that if the Bureau of Reclamation builds this dam at Marble Canyon, then the western portion of the Navajo reservation would get power; while, if the Arizona Power Authority builds that dam, the western Navajos would be left out entirely.

The Navajo Tribal Council voted 56–0 in favor of the resolution. In so doing, the council endorsed a hydroelectric dam project on the Colorado River because it would prevent Arizona energy corporations from locking the Navajo people out of access to water and land. Delegates believed federal control of the project would provide more assurances than state authority because the federal government would incorporate Diné claims to the area. As is evidenced in Gorman's testimony, the Navajo council encouraged the Bureau of Reclamation (BOR) to take over the project for this reason. The decision by the council to side with BOR and other federal entities was the outcome of state government hostility toward tribes, especially in the late 1950s and early 1960s during the era of termination, when whole tribes were extinguished.

In this political context, the Bridge Canyon and Marble Canyon Dams weren't central; they were a means to an end, and that end was a fully funded and powered Central Arizona Project. After the council passed the resolution supporting both the Marble Canyon and Bridge Canyon Dams in 1961, Secretary Udall pushed large federal projects meant to bring water and power throughout the West. He envisioned a series of pipes and large water projects that would bring water from the Columbia River Basin in the northwest to the southwest. Udall's ambitions were checked by the political reality of the Colorado River, a hotly contested idea that defined state sovereignty and environmental governance. The network of large canals was impossible, and it would be unlikely he could get the Central Arizona Project off the ground (Einberger 2018; T. Smith 2017).

A SHIFTING POLITICAL CONSCIOUSNESS

At the beginning of the decade, sovereignty was wed to the goals of modernization and development. This was part of the original vision of the Indian Reorganization Act of 1934 that restructured federal Indian policy from forced assimilation to nation building. For decades, this project failed. The federal government forced livestock reduction. It also undermined the authority of traditional leadership for partners on the ground who would implement the government's agenda.

The Diné people's understanding of sovereignty changed with the rise of Diné nationalism and the rhetoric of tribal sovereignty and self-determination that was part of a changing political consciousness in the United States. Younger Diné people organized across the reservation (see figure 8). They were radicalized by the civil rights movement and the antiwar movement. Many younger Diné people read about the Black Panthers and Malcolm X. John Redhouse, a Diné radical by the early 1970s, quoted Malcolm X in a *Navajo Times* opinion

Page B-1 NAVAJO TIMES April 5, 1973

Hundreds March In Peaceful Protest

FIGURE 8. "Hundred March in Peaceful Protest," *Navajo Times*, April 5, 1973.

editorial against the emerging coal industry. He said to then tribal chairman Raymond Nakai, "But I don't like the way you've been running our government. You change things or we'll change them. I don't care. Malcom X once said, 'The Ballot or the Bullet.' And I say after Mr. X, let us sound off at the polls or we'll sound off in the streets. At any rate, the choice isn't going to be yours much longer."[4] Some Diné men were radicalized from the experience fighting in Vietnam. They returned to the United States skeptical of federal Indian policy.

This emerging political consciousness within the Navajo Nation matched developments happening in resource politics across the West. Water users from the Upper Basin believed that the proposed dams would give Arizona users more water than they were entitled to. They petitioned their representatives in Utah, Wyoming, and Colorado to oppose any additional dams along the Colorado River. They also opposed the construction of a proposed water canal that would bring waters from the Colorado River to Phoenix and Tucson. Up until this point, most of the political drama over the Colorado River concerned fights between California and Arizona. The Upper Basin states had smaller populations and less political leverage. They simply wanted to ensure downstream communities didn't take all the water—while they ignored Indigenous water needs.

For California, in the Lower Basin, the Boulder Canyon Act in 1928 initiated the legal-political work needed to build the Hoover Dam, which included water diversions to the Imperial and Coachella Valleys. For California, the Hoover Dam helped guarantee the state its share of the Colorado River. Arizona got nothing from this. The state objected to the division of waters in the Colorado Compact six years earlier. It felt the compact leaned too heavily in favor of California. The Boulder Canyon Act and the expansion of agricultural production in low-lying valleys in southern California were a threat to Arizona's water interest. In 1948 the Upper Basin states formed their own agreement over the distribution of the Colorado River and its tributaries. This became a governing law operating within the framework of the 1922 Colorado Compact. In 1952 Arizona sued California, and the Supreme Court appointed a legal expert, called a special master, to work through Arizona and California's competing claims. The report took years to complete but was issued in 1963 largely recognizing Arizona's claims.

By the 1960s, the Upper Basin users were worried about Arizona's designs on the Colorado. This ambitious project that the state's political elite proposed would drain the river of most of its waters. Representative Wayne Aspinall of southern Colorado was especially worried. He wanted better guarantees outside of the existing Colorado Compact. He was also the chair of the House Interior and Insular Affairs Committee and used this position to prevent CAP legislation from moving froward in Congress. As mentioned earlier, much was working in Arizona's favor at the time. Senator Hayden was the majority leader in Congress. Stewart Udall, a former representative from southern Arizona, was Kennedy's secretary of the interior. The Supreme Court, after nearly a decade of litigation between California and Arizona over rights to the Lower Basin waters, ruled largely in favor of Arizona. The momentum toward water development along the lower Colorado swung heavily in favor of Arizona in the early 1960s. By that time, Arizona had overcome many of the legal and political challenges preventing its exploitation of the Colorado River. What it didn't count on was the role of environmental groups in opposing Arizona's designs.

Another difference between 1961 and 1966 was the new role of environmental groups, particularly the Sierra Club, which now vocally opposed the dam projects. The organization launched a new style of campaigning to oppose the project, buying an advertisement in the *New York Times* comparing the inundation of the Grand Canyon from the proposed Bridge Canyon and Marble Canyon Dams with the flooding of the Sistine Chapel. This was unprecedented in U.S. environmentalism at the time. The Sierra Club asked its members to write to their congressperson to end the dam project and to expand the official boundaries of the Grand Canyon National Park to include sections that would be flooded in the proposed dam projects. This was one of the most successful and famous Sierra Club campaigns and is seen now as a milestone of U.S. environmentalism (Gottlieb 2005).

Pressure from environmentalists created impossible barriers for the Marble Canyon and Bridge Canyon Dams. Up until 1965, Arizona's political elite believed California was the main threat to Arizona's water ambitions. Suddenly, Upper Basin users and environmentalists added new challenges. It was a breaking point for Arizona, and its political leadership complained loudly in editorials in local papers.

From Phoenix, developers, representatives, and others threatened to build the project with or without federal assistance. The state took on a bellicose attitude even though it didn't have the political or financial capital to go it alone. It was emboldened reactionary politics, epitomized in Barry Goldwater and his rebranding of conservatism in his 1964 presidential run. Lyndon B. Johnson famously insinuated Goldwater would lead the United States into a nuclear war if he was elected. He was a threat to the country. He was also a representative from Arizona with direct influence over Indigenous nations and federal Indian policy. The state's public threats to build CAP without federal approval didn't help Udall's efforts to appease California's governor at the time, Jerry Brown. Udall took an approach to appease a more general political interest, promising funding for projects outside Arizona alongside the building of CAP. Phoenix blasted California, the federal government, upstream users in Colorado, and tribes.

In 1966, only five years after the tribal council voted to support the construction of the Marble Canyon and Bridge Canyon Dams, the council revisited these proposed projects. Again, Little initiated the review. He used his position as the tribe's main attorney to play politics in Washington, D.C. By 1966 he and others saw the dams as a threat to tribal sovereignty. He convinced the council that it should rescind the 1961 resolution supporting the two dams and replace it with a resolution supporting a coal-fired power plant instead. For the first time, the council spoke in support of a coal-fired power plant on the western end of the reservation—what would become the Navajo Generating Station (NGS).[5]

By the time I did my field research nearly fifty years later, coal was an entrenched industry in the Navajo Nation. In 1966 coal existed only on the eastern end of the reservation and the tribe was already seeing the benefits. The council believed the development of coal would spur more economic development in the western end of the reservation and guarantee energy security. The dam projects were designed in a way that would provide the tribe little benefit. Coal, it was thought, could supply outside interests, and provide power to Navajo homes.

On August 3, 1966, the Navajo Tribal Council considered resolution CAU-97–66, "Opposing the Construction of Dams in Marble Gorge and Other Portions of the Grand Canyon." The resolution condemned the Udall brothers, Representative Morris Udall (AZ) and Secretary of the Interior Stewart Udall, for not considering the interests of the Navajo people in their efforts to secure the construction of a dam on the Colorado River. The premise of the resolution, the "whereas" section of it, reads like a polemic against the Udall brothers and others in the federal government. It "condemn[s] the ruthless character of the promoters of the Lower Colorado River Basin Project." It also emphasizes coal as a cheaper alternative to hydroelectric power—which the resolution characterizes as "a waste of public funds." In the resolution, the Navajo Tribal Council "urges and memorializes the Congress to consider favorably" the enlargement of the Grand Canyon National Monument to prevent the Bureau of Reclamation or anyone else from constructing a dam on the western rim of the Navajo Nation. But when Navajo Tribal Council delegates spoke in favor of it, again they demonstrated that their own thinking on the issue often diverged in important ways from the language of the resolution.

Carl Todacheene, a delegate from Shiprock, said in no uncertain terms, "We have to sell our coal." For him, coal was the primary concern. "I think we would be jeopardizing that thing [Navajo coal] if we don't withdraw that resolution of

1961"—the resolution that supported the Marble Canyon and Bridge Canyon Dams. In Todacheene's view, if hydroelectric power were developed, there would be no place to sell the tribe's bounty of coal reserves. Norman Little informed the tribe that it should support coal development because coal and nuclear energy were cheaper to produce than hydroelectric power. Little said, "Long after all of us have left this mortal world coal will still be going strong but when it does run out you have thermo-nuclear power which can create and generate electric power far cheaper than hydro power."

The resolution reversed the council's earlier support for the dams. Council Delegate Howard Gorman, from Ganado, spoke the most passionately in favor of the tribe's opposition to dams along the Colorado River. He expressed frustration in colonial indifference to tribal needs. He believed the tribe needed to act in order to preserve tribal resources, whose taking away was inherently wrong and unfair. Gorman said:

> We're talking really about Navajo property or recognized something which rightly belongs to the Navajo people, the river, the country. . . . The Federal Government has been taking lands away from us right and left and it has been repeated so many times that the Navajos have just been pressed into a small area. . . . Everybody forgets the Navajo Tribe. Nobody remembers our interests. For that matter these people who are promoting this have apparently no respect for our existence or that we have a legally operated Tribal Council with legal advisors. They ignore all of this.

Here Gorman expresses his sense of how the Navajo Nation was treated unfairly in mineral leases. He went on to say, "We have a right to fight for our rights." Gorman's testimony suggests that the tribal council wasn't deluded or tricked into signing coal leases. Diné leaders made pragmatic concessions to support one form of energy development over another in the interest of self-determination. The political climate around energy disfavored more damming on the Colorado River. Coal was the environmentally friendly choice and one that had the benefit of strengthening the tribe's position. It is the origin for carbon sovereignty in modern practice in the reservation. Carbon sovereignty—with its limited rights and forced partnerships with federal institutions—was the vehicle through which the delegates exercised the Navajo people's collective "rights," or sense of control, over their land and water. The need to develop the tribe's carbon resources in order to modernize the reservation created the dynamics of carbon sovereignty shown here. Fifty years later, these dynamics persist.

MOVING TOWARD SOVEREIGNTY AND SELF-DETERMINATION

The Diné people elected Peter MacDonald, a new kind of popular leader, in 1970, a year after the SRP contract was signed. He championed the different language of activism, social justice, and tribal self-determination. It was a discourse in conversation with radical movements forming throughout Indian Country. Although the American Indian Movement (AIM) is the most well-known group from this period, a new spirit of organizing and critique of the federal government permeated throughout Indian Country and within urban diasporic Indigenous communities. For decades, tribal leaders were ignored, only able to voice enough opposition to mitigate the destruction of land theft, river diversion, and ecosystem destruction that followed new settlements, technologies, and settlement. At best, tribal leaders could mitigate outright land theft. For Diné people, the Treaty of 1868 wasn't a compromise as much as an ultimatum—Diné people had to live within the physical and social boundaries established by the United States or face destruction as a people.

In 1972, three years after the Navajo council signed the lease with the Salt River Project, AIM activists and Indigenous community members walked hundreds of miles from one end of the country to the other in the "Trail of Broken Treaties." The march took its name from both the infamous "trail of tears"—the 1830s ethnic cleansing of Cherokee, Choctaws, Creeks, Seminoles, and Chickasaws from what would become the U.S. South, where slavery would expand in new and brutal forms—and the hundreds of treaties the United States signed with Indigenous nations but casually disregarded in imperialistic landgrabs throughout the nineteenth century.

Tribal organizers throughout Indian Country petitioned for major reforms in federal Indian administration. There was a growing awareness that the BIA was paternalistic and many officials openly racist. Indigenous leaders, both old and young, witnessed civil rights activism and antiwar protests (Wilkinson 2005). In response to this activism, Congress passed the Indian Self-Determination and Educational Assistance Act of 1975. The legislation allowed tribes to take over functions of the federal government on reservation lands. Public Law 93–638 (the Indian Self-Determination and Educational Assistance Act) devolved to the tribal government authorities and administration. This allowed tribal leaders to oversee their own institutions. One of the first institutions that the Navajo Nation took over were the tribal courts and police.[6]

In 1973 Egypt and Syria went to war against Israel to recapture territories Israel took in 1967. The United States and other capitalist countries supported Israel. OPEC issued an embargo against Israel's allies to pressure them to the negotiating table. The price of oil increased substantially in the United States in late 1973 and early 1974. Gas stations ran out of gas. The media at the time characterized these events as an oil crisis. For the U.S. public, the question was one rooted in energy consumption, not colonialism.

Peter MacDonald and other Indigenous leaders in the United States saw the power of international organizations like OPEC. They recognized that their own nations also exported the raw materials for U.S. energy infrastructure, including oil, coal, and natural gas. In 1975, after a series of meetings and conferences, the Navajo Nation and twenty-four other tribes founded the Council of Energy Resource Tribes (CERT). CERT was meant to act like a "cartel" and coordinate a united voice of tribes with resources against the divide-and-conquer approach of the federal government. CERT is an important example of how the self-determination era ushered in a new sense of Indigenous nationalism with concomitant efforts to "develop" along capitalist lines.

Just as Peabody Coal started mining on Black Mesa in 1974, Congress passed the Navajo-Hopi Land Settlement Act. It was not just a coincidence. Peabody needed Hopi and Diné boundaries to be established so it could enter contracts with either and both nations to mine coal on Black Mesa. The legislation created a land swap, whereby Diné families were displaced from their homes on Black Mesa and relocated to "new lands" purchased by the federal government and held "in trust" for the tribe. While the Navajo-Hopi Land Settlement Act was passed in 1974, the process of relocation did not begin until Peterson Zah took office in 1983, nine years later. The relocation was delayed because many Diné families refused to move from their homelands onto these new reservations created in places unknown to them. Hopi police impounded Diné livestock and harassed Diné families who refused to leave. The BIA prevented Diné people from performing routine house maintenance and from building on family lands. This "freeze" on simple home repair amounted to policies of ethnic cleansing that were euphemistically called the Navajo–Hopi land dispute. With limited options, the Navajo Nation believed it could challenge colonial policies like the forced removal of Navajo families by exerting greater control over its resources. With money from resources, the Navajo Nation could gain leverage in the policy-making process and protect families who resisted resettlement.

Concluding this transformative decade was a reminder of the toxic nature of extractive industries for tribes. By this point, Diné miners who worked in uranium mines in the 1950s and early 1960s started developing unusual cancers. Most didn't smoke, but they were diagnosed with lung cancer. One thing they had in common was that they worked underground with uranium and often without masks or any kind of protective gear other than a hard hat. The cancer epidemic among Diné uranium workers was one of the first wake-up calls about the dangers of extractive industries on the people. Then, in 1979, the United Nuclear Corporation, a uranium company, spilled hundreds of gallons of radioactive water into the Rio Puerco, which served Diné communities downstream. The permanent contamination of this river was the greatest nuclear accident in U.S. history. The disaster marked the end of uranium mining for the tribe. Most of the mines from the 1950s and 1960s closed by this time (often haphazardly), and the increasing scale of nuclear contamination was too much for the tribal government to handle. The physical destruction of Black Mesa for coal mining and the health implications of uranium mining shaped the practice of Diné carbon sovereignty going forward.

NEOLIBERALISM IN THE NAVAJO NATION

The Navajo Nation renegotiated its mining lease with Peabody Coal in 1986. It tried to rework the royalty rates for Black Mesa coal. In the 1960s and 1970s, when the first mine leases were signed, Peabody paid eight cents per ton of coal. This was the federal rate for mining on public lands. It was also a dismally low rate that undervalued Diné coal for decades. In the language of sovereignty, the tribe asserted that it wanted more from its leases. It worked to move away from the cents-per-ton model to a percentage of the coal sold.[7]

In 1980 Ronald Reagan was elected president and reduced federal spending toward tribes (Kotlowski 2008). At the same time, the Navajo Nation passed its first comprehensive energy policy. This was in response to the changes in attitudes toward both uranium and coal mining. In this new perspective, coal was the future; uranium was poison. Energy took on new importance in the imagination of the U.S. public following the OPEC embargo and oil crisis of the late 1970s. A concern about the future of U.S. energy and a renewed sense of Indigenous nationalism fueled Navajo carbon sovereignty at the time.

The language of the Navajo Nation's 1980 energy policy was largely rhetorical, but it was also assertive. The energy policy emphasized the role of tribal sovereignty in controlling natural resources. The tribe adopted the energy proposal to emerge from an era when it felt it was exploited by mineral and leasing contracts with large energy companies like Peabody Coal and BHP Billiton. The first assertion of sovereign power over resources was to own the means of energy production.

In 1985 the Navajo Nation won a legal challenge against Peabody Coal for its undervaluing of the coal extracted from the Navajo Nation, depriving the tribe of hundreds of millions of dollars. The suit procured a windfall of money for the tribe. Then Navajo Nation chairman Peterson Zah created a permanent trust fund in which to invest the money. The idea was to expand the money so that it would increase in value over time. The Navajo Nation was trying new ways of securing its future, including new forms of financialization of its resources and assets. The same year, the Navajo Nation Tribal Council created the Diné Power Authority to build a coal-fired power plant and high-capacity transmission lines. The council wanted to capture more value from the energy economy. Leaders realized that the power plants captured most of the profit in closed-market energy economies. If the tribe wanted to advance into a wealthier nation, it needed to move beyond the revenues of coal.

Also that year, the tribe initiated a project to build a coal-fired power plant on lands it was swapping via the Navajo-Hopi Land Settlement Act from 1974. The tribe had the right to select thirty-five thousand acres of federal land in New Mexico to relocate Diné people who lost their homes on the expanding boundaries of the Hopi Reservation. The tribe's strategy was to use the land in New Mexico to secure new sources of coal, namely at Paragon Ranch. Although the land title and mineral rights weren't transferred as quickly as tribal lawmakers thought was possible, the tribe nonetheless created an institutional apparatus to realize a future power plant project on this land—the Diné Power and Light Authority, eventually Diné Power Authority (DPA). DPA evolved over the next twenty years. Paragon Ranch faltered. New Mexico and other energy developers challenged the tribe to the right to acquire that land. The Navajo Nation had to wait. In the meantime, it continued to staff and fund DPA.

In 1989 the Navajo Nation Council removed Peter MacDonald as chairman of the Navajo Nation because of his abuses of authority. The council also restructured the tribal government to resemble the U.S. three-branch system of federal power, replacing the title of "chairman" with "president." Peterson Zah was elected again in 1992 as the first president of the Navajo Nation, and in 1994 the Navajo Nation created the Navajo Environmental Protection Agency (Navajo EPA), mirroring the federal agency. Zah brought together organizers working on environmental issues and asked them to form an organization. This became the Diné Citizens Against Ruining our Environment (Diné C.A.R.E.). Some of the members had worked against proposed projects on the reservation, like a waste incinerator factoring on the western end of the reservation. Others came to the organizing through work against border-town violence in Gallup—centering social and racial justice advocacy in the work of Diné environmental activism.

During the 1990s, the Navajo Nation created a water rights unit in its tribal Department of Justice. The strategy of its lead attorney, Stanley Pollack, has been to settle the Navajo Nation's outstanding water claims. Pollack has been both praised and criticized for his approach to water rights advocacy, relying on negotiating settlements over court litigation. He was the lead attorney to settle a Navajo water claim to the San Juan River in 2005. I was in the Navajo Nation Council chambers in 2005 when the council agreed to this settlement. The goal of these settlements has been to secure adequate amounts of water and ensure funding for large water infrastructure in the Navajo Nation.

The Navajo tribal government responded to emerging environmental activism. It created institutions that mimicked federal environmental laws. The similarity between tribal law and federal law wasn't accidental; the tribal government passed laws that would make it easier for the federal government to devolve its authority to the tribal level. The Navajo Environmental Protection Agency was the first in a series of environmental laws passed. The Navajo Nation strengthened its institutional authority over resource questions during this time. The Navajo Nation Council created a version of a tribal institutional review board within the Division of Health to protect Diné people from exploitative research. Albert Hale, the Diné attorney who helped restructure the government in 1989, also worked with former secretary of the interior Stewart Udall to get federal compensation for the widows of former uranium mine workers. When he was president, he helped initiate local governance as a political project. Local governance referred to the more than one hundred community centers, or chapter houses, throughout the reservation. Udall wanted to devolve certain forms of decision-making to these governments and away from Window Rock. President

Kelsey Begaye signed the Local Governance Act (LGA), or Title 26, to the Navajo Nation Code in 1998. LGA provided conditions for chapter houses to do business development and land-use planning. Sovereignty was reimagined to work at different scales, against the centralization of tribal governments and something imagined as a "traditional" form.

These changes culminated in the 2002 passage of the Fundamental Laws of the Diné. The laws were an attempt to codify traditional Diné teachings into the structure of the Navajo Nation government. One-quarter of the Fundamental Laws are dedicated to "natural laws," or laws that deal with the Navajo people's traditional relationship with the environment. In 2005 the Navajo Nation Council permanently banned uranium mining in the Navajo Nation because of its legacy of harm to the environment and health of the Navajo people. The Navajo Nation Council did this at the same time it pursued new and expanded forms of coal mining in the reservation, talking about negative environmental and health effects with respect to uranium mining but focusing on jobs and revenues when it came to coal.

Since 2005, environmental organizations and others have developed a strong critique of carbon sovereignty in the Navajo Nation. Much of this critique is immersed in the changed contextual circumstances of our time. As in the 1960s, profound social change has occurred in the early 2000s, with consequences not fully appreciated at this time. Following the September 11, 2001, attacks on the World Trade Center, the United States has been involved in two wars across the world, one in Afghanistan and the other in Iraq. Many members of the Navajo Nation circulated through this military experience. It was also during this time that the decennial census found that more self-identified "Native American" respondents lived outside reservations than inside them. A new kind of anxiety informed tribal lawmakers and everyday Diné people in the early 2000s: younger people weren't speaking the Diné language, and the jobs of the 1950s and 1960s never materialized. Coal work, education, and government were chief employment sectors (Henson 2008). Lawmakers sought new sources of employment to keep people living on the reservation, including more coal mines and new power plants.

Also in 2005, the Houston energy firm Sithe Global approached the Navajo Nation with a proposal to build a power plant in the reservation. The project immediately generated opposition. By this point, the Navajo public was largely aware of the environmental costs of strip mining. Many Diné environmental groups pointed out that coal power contributed a large portion to the greenhouse gasses causing climate change. This was a different social landscape than when coal was an exciting new source of jobs and revenues for the reservation. In 2008 the U.S. economy nearly collapsed. President Barack Obama proposed changes to the U.S. economy that would prioritize green energy. When I started looking at these issues of coal and development in the Navajo Nation in the mid-2000s, this was the context of the debate.

In 2010 Navajo Nation president Ben Shelly, whose largest campaign contributions came from the United Mine Workers, declared that the Navajo Nation must invest in "sustainable" and "alternative" energy technologies. In October 2013 the Navajo Nation Council rescinded its 1980 energy policy, which acknowledged that the tribe must "transition" out of the coal economy. This was a point first offered by environmental organizations in 2005. Yet this new energy policy defined new uses of coal, such as coal liquification and clean coal technologies, as "alternative" energy technologies on par with "sustainable energy." The 2013 energy policy actively worked to redefine coal as an alternative to itself. Although the policy still embraces coal, it has qualitatively changed. That year, the Navajo Nation Council voted to change its energy policy. The rhetoric and tone moved from the resource nationalism of the 1980s into the language of transition and alternatives that exist today and that are part of a burgeoning politics of alternatives. In 2019, in a desperate effort to keep NGS open, the Navajo Nation Council briefly considered rescinding the 2013 energy policy.

These developments signify that a new Navajo nationalist resource consciousness that had matured by the mid-2000s was in full practice in the Navajo Nation. New environmental laws and regulatory agencies, such as Navajo EPA or the Fundamental Laws of the Diné, although seemingly about conservation of natural resources and not their exploitation, are nonetheless expressions of this resource nationalism. Both exploitation and conservation exert a claim of Navajo ownership over its resources that conform to the political and legal boundaries of the tribal government. As we saw in chapter 1, Diné conceptualization of space changes into the legal and political boundaries of the Navajo Reservation that the U.S. government recognized. As we will see in the next chapter, a critique of these practices emerged concurrent with and against this resource nationalism that built on critiques of tribal sovereignty as both corrupt and exploitive in nature. I discuss this emergent ideology—one actively engaged in the construction of a culture of alternatives to both resource nationalism and development—in the concluding chapter of this book.

CONCLUSION

When the federal government established the Navajo Nation as a reservation (consistent with federal Indian law and policy), it created extractive spaces, a territorializing that emphasized mining, leasing, and energy development. This is the consequence of reservations and the authorities they were given. It is easier and quicker to get a coal mine established than to build a home on tribal lands. Other industries have not established themselves in the reservation because of the difficult legal-political terrain they encounter that is the result of colonial policy.

Over time, fossil fuels defined a new expression of sovereignty, a *carbon sovereignty* that has come to define the goals and objectives of tribal governance in the Navajo Nation. Fossil fuel extraction, primarily coal and oil, gave the Navajo Nation the possibility to expand its governance and sense of self-determination. Coal was defined against colonial control, an irony because it is today understood as a function of colonial governance. What is important here is that carbon sovereignty became a baseline for governance. New projects were judged against the way coal and other extractive industries worked on the reservation. The possibility for decades of revenue and hundreds of good-paying jobs made coal a solution to many of the colonial problems reservations created.

CHAPTER 3

CARBON TREATYMAKING

SHORTLY AFTER BLACK Mesa Mine closed on January 1, 2006, then Navajo Nation president Joe Shirley Jr. proposed that the Navajo Nation build Desert Rock, a brand-new coal-fired power plant, on the eastern end of the reservation. Coming off the heels of the Diné Natural Resource Protection Act of 2005, which banned uranium mining in the Navajo Nation, this was seen as contradictory. In an interview that year on *Democracy Now!*, president Joe Shirley defended the Navajo coal economy. He said, "In the case of the uranium, we don't want any more companies coming in, so that's where this ban has been put on the books, and we're going to stand our ground as a sovereign nation to try to preserve our ability to not let it happen. But as far as coal and natural gas, we're continuing to mine those, albeit, you know, there are some things that are not good about it" (Curley 2008, 12).

The power plant would be the most ambitious extension of the Navajo coal economy in thirty years and in some ways was a response to the closure of the mine earlier that year. The debate Desert Rock generated was a forerunner to what would occur in 2013 (Curley 2018; Powell 2017a, 2017b). The tribe argued that the plant would create more jobs for Diné workers and increase revenues in tribal coffers. However, the project failed. The Navajo Nation Council stopped funding studies that supported the plant and ended meetings with potential partners. The project quietly faded from possibility and from memory. It was an example of carbon sovereignty unfulfilled.

At the height of the debate in 2007, I was working as a research assistant at Diné College, a tribal college whose main campus is in Tsaile. During this time, I realized that the politics of development in our nation was between environmental organizations and the Navajo tribal government over the issue of mineral extraction and resource development. In the case of Desert Rock, several environmental organizations publicly opposed the proposed power plant. Ojibwe activist and environmentalist Winona LaDuke published an op-ed in the *Navajo Times* pleading to the Navajo Nation Council to not build the plant. As a confidential interviewee in the tribal government told me, New Mexico killed the project in 2008 when it denied the project the necessary air permits to operate (TG14; see table 1 for a list of 2013 interviews). This action by the State of New Mexico, more than the protests of environmentalists or the misgivings of the council, ended the project. With the closure of Black Mesa Mine and the death of the Desert Rock project, the Navajo coal economy experienced its biggest setback in its fifty-year history.

TABLE 1. Tribal government interviews, 2013

	AGE*	GENDER	EDUCATION	OCCUPATION
TG1	40s	F	College	Auditor
TG2	40s	M	Graduate	Division director
TG3	40s	M	Graduate	Advisor
TG4	40s	M	High school	Advisor
TG5	60s	M	Graduate	Attorney
TG6	50s	M	College	Elected official
TG7	50s	F	Graduate	Attorney
TG8	50s	M	Graduate	Attorney
TG9	60s	F	Graduate	Attorney
TG10	40s	M	Graduate	Advisor
TG11	50s	M	Graduate	Elected official
TG12	50s	M	College	Elected official
TG13	60s	M	Graduate	Attorney
TG14	50s	M	College	Advisor

*exact age and occupation withheld

In the past, coal leases were passed almost unanimously and with little debate. As discussed in the previous chapter, white lawyers from the Navajo Department of Justice such as Norman Little persuaded the Navajo Tribal Council that pursuing coal development was a good idea to preserve Diné control over its resources. Little explicitly said that coal had a limited life in the reservation and that the Navajo Tribe should pursue it before nuclear energy eventually replaced it. This was before the science of climate change was well established. For conservation groups opposing hydroelectric dams at the time, coal was a better alternative. Once established, coal became an important source of revenue for the tribal government and a source of livelihood for workers in the industry. Unlike the oil industry, coal employed hundreds of workers.

In 2009, the year after New Mexico killed Desert Rock, the Chevron Corporation announced that it would close the McKinley Mine, which was located between Window Rock and Gallup and had been in operation since 1962. On the side of the tribal government, there was no effort to save the mine from closing. The Navajo Nation accepted the closure of the mine with little ceremony. The workers at the mine were let go. I asked a former Shirley official why the Navajo Nation did not try to save the McKinley Mine and that person told me coal there was "exhausted." Some of these workers, as a Kayenta resident told me, moved to Kayenta to look for work at the mine (KR10; see table 2, next chapter). Others simply left the industry altogether.[1]

The next year, on the eve of the next presidential election, the tribe's attention turned to the question of government reform in the form of council reduction. As a referendum vote, reduction would decrease the size of the tribal council from eighty-eight members to twenty-four. Like the literature on resource curse, community members blamed governing officials for the lack of progress in the nation. As the son of a council delegate, I was opposed to the effort. I thought it was shortsighted and didn't address problems more fundamental to tribal governance.

With the closing of two of the four long-standing coal mines in the Navajo Nation in a three-year span, and the failure of the tribe to build a new power plant on the eastern end of the reservation, it looked like coal would experience a fast exit from the reservation. In 2010 BHP, the Australian mining company that had operated Navajo Mine since 1963, announced that it could not come to a coal supply agreement with the New Mexico utility PNM, which owned and operated the Four Corners Generating Station, fifty years old at this point. With BHP unable to come to terms with PNM, it seemed that Navajo Mine would close alongside one of the region's most polluting power plants.[2]

Unknown to outside observers at the time, including myself, outgoing president Joe Shirley Jr. had created a negotiating team in 2010 to renew the lease of the Navajo Generating Station (TG3). For two years, the NGS negotiating team met in secret and negotiated the lease with the Salt River Project.[3] It was during this time that members of this team proposed the idea of buying Navajo Mine from BHP (TG12). This was a pipe dream at the time, but a pipe dream that complemented the ideals of an entrenched political interest in the Navajo Nation. This dream quickly gained political momentum. Soon, it was a reasonable position among elected lawmakers and tribal officials. According to one council delegate, a former member of the Natural Resources and Economic Development Committee, the president's advisor on energy introduced this idea of purchasing the mine for the first time in a meeting between BHP and the Navajo Nation about the potential closure of Navajo Mine sometime in 2012 (TG12). This information was relayed to me in passing, and crucial details are missing, such as the meeting time, date, and agenda. But information of this sort—anecdotes, gossip, and other informal conversations—plays an important function in constructing a narrative about the behind-the-scenes politics involved on an issue, as these backdoor politics reflect real motivations for coal renewal.

CARBON TREATIES

The renewal of the Navajo Generating Station lease in 2013 was an example of modern-day treatymaking. Navajo Nation Council delegates were concerned about land leases for strip-mining, water rates for coal production, the land lease over the railway that connected the mine to the power plant, and the land lease for the actual power plant itself. This combination of revenues from land leases and water leases accounted for a quarter of the Navajo Nation's nonfederal revenue at the time. Tribal sovereignty was understood but performed in the context of colonial capitalism.

The Navajo Nation Council signed the original land lease for the Navajo Generating Station in 1969. It was an agreement between the tribe and several regional utilities, the Bureau of Reclamation, and the Navajo Nation. The life of the lease was fifty years but with the option to extend it for another twenty-five if the utilities wanted to. An extension would take the life of the power plant to 2044.

In 2013 the Navajo Nation and SRP were interested in extending the lease, but other owners of NGS, Los Angeles Department of Water and Power (LADWP) and Nevada Electric, said they would not continue with the power plant beyond 2019 and would no longer buy power from it. LADWP and Nevada Electric had ambitious goals to move out of coal and into renewable energy production. LADWP was even subject to a State of California mandate to do it.

In the previous chapter, I discussed the ideological and material basis of carbon sovereignty. But the flipside of sovereignty is concession. For many Indigenous nations in the United States, concession comes in the form of treaties. Colonial governments and corporations looking to take advantage of the limited political power of tribes force Indigenous nations to adhere to the political, legal, and social limitations of tribal sovereignty that are built into federal Indian law and policy. For colonizers, these powers need to access resources in and around reservations. I refer to this concession process between tribes and colonizers as *carbon treatymaking*—an extension of the idea of carbon sovereignty and its inherent limitations.

Carbon treatymaking is not simply an abstract, theoretical idea but an observable phenomenon. It is embodied in practices recognizable to anyone who has spent any time with tribal officials trying to carry out everyday functions of governance. It is not just the "agency" in a social structure; it is an explanation of how agency works within a colonial context. The research and ideas in this book are something of a grounded approach to tribal sovereignty, focusing on how Indigenous actors understand and practice "sovereignty," and what they believe they can do with the powers and authorities of tribal governments.

During the nineteenth century, Indigenous nations were compelled by force to give up land and territory and move to much smaller reservations out of the path of westward expansion. Colonizers continued a pattern of land theft into the twentieth and twenty-first centuries through leases, intergovernmental agreements, and settlements. Like the treaties of the nineteenth century, these modern agreements often involve the use of or access to natural resources. I have written about Indian water settlements as colonial enclosures elsewhere (Curley 2019a, 2021b).

This chapter illustrates some of the ways in which extractive industries perpetuate colonial difference through modern forms of treatymaking that are aimed at placing limitations and concessions around Indigenous resource claims. Although we can look to the past for examples of outrageous colonial indifference in the sordid history of U.S.–Indigenous relations (from the Trail of Tears to Wounded Knee), it is in the present where the renewal, expansion, and evolution of colonial limitations are harder to see and identify. In the present tense, colonial institutions are in full public relations spin. This is the case in contract renewals, water settlements, policing agreements, and land-use agreements where political inequality is perpetuated and expanded.

To get a sense of this larger phenomena, we will look in detail at one such event—the renewal of a land lease between the Navajo Nation and the owners of the Navajo Generating Station in 2013. I suggest that the renewal of the NGS lease in 2013 was another process of treatymaking between the Navajo Nation and colonial governments. In the 2013 lease renewal, the Navajo Nation was asked to forego water claims to the Colorado River. It was also asked to exempt the owners of the power plant from Navajo Nation law, which in effect exempted the lease site from tribal sovereignty. The renewal of the lease between the tribe and the owners of the power plant renewed key political limitations on the Navajo Nation. Some might rightly argue that there is a difference between treaties and leases. Treaties are agreements often over territory between independent nations. This is the reading of many Indigenous scholars to argue that tribes are deserving of more political freedoms. Another reading of Indian treaties is that they imposed limitations on tribes in the interest of colonial westward expansion. Tribes didn't come to the treatymaking table as equal partners or even as willing participants. We don't need to get into a pedantic and legal discourse on treaties and leases to focus on one commonality: treaties and leases set land, water, and other resource limits on the collective rights of Indigenous nations in the interest of colonial, corporate, and capitalist expansion.

The 2013 lease between the Navajo Nation and SRP required active participation from tribal lawmakers to legitimize these limitations (figure 9). The lease, like treaties before it, set conditions on Navajo jurisdiction and the use of Diné resources in exchange for monetary goods and investment in infrastructure. Functionally, the lease operated like previous treaties, but it gave fewer rights to Diné people as benefits had temporal end points (whereas the costs became permanent). The two major limitations the 2013 lease imposed were labor rights for Diné workers and rights to thirty-four thousand acre-feet of Colorado River waters. I will explain both conditions and how they were reproduced in a 2013 lease throughout the remainder of this chapter.

The land lease, which alienated tribal lands from tribal control and preserved water for colonial institutions instead of tribal interests, had the same effect as

FIGURE 9. Former Navajo Nation attorney general Harrison Tsosie addressing a gathering of coal workers before the Navajo Nation Council vote on April 11, 2013, to extend the lease for the Navajo Generating Station for an additional twenty-five years. Photograph by Andrew Curley.

nineteenth-century treaty agreements that reduced and restricted Navajo land claims and deferred to federal policing over criminal jurisdiction issues. The 1885 Major Crimes Act built off the spirit of the "Bad Man" clause found in treaty language and deferred policing and punishment to the criminal codes of the federal government. The lineage of this law is in effect today—making the FBI responsible for murders on reservations.

But the lease renewal was also a cultural event. It was an expression of the values and ideological understandings of colonial forces against the internal desire for enhanced rights and self-determination. The lease was a structure through which agency was performed. The degree to which actors such as SRP could impact the terms of the lease compared to the Navajo Nation speaks to the power differentials existent between colonizing forces and Indigenous resistance. SRP could walk away and abandon the lease if it didn't like the terms the Navajo Nation put forward. For the Diné people, much more was at stake.

The *renewal* of a lease taken as a social phenomenon is intriguing because it tells us something different about the social, cultural, and political dimensions of the actors over time. It is different from the initial signing of the lease—in this case nearly fifty years prior—and demonstrates social change; that is, what were the new priorities of the tribal government in 2013 compared to 1969? Renewal speaks to the social, political, and economic dependency, to colonialism and new forms of paternalism and racism. Renewal brings in the politics of climate change and the consideration of carbon that was not part of the debate during the signing of the original lease in 1969. It asks uncomfortable questions about the limitations of tribal sovereignty, as most of the terms of the lease were unaltered in 2013 from the midcentury original. The process of renewal is the object of analysis here. What were its social components? What does this tell us about the state of U.S.–Indigenous relations? What does the event inform us about the prospect for development in reservations? What is the collective but fractured legacy of extractive industries in the Navajo Nation and how do these inform the way different groups responded to the prospect of renewal—both socially and politically?

Through participant-observation research in 2013, I observed Diné lawmakers debate the meaning and importance "for the tribe" of the Navajo Generating Station and coal industry in general. Tribal lawmakers described in detail the social forces that keep coal in the reservation.

2013 COAL RENEWAL

To understand carbon treaties, we must appreciate how they are both different and similar to nineteenth-century treaties. In the era of treatymaking between the federal government and Indigenous nations, control over land was a key obstacle of control. The United States was interested in expanding its absolute territorial claims, and a key strategy was the displacement and confinement of Indigenous nations. Tribes were confined to reservations in the process. This history is well understood among Indigenous critiques and historians and forms much of the basis of settler-colonial theory.

As was discussed in the previous chapter, the 1934 Indian Reorganization Act replaced parts of the assimilationist program while replicating core assumptions of it. An aim of the IRA was to address tribal land loss, especially lands lost through the 1887 General Allotment Act. The IRA consolidated territorial rights of tribes within remaining treaty lands. This, it was believed, would prevent further alienation of tribal land. However, the IRA retained Congress's plenary power over tribes. The IRA also ensured that title for all Indian lands was in the hands of the federal government. Within the U.S. federal system, tribes became use-occupants of their own lands, with the United States holding ultimate ownership and power.

Although the United States claims title over the continent—including reservation lands—in practice, within their territories Indigenous nations continued to live socially, culturally, and politically under their own institutions. Of course, there were continued campaigns of social and cultural intervention and each Indigenous nation had a different configuration of settler pressures.

The land arrangements between Indigenous and settled societies were fostered through treaties, which we can understand as contracts of colonialism. The Navajo Treaty of 1868, signed almost exactly one hundred years prior to the signing of the NGS lease, was one example of a colonial contract. Diné people, who were forced to agree to the treaty under the threat of starvation at Bosque Redondo, surrendered much of their former territories simply to return home.

Congress passed the Indian Reorganization Act in 1934 and the Indian Mineral Leasing Act in 1938. The development of resources was a kind of assimilationist project. The labor historian Colleen O'Neil (2005) documents the BIA's efforts to place Diné men in regional mining employment during the 1930s and 1940s in an attempt to teach them how to work. Coal mining had existed in small-scale, scattershot form throughout the reservation prior to the 1930s, but with the introduction of coal as an industry into the Southwest, BIA officials saw an opportunity for cultural assimilation. They encouraged Diné men to become laborers within an expanding capitalist society. The Indian Reorganization Act and the Indian Mineral Leasing Act of 1938 imagined reservations as sites of development. Peter Iverson (2002) writes about the expansion of uranium mining in the 1950s as a key to Navajo economic growth. By the 1960s, new resource challenges confronted tribes. State governments needed water for dams, development, or other kinds of diversions. Water use and water rights took on new importance. At the same time, settlement in the West expanded. Cities in the Southwest such as Los Angeles, Las Vegas, and Phoenix grew exponentially.

We often remember the IRA for setting up tribal councils. This is true and is an important change in Indian Country. But the act also created the conditions for modern forms of contracting throughout reservations. It made tribal governments the official interface between an Indigenous people and the federal government and mining companies. The IRA contained provisions for the tribal government to start corporations. The idea was to move Indigenous nations out of traditional economies and into capitalist ones.

It was this function of the IRA that created the opportunities for sovereignty and self-determination within tribal governments but also contained the exploitative framework for political and resource concessions. The mineral contract extended core features of treatymaking into performative functions of tribal governance. It set the conditions for concessions. It dealt with a people living on a land but without title to it. It is true that mineral contracts set conditions for any land use, but the contracts assumed unique features in Indigenous communities compared to contracts between private actors, like bank loans and borrowers. These contracts recognized and perpetuated U.S. colonial control over Indigenous lands and resources. Mineral leases recognized not only the authority of the new IRA tribal governments but also the authority of the federal government as ultimate decider over the fate of reservation lands.

During this period, all mineral and leasing contracts still required the signature of the secretary of the interior to go into effect. In contrast, no private landowner is required to get approval from the secretary of the interior before entering a leasing contract. This signature requirement was a form of paternalism. It was a key feature of colonial administration preserved in the contract. It built on the legacy of treaties and created the legal and political limitations of traditional land use. The antecedent of many provisions found in mineral contracts was in federal Indian law. Contracts were not the same, and some contained very different kinds of provisions, restrictions, and opportunities.

The language of the 1969 lease allowed for the owners of the NGS to unilaterally renew the lease in 2019 for another twenty-five years. The provision to extend the lease was described as a "right and option" for the land lessees, the utility owners of the power plant. It was this provision in 2013 that the Salt River Project utility said gave it authority to extend the life of the plant, even if the Navajo Nation Council ultimately didn't agree to continue the lease. SRP said it was operating in good faith by seeking Navajo Nation Council approval. As it turned out, this was largely a political performance by SRP.

A key provision of the lease that most resembled nineteenth-century treatymaking processes was the way the lease legally removed Navajo Generating Station from the territorial control of the reservation. The lease prevented the tribe from enforcing the Navajo Preference in Employment Act and other tribal laws in the areas leased for the construction and operation of the station. Removing the land from tribal jurisdiction, even if it was still part of the Navajo Reservation, had the effect of creating a zone of exception akin to export-processing zones in developing countries abroad. Unlike the treaties of the nineteenth century, however, the lease involved multiple actors, serving both settler-colonial publics and private capital. These actors were utilities, such as the Salt River Project, Tucson Electric, Los Angeles Department of Water and Power, and Nevada Electric. The lease also created a contract between the Navajo Nation and the Bureau of Reclamation, a desk in the Department of the Interior that was also the department of government where the Bureau of Indian Affairs was located. This blurred the line between lessee and the government's "trust responsibility" oversight role over tribes. In short, the provisions in the lease transformed treatymaking from the nineteenth-century era of settlement and displacement to twenty-first-century neocolonialism in anticipation of the era of neoliberalism.

EMBEDDED WORK

During this period of the NGS lease renewal, I was living in Kayenta, Arizona, and trying to meet with and interview coal workers. My research was initially focused on understanding the meaning of coal and coal work for a community that was largely understood to benefit from the industry. When designing my research prior to returning to Arizona, I did not anticipate a lease renewal for the Navajo Generating Station. The lease renewal was not made public until the lease was ready for approval by the Navajo Nation Council. Prior to this point, it was negotiated behind closed doors between representatives of the tribe and the Salt River Project.

In 2013, as the council considered the lease renewal, I made regular trips to Window Rock. Across the street from the council chamber are the offices of the president and vice president. The office for the speaker of the Navajo Nation Council, a position created in 1990 after the tumultuous 1989 Navajo government reforms, sits between the council chamber and the president's office. These buildings comprise the core of the Navajo government. Modeled after the U.S. government, the Navajo Nation government is also a three-branch government, based on the Navajo Nation Code (the laws passed by the council) with no constitution. I had done work prior to graduate school with Diné College for the council. With other researchers, we wrote a series of reports about the history of the tribal council, the president, the judicial branch, and other areas of tribal governance.

I also remembered the council from when I lived in Window Rock in the late 1980s. I started school down the road from the tribal complex at Window Rock Elementary School. Of course, as a six-year-old, everything seemed bigger and newer then. All these buildings were big and felt imposing. I saw Diné men and women in dress clothes, looking busy and serious as they walked through hallways or between the sandstone buildings of the capital. My mother, who is white, worked as a secretary in the Department of Justice. This was during the time when Peter MacDonald was chairman of the tribe. He was the most famous and controversial tribal leader across the country—organizing the Council of Energy Resource Tribes (CERT) in an OPEC-like model to pressure for better energy deals for tribes. He was part of a new Navajo nationalism. In my memory, the tribal headquarters in the 1980s was a place of possibility—infused with a sense of Diné independence, sovereignty, and national self-determination. As a kid, I was at the tail end of the urbanization of Window Rock—an experiment to modernize a reservation community. During that time, the grocery chain Bashas' opened a store in town. The grocery store was brand new and had video cassettes for sale.

There are only a handful of large communities like Window Rock where I lived in the Navajo Nation. These tend to be the "agency capitals," or places where the Bureau of Indian Affairs created managerial posts and sites to distribute food and other supplies originally mentioned in the Treaty of 1868. They were products of long-standing efforts to centralize the life of Diné people. The other communities comparable in size to Window Rock are Crownpoint, Shiprock, Chinle, Tuba City, Dilkon, and Kayenta. As discussed in chapter 1, Window Rock was created as a capital city for the reservation, the only example of a capital city in any reservation. Today, there are many businesses that cater to the needs of workers in the tribal government. There are two hotels, restaurants, and a museum with conference rooms. It is in these auxiliary places where governing meetings are held.

By any other capital standards, these hotels would be modest. But for the Navajo Nation, the community of Window Rock is big, and the amenities are comfortable. The hotels also target tourists who are visiting the Navajo Nation. People from throughout the world travel to the capital city to visit the Navajo Nation Museum, the Window Rock sandstone arch, and the adjacent Veterans Memorial Park dedicated to World War II Code Talkers and other veterans.

When the Navajo Nation Council holds official meetings or work sessions, it often arranges to use one of the large conference rooms of the Quality Inn down the street. It is as if Congress did work sessions in a Best Western. It was in these conference rooms, for example, that the twenty-four delegates of the Navajo Nation Council met in 2009 and came up with a new government after Diné people voted to reduce the size of the council from eighty-eight to twenty-four. My father was one of the delegates, elected to the first twenty-four-member council, and I attended many of these meetings—snapping photos of the presentations and making jokes with my friends who worked at Diné College or the *Navajo Times*.

In the early 2010s, the Salt River Project, the most powerful utility in Arizona, combined forces with the federal government to push for a renewal of the Navajo Generating Station—the largest source of carbon emissions for all of Indian Country at the time. The Navajo Nation was keen on renewing the contract, not wanting to lose critical revenues for the operation of the government. Tribal officials also felt pressure from Navajo coal workers, who were insistent that the tribe renew the lease.

From informal conversations I had with tribal officials in Window Rock, I learned that the renewal of the 2013 leases started as early as 2010. I caught people walking between offices, going from one meeting to the next—much like it was in 1989, except by 2013 I had a better idea of what was happening. From what I learned, Salt River Project management decided in 2010 that they wanted to renew the lease and anticipated it would take some time to clear the council and the secretary of the interior. SRP wanted to start the process early because it takes a long time to get the lease through the tribal council and the federal government. Later on, there was discussion as to whether SRP actually needed the tribe's approval as the terms of the 1969 lease can be read to suggest SRP and the other owners of NGS can extend the lease by twenty-five years if they want to. SRP, for whatever reason, thought it would be best to get the tribe's endorsement and to offer some monetary incentives to convince the council it was a good idea. Perhaps SRP thought the federal government would turn down the renewal without the tribe's consent.

PRELUDE TO SETTLEMENT—APRIL 2012

This was not the first time I had seen tribal officials in the Navajo government act in this manner. I first saw this tendency when I sat outside a high-profile meeting about Diné and Hopi water settlements in the Hogan Family

Restaurant in Tuba City in 2012. Like the Quality Inn restaurant in Window Rock, the Hogan Family Restaurant has a conference room kept separate from the public where attendees can have a private, catered meeting. Although there was no food at this event, it was a space concealed from the public. Arizona's then senators John McCain and Jon Kyl met with members of the Navajo Nation Council and President Shelly to try to persuade them to agree to a water rights settlement with the State of Arizona (figure 10). My father was in the meeting as a council delegate and gave me his impression of the conversations. He felt nothing was really discussed or decided.

I drove to the meeting from Flagstaff with my friend Natasha Johnson, who worked for the environmental conservation organization Grand Canyon Trust, was formerly a staff assistant at the office of the speaker, and knew most of the political actors in Window Rock. We sat at a table and drank coffee while protesters gathered outside to demonstrate against the water settlement. They held signs that read, "No Deal" and "Stop Stealing Our Water!" The fact that the meeting with two high-profile senators was scheduled in secret only added to people's suspicions about it. At that point, Johnson and I approached the president's chief advisor and asked him why he excluded the public from the meeting. He said tribal leaders could not make the hard choices necessary for the tribe if they knew the public was watching them. He said that with the

FIGURE 10. Former Arizona senator John McCain entering a water rights meeting with Navajo Nation Council delegates, April 5, 2012. Photograph by Andrew Curley.

media there, elected officials would grandstand and not make "tough decisions." This statement reflected how some in tribal government view the role of the elected official. In his view, tribal leaders were vetted by the public to make decisions on behalf of the tribe, but not in conversation with their constituents.

In the meeting, the senators were blunt about the meaning of the proposed water settlement and told the Navajo Nation that they would not get a better deal than what was offered. McCain talked in generalities, saying other tribes were happy with their settlements, and that it was good for the Navajo Nation (TG11). Like the later meeting on coal, this one was held in executive session and journalists were barred from documenting it (although I managed to hear a copy of an audio recording of the meeting). McCain and Kyl appeared surprised by the protesters. McCain started the meeting with the following statement:

> Frankly, I am amazed because we have never forced a water settlement on any tribe. Jon and I were talking on the way up. . . . We have seven water settlements with tribes in the State of Arizona. If you went to the tribal leadership, they would tell you in retrospect, some as long ago as twenty years, some [a] shorter time ago—just a couple of years ago—water settlements, that . . . they are very happy with the results of these water settlements, thereby preventing twenty, thirty, forty, fifty years of litigation in the courts. We have ensuing prosperity on these reservations that has been a result of the water settlements. So, to somehow see these demonstrators out here—everybody is free to demonstrate—but I say, Mr. President, in all sincerity, [you] don't want to have a water settlement? Fine, stay in court. That's [a] decision to be made by the leaders, the elected leaders of the Navajo and Hopi tribes. We have no interest whatsoever in imposing any kind of settlement.

Navajo tribal leaders and the senators discussed a range of topics, including a proposed Utah Water Settlement and the long-standing Navajo–Hopi land dispute. In this proposed settlement, Arizona wanted the Navajo Nation to renew the lease with NGS and settle water claims to the Little Colorado River. Although tribal lawmakers weren't opposed to either proposition, they felt that the items shouldn't be combined. Council Delegate Katherine Benally put it this way:

> Two things: As long as [the Little Colorado River Settlement] truly does not have us waiving our rights to claim the main stem of the Colorado River. . . .

> The other thing is, *keep Navajo Generating Station agreement out of this bill.* That's all we ask.

Eventually this was a moot point. The settlement and its enabling legislation failed in two tribal councils and in congress. Although the proposed settlement existed, it didn't go anywhere. For our purposes here, in understanding carbon treatymaking and resource negotiations, the meeting was an example of negotiations done in secret. Members of the Navajo Nation Council would conduct the same type of negotiations with SRP nearly a year later. The secret nature of the dialogue was made possible through the skilled coordination of Attorney General Harrison Tsosie, President Shelly, and Speaker Naize. It was also the overwhelming preference of private actors, such as the Salt River Project or BHP Billiton. It was an imposed condition for the making of modern treaties.

MEETINGS BEHIND CLOSED DOORS—THE FORMATION OF NTEC

While the lease renewal of SRP loomed, the fate of Navajo Mine on the eastern end of the reservation was also under consideration. The mine was on the opposite end of the reservation from Kayenta. It was owned and maintained by the Australian company BHP Billiton. The buyers of the coal and BHP couldn't come to a fuel supply agreement, that is, the price at which BHP wanted to sell its coal vis-à-vis the price power plants were willing to spend. Negotiations between BHP and SRP had broken down. BHP was going to close the mine at the end of its lease with the Navajo Nation and move on. The Navajo Nation, under the leadership of Council Delegate LoRenzo Bates, worked to create a front company that could buy the mine and sell it to the Four Corners Generating Station at a price the utilities were willing to pay. Navajo lawmakers figured that the company would save money on taxes and be able to sell its coal cheaper.

On January 31, 2013, Harrison Tsosie met informally with delegates at the Quality Inn in Window Rock, Arizona. The room was on the same floor as the restaurant. But at some point, the inn added partitions to the back half of the restaurant and made these into conference spaces that the council could reserve for official business. Because it shares the same space as the rest of the restaurant, one could hang out at a table just beyond the partition, order a coffee, and see who goes in and out. Other patrons are people who work in Window Rock, younger Diné people on strange business like me, or white tourists who happened to stay at the inn the previous night. It always struck me as strange that visitors were able to eat and stay so close to where our official business is being done—they get instant access to our most important sites of deliberation. Of course, hardly any of them knew what was happening around them. We had also allowed this to happen, to set our meetings so close to people coming from the outside. The half of the restaurant that was partitioned for official tribal business had framed pictures of past tribal chairmen hanging on the wall. I remember these same portraits from when I was in elementary school, the same official representation of leaders from as far back as the 1920s. Their presence in the room spoke to the continuity of governance at work. It was ideological nation building, an imagined history, leaders from a past era setting into motion the very structure of decision-making at work in the cheaply partitioned rooms where consequential decisions were made.

I let myself in and sat where people were gathering, in the back row of a long, semicircular arrangement of tables and chairs. I took out my laptop to take notes. In the room was Suzanne Baldwin, who represented the Four Corners Power Plant, and council delegates Alton Shepard, Roscoe Smith, Mel Begay, and Leonard Tsosie. Also in the room were Amber Crotty and Lambert Benally, legislative assistants to Nelson Begaye and Russell Begaye. Today, Crotty is a three-term delegate. Representing the president's office was the communications director, Erny Zah, and the office's attorney, Heather Clah. Attending for the speaker's office was the chief of staff, Jarvis Williams, and the energy advisor, Anthony Peterman. Also in the room was a representative for Arizona Public Service whose name I did not catch. I sat next to him and when I introduced myself to the audience, I joked that I represented the U.S. Environmental Protection Agency. The utility representative's eyes nearly jumped out of his sockets. But everyone else in the room laughed because they already knew who I was.

I learned about the meeting from my father, then a council delegate, who said I should attend. He was probably not aware that the meeting was supposed to be private because he was surprised when he learned that I was kicked out shortly before the meeting started. I was allowed to sit in for a while and talk with attendees, but once Harrison Tsosie recommended that the council delegates go into "executive session," I was forced to leave. I was the only one who had to leave. It was mildly embarrassing. But in the privacy of a closed space—executive session—Tsosie was able to maintain an exclusive audience with Navajo lawmakers and push his proposals forward without countering claims. In explaining why he wanted to move the meeting into executive session, he said that BHP Billiton, the owner of the mine, did not want to release sensitive company information that might give its rivals an advantage in the coal market. Instead, he preferred a closed meeting with lawmakers. In my opinion, it was a blurring of the public mission of the Navajo Nation government and eschewed the question of democratic deliberation about an important resource related to the long-term viability of the Navajo people. Also, what do we care if other coal companies learn about BHP's deal with the Navajo Nation? Maybe they would offer us a better deal.

NGS IN COUNCIL, FIRST ATTEMPT—FEBRUARY 2013

The next month, February 2013, the Navajo Nation Council made its first attempt to pass legislation to extend the Navajo Generating Station's lease. Those of us looking at the question of coal in the Navajo Nation had a vague sense that something was in the works. I talked to a council delegate in 2012 who said this was the next big issue that the Navajo Nation Council was to consider (TG11). Up until that point, the lease renewal was kept out of the public spotlight. Beginning in 2010, a select "negotiating team" was put in charge of working out the details of the renewal (TG3). This lease was between the owners and operators of the Navajo Generating Station, several public and private utilities in the region, and the Navajo Nation. The people on the negotiating team included the Navajo Nation's attorney general, the president's energy advisor, members of the Navajo tax commission, and a number of others the president selected from the executive branch. Noticeably missing were Navajo Nation Council delegates who were supposed to be there according to Navajo Nation law. The lack of council representation proved critical in this first attempt to pass the lease.

On any given day, the Navajo Nation Council will consider mundane issues. Delegates might talk about spending for a particular program or even approve a business site lease. Sometimes they are asked to enroll former members who lost or opted out of tribal membership.[4] Chairman Sam Ahkeah, in a foreword to a book on Navajo resolutions between 1922 and 1951, wrote, "It will be noted also that the complexity of the subject matter of resolutions increased greatly in the latter years as we have come to grips more and more with the complex problems of the reservation involving coal, oil, timber, water, uranium, grazing, employment, law and order, domestic relations, and many many other subjects" (Navajo Tribal Council 1952, i).

The Navajo Nation Council considers a wide range of issues. But mineral leases are among the most important. In 2013 these leases constituted half of the tribe's income. Hundreds of members of the Navajo Nation were employed in coal mining. Powerful regional interests applied pressure on the tribe to pass leases and ensure the continuation of energy production on and around the Navajo Nation.

The speaker of the Navajo Nation Council sets the council's meeting agenda and is the most powerful delegate. In 2013 the speaker of the Navajo Nation Council was a two-term delegate named Johnny Naize from the community of Cottonwood, between Chinle and Black Mesa. Naize once worked for Peabody Coal and strongly supported the renewal of the NGS lease. By 2012, the negotiating team had concluded its work and brought the completed lease agreement to Naize, who put it in the form of legislation and scheduled it for the full Navajo Nation Council to consider. Once proposed as legislation, the terms of the lease were made public for the first time.

The parliamentary rules of the Navajo Nation Council require that the speaker step down when he or she is the sponsor of legislation. They must then select a speaker *pro tempore* (Latin for "for the time being" and often shortened to "pro tem") to take over their duties. Council delegates, including my father, gave me their take on how politics in the council works. They felt the speaker selects delegates whom he knows will help him pass his legislation. The speaker or speaker pro tem controls the debate on the floor and can recognize a call to cease debate and vote on an item. Speaker Naize was the sponsor of the legislation to renew the NGS lease and asked Council Delegate Elmer Begay to sit in as speaker pro tem on the legislation. Begay was a first-term delegate, low in seniority among the delegates, and still somewhat unfamiliar with the cumbersome rules of council.

Yet Naize selected him as speaker pro tem. Begay's job was to move the debate in a way to pass the legislation. Even when delegates maintain strong reservations about a particular issue before them, the speaker and his allies can introduce the item, limit discussion, and call for a vote. If they feel they have the numbers to pass legislation, they prefer to vote rather than discuss. This is not so different from what happens in other parliamentary bodies throughout the world, including the U.S. Congress.[5]

Speaker Naize called up the legislation and then surrendered his seat to Speaker Pro Tem Begay. Naize took his seat at a chair, physically a level below the speaker's chair, to present his legislation. He probably did not realize at the time that several outspoken delegates would challenge the legality of the entire lease negotiation process because no council delegate was an official part of it.

When Begay took over the speaker's responsibility, he acted nervously. This was consequential legislation. He looked flustered while responding to delegates as they initiated their legalistic dance of motions, points of order, and other forms of objections from the floor. Many of these objections were technical in nature. Did the legislation go through the proper process to be introduced for debate and vote on the council floor? Begay deflected many of these questions to the council's legal team—lawyers from the Navajo Nation's Office of Legislative Counsel who interpret the legalities of council actions for the delegates to answer.

As soon as Begay opened the floor for debate, several council delegates pushed the red buttons on the desks to raise a "point of order." They asked Begay to rule the legislation "out of order," meaning it is not in proper form for the council to consider and vote on because it was negotiated improperly according to Navajo Nation law. This request required Begay to give a legal interpretation of the process. As a freshman delegate, not quite understanding the parliamentary process, and with limited legal acumen, he ruled it "out of order" probably because this was the least controversial action he could have taken on it.

Ruling the legislation "out of order" allowed opponents of the renewal to redouble their efforts and to mount an effective challenge to the negotiated lease. Naize's strategy to get this item passed as quickly as possible with the least amount of debate and public attention had failed. The legislation returned to the bureaucratic underground. It disappeared into the rhythm of the law-making process in Window Rock.

The public rarely knows how legislation is drafted, considered, and passed in the Navajo Nation. Most people do not regularly witness the legalities that shape council actions. Legislation is discussed among delegates, lawyers, and industry officials in private meetings, and often these meetings are held in places outside the reservation, like in hotel conference rooms in Albuquerque or Phoenix. It is here where the political reproduction of carbon sovereignty occurs. The proposal reproduces existing industries, existing approaches, and—in this case—much of the language of existing contracts. The spectrum of possible development is reduced to the proposal at hand. Whereas environmental groups prefer that the tribe think about renewable energy as an alternative to coal, these are not the proposals that the tribe must decide on. The disconnect between popular sentiment, or the ideas of groups like Diné C.A.R.E. or Black Mesa

Water Coalition, and the work of the tribal government are shaped by proposals, enabling legislation and the work of outside industries in presenting these options to the tribe.

MARCH 2013

During these negotiations, Tsosie threatened Navajo Nation Council delegates with legal action if they "leaked" details of the lease renewal to the public. On Thursday, March 21, 2013, the Navajo Nation Council held a secret meeting with representatives from SRP in Phoenix, Arizona. During this meeting, I was told that the Salt River Project informed members of the Navajo Nation Council that if they refused to renew the twenty-five-year lease extension, SRP was prepared to buy energy from other facilities and would have an alternative natural gas power plant online to compensate for the energy lost from NGS within a couple of years (TG11).

The Navajo public was not made aware of these conditions. And it is interesting to note that SRP told the U.S. EPA at the time that shutting down the power plant would be a terrible economic loss for the region and jeopardize energy for users in Phoenix. To the EPA, SRP management suggested there would be economic catastrophe and sudden increases in water prices if the Navajo Generating Station was forced to shut down due to environmental regulation. But to the Navajo Nation, SRP officials said it would be easy for them to transition out of NGS should the tribe refuse the renewal, insinuating that the Navajo Nation was at jeopardy of losing out (TG11). According to my interviewee, the meeting was a combination of carrots and sticks, incentives, and threats. After the failed February meeting, the Salt River Project and its lawyers agreed to meet confidentially with members of the Navajo Nation Council to discuss the terms of the lease. SRP extended the deadline for a $1 million signing bonus. They did this at SRP's headquarters in Phoenix, Arizona, without any public notice or input.

This makes the whole law-making process murky and suspect. During this time, Naize lobbied skeptical delegates to support the renewal. Coal workers in Kayenta also noticed the council's pause and anticipated trouble. One of my coal-worker sources told me as much. In 2005 the Navajo Nation Council failed to renew the lease to the Black Mesa Mine because of concerns tribal members had with the use of fresh water to slurry the coal 273 miles northwest of the mine site to the Mohave Generating Station in Laughlin, Nevada. Due to this pause, the lease failed, the power plant closed, and the mine shut down, putting hundreds of miners out of work. There were other considerations, but that was the impression of one of my informants (CW3).

It was also clear from the conversations I had with council delegates that their concern was primarily for the revenues—jobs never seemed to be a central issue. Some delegates disliked the tactics of the coal workers and felt that they were already a privileged class who could afford things most Navajos could not. Some non-coal Kayenta community members expressed similar sentiments. There was a general impression that the families of coal workers were better off than the rest of the Navajo Nation. Coal workers felt an equal animosity toward council delegates.

In my interviews and conversations with tribal officials in Window Rock, however, they spoke of a utilitarian understanding of coal—a question of cost versus benefit of the industry. For the tribal lawmaker and governing official, the risk of coal shutting down was too high to assert strong claims of sovereignty over the resource. I learned this when observing the Navajo Nation Council deliberate the lease. On the dust-filled streets of Window Rock, I stopped one day at one of the tribe's aged administrative buildings located a half mile down the road from the tribe's council chambers and president's office. I was doing other business and ran into Martin Ashley, executive director of the Navajo Tax Commission and someone I had previously met through my father. I asked him informally about coal; he told me it was important for the Navajo Nation to renew the resource. He told me that most of the Navajo budget depended on coal as a source of revenue. In another report prepared for the council, coal accounted for 24 percent of the Navajo budget, with land leases making another significant contribution. The financial importance of coal revenues for the Navajo Nation was well understood by tribal lawmakers

APRIL 2013

I spoke with the Navajo Nation's energy advisor, Sam Woods, on April 23, 2013, after the failure of the Navajo Nation Council to renew the lease in February and a few days before the Navajo Nation would revisit the issue in an all-night session in which delegates made several amendments dealing with questions about water and labor. Woods did not mention the jobs of the coal workers during my interview with him. I did not interpret this to mean he did not care about the jobs of the coal workers. I interpreted it to mean his interest in the renewal of the lease dealt primarily with issues other than jobs, for example, the revenues the renewal represented for the tribe. This was a subtle and important distinction. For Woods, the leverage that the tribe gained in terms of the potential for ownership over the energy infrastructure, such as power transmission lines, was key.

On Monday, April 29, 2013, Speaker Johnny Naize scheduled a special council meeting to consider two pieces of legislation that had some urgency to them. These were coal-related resolutions. The first involved the formation of a company, NTEC, that would buy and operate Navajo Mine on the eastern end of the reservation after BHP Billiton left at the end of its lease with the Navajo Nation in 2016. This was the result of planning and contracted analysis to LA-based legal firms. It was also the result of the conversation Harrison Tsosie had with delegates behind closed doors, mentioned previously. The second issue was a twenty-five-year lease extension on the Navajo Generating Station.

Naize presented two coal legislations to his colleagues on that day, one renewing the NGS lease for another twenty-five years and the other setting into motion the purchase of Navajo Mine on the eastern end of the reservation. These legislations would put new life in the Navajo coal economy. In controlling the timing of the council sessions, Naize was also able to prevent "grassroots" groups and environmental organizations from mounting an effective challenge to them.

For Naize, as with many coal workers with whom I spoke, the bitter memory of the 2006 closing of the Black Mesa Mine loomed large over the proceedings. Although the closing of the mine had more to do with circumstances largely out of the hands of the environmental groups and Navajo Nation Council, particularly California's move away from coal in 2006, coal workers still blamed the environmentalists and the tribal council for the closure of the mine. At the time, environmental groups challenged Peabody Coal's water use on Black Mesa, pointing out sinkholes that had developed over time. When the mine closed, several hundred mine workers immediately lost their jobs, and some left the reservation to look for other work. The memory from eight years earlier of environmentalists from Black Mesa who testified to the Navajo Nation Council about sinkholes near the mine site still burned in the memories of some of the workers who had lost their jobs.

When the Navajo Nation Council schedules a "special session"—an ad hoc meeting of the council—the Navajo public is given only a five-day notice of the meeting. This makes it difficult to organize a challenge to it. But no challenge was coming. The major environmental groups from 2005 had been noticeably absent during the entire NGS renewal debate. Some core organizers had left the region, leaving their organizations a shell of their former selves and with foci far from the oppositional politics of the mid-2000s.[6] The only groups present were the coal workers and a handful of activists I knew from Diné College and who were there to oppose the lease extension. The coal workers clearly had the power. They chartered a bus for the 140-mile trip from Kayenta to Window Rock. They had printed and distributed professional political signs that read, "Yes to NGS" and "Support Families, Vote NGS."

That morning, I left Phoenix at about 3 a.m. It is perhaps the only time when the streets of the city appeared empty. When I finally arrived in Window Rock seven hours later, I saw what I had seen before—coal workers gathered in front of the council, a large Navajo police presence assembled, and tribal workers moving quickly between buildings with bundles of papers in hand. By this point, the social spectacle of coal had become routine in the tribe's capital. The Navajo Nation Police had closed the main road toward the Navajo Nation Council chambers. The only vehicles allowed into the area were buses for the coal miners. Everyone else had to park outside and walk in. This was already a bias that foreshadowed how the evening would play out. The police created these roadblocks at all the major entrances. Even the dirt paths going between the famous sandstone formations that define Window Rock were now blocked or monitored by police. I used to ride my bike on those trails as a child in the late 1980s. There were never boundaries between where people lived on one side of the rocks and the Navajo Nation Council complex on the other. On that unusual day, police checked foot traffic and patrolled the footpaths.

Although foot traffic was allowed, everything else was restricted. I walked over the hill to the chambers and saw that the coal miners and power-plant workers were already gathered en masse. This was a crowd with disparate interests. There were the Kayenta coal miners supporting the extension of the NGS lease. But BHP miners and Four Corners Generating Station employees from the other end of the reservation were there to support the purchase of Navajo Mine. The two groups did not know one another and they supported different projects, but they were all there for the same reason. After I arrived to the front of the Navajo Nation Council chamber, I spotted one of the few white people in attendance. He held a sign supporting the acquisition of Navajo Mine. I was curious why a non-Navajo would come to the Navajo Nation Council chamber and ask the tribe to buy a mine in the reservation. I thought this was (and should remain) an exclusively Navajo question. I asked him what he was doing there and for whom he worked. He said he worked at the Four Corners Generating Station (FCGS) based in Farmington, New Mexico, just beyond the northeastern border of the reservation. He wanted the Navajo Nation to buy Navajo Mine so that the power plant would remain open to keep his job.

At the time, there was already some serious doubt about the life of the future of the FCGS plant. It was one of the oldest in the region and one of the most polluting. Most of its technology predated federal environmental laws and made it likely to be one of the first power plants to completely shut down soon. In fact, part of the argument for the Navajo Nation to build a new power plant in the area in 2007 was that it would replace the dirtier FCGS (Powell 2017a). It was "jiní," or "gossip," at the time. But after the Navajo Nation agreed to buy Navajo Mine, the utility companies who own FCGS—Public Service Company of New Mexico (PNM) and Arizona Public Service (APS)—announced they would shut down three of the four reactors at FCGS.[7] Anticipating this shutdown might have contributed to BHP Billiton's decision to withdraw from the mine when its fuel-supply contract was scheduled to end in 2016.

Opposite these circumstances was the future for the Navajo Generating Station and the Kayenta Mine. Both operations were more politically secure. NGS was a decade newer than FCGS and was already in compliance with several environmental regulations, such as the U.S. Clean Air Act. It was built during the passage of the first environmental laws in the early 1970s. The coal from Kayenta Mine that supplies NGS is also of higher quality and is less polluting than the coal mined in Navajo Mine. Importantly, NGS enjoys a unique configuration of ownership between private and public utilities and the Bureau of Reclamation, which use the power generated in the plant to power the Central Arizona Project that supplies Colorado River water to Phoenix. This special session of the council was scheduled somewhat quickly and done with little public notice. I learned about it not from people I knew in the tribal government, who were also somewhat oblivious to the meeting, but from a coal miner who told me casually while I was trying to schedule an interview with him that he would be in Window Rock that next Monday for the Navajo Nation Council meeting. This meant that elements within the tribal government were coordinating with the coal workers to ensure they were there to pressure otherwise hesitant Navajo Nation Council delegates to follow through on the renewal.

Navajo Nation Council meetings can be long and sometimes boring for audience members. I have observed people slouch, yawn, and sigh when a delegate introduces a technical objection to a motion or legislation under discussion. For audience members who are not versed in the parliamentary procedures of the Navajo Nation Council, this process can seem excruciating and frustrating. When I talked to coal miners standing outside the council chambers and asked them what was happening inside, they told me, "Talking B.S."

Several council delegates with amendments to the lease immediately voiced objection to legislation approving it. Delegate Leonard Tsosie was the most adamantly opposed to it. He had objections to how the language of the lease read. Naize and his allies wanted the lease to pass as it was written. They believed that adding amendments to it was a risk. They were not sure that SRP and the other owners would agree to what the Navajo Nation Council amended. They had negotiated for nearly four years before the Navajo Nation Council considered the matter. The negotiating team and the owners of the power plant said they had talked through all the possible points. Now individual members of the Navajo Nation Council were attempting to change the language of the lease. This was a serious concern among proponents of the lease extension. They thought these delegates would sabotage the lease.

When the council agreed to "discussion" on the legislation, the delegates with concerns about the lease added their amendments to the agenda. These amendments included a number of topics but focused primarily on "Navajo preference" for job openings at the plant and Navajo water rights. On Navajo preference, the owners of NGS had previously contested the Navajo Nation's claim that it could enforce Navajo preference laws in the Navajo Generating Station (TG7). The facility was exempt from Navajo law even though it was territorially in the reservation. In the original 1969 lease, the council waived its right to enforce any form of regulation on the plant. Now Navajo Nation Council delegates wanted to change this circumstance. Council Delegate Russell Begaye (who was later elected Navajo Nation president and served from 2015 to 2019) offered an amendment that read, "The Navajo Nation hereby approves that the Navajo Business Opportunity Act will apply for all contracts considered by Navajo Generating Station." Basically, this amendment would make Navajo hiring preference a term of the lease. Council Delegate Dwight Witherspoon, from Black Mesa, offered an amendment on water rights, which read:

> The Navajo Nation hereby recommends and approves the Amendment to the Indenture of the Lease on the condition that nothing in this lease modification agreement hinders the Navajo Nation from legally obtaining water rights, beyond the end of the year 2019, to the 50,000 acre feet or to assert claim to more than 50,000 acre feet from the Arizona Allocation of the Upper Colorado River Basin per the 1948 [*sic*] Compact.[8]

The amendment simply asked the Salt River Project utility not to challenge any future claim to the Colorado River that the Navajo Nation intended to make. It was a much more radical departure from existing water law than perhaps Delegate Witherspoon realized at the time. He was not aware of the politics of water in the 1960s and the claim that the Colorado House of Representatives agreed, in Congress, to federal spending on the Central Arizona Project so long as the Lower Basin states did not impede on the Upper Basin states. William Greider (1969) wrote at the time of the original lease's signing that the Central Arizona Project was passed at the expense of Navajo claims to Arizona's fifty thousand acre-feet allocation in the 1922 Colorado River Compact. Witherspoon's amendment ignored these circumstances and suggested that the Navajo Nation might claim *more* than fifty thousand acre-feet, which would throw water rights claims in both basins into chaos. It was the least politically possible assertion of Navajo rights, and the most radical.

Naize, Shelly, and others in the Navajo Nation government trying to get the lease passed would not tolerate it. Their perspective was that any amendment to the lease that the NGS negotiating team had negotiated would jeopardize the entire thing. During this special session, the Navajo Nation Council approved a total of ten amendments to the Navajo Nation Council Legislation 0042–13 after six hours of debate, which in effect added the Navajo Nation Council's concerns to the lease.[9] Most of these amendments were technical, having to do with the language and phrases used in the lease. In one amendment, Council Delegate Walter Phelps added the Bureau of Reclamation to the lease—its absence had been an oversight in the drafting of the document. But significant amendments pertained to water, labor, and what some delegates felt was the conflicting role of the federal government as both trustee for tribes and part owner of the power plant. As discussed previously, this feeling harkened back to the Supreme Court's decision in *United States v. Navajo Nation*, where the Navajo Nation felt the secretary of the interior deliberately undermined the tribe's renegotiation of royalty rates for coal mined on Black Mesa. Now the delegates believed that the federal government had an inherent conflict of interest because of the role of the Bureau of Reclamation as a part owner of NGS and the Department of the Interior maintaining ultimate control over tribes. This was an amendment Kayenta's council delegate Katherine Benally made. It read:

> The Navajo Nation hereby declares that the United States' contractual interest, held by the Salt River Project for the Bureau of Reclamation, to the power generated by 24.3 percent of the Navajo Generating Station's capacity is in direct conflict with the federal government's trust responsibilities and duties to the Navajo Nation and the Navajo people.

I sat in the east conference room of the Navajo Nation Council chamber through the entirety of the debate. I was with friends from the Diné Policy Institute who were there to witness the renewal of the lease.

The Navajo Nation Council passed most of these amendments pertaining to hiring preference and water rights. It wasn't until 11:17 p.m. that the Navajo Nation Council passed the legislation extending the Navajo Generating Station lease for another twenty-five years. The final vote was 21–1. Many of the coal miners stayed until the bitter end. But by that time everyone was too emotionally tired to celebrate or protest. Despite the momentous occasion, everyone left unceremoniously. The single delegate who voted against the lease extension was Dwight Witherspoon from Black Mesa. When I asked him as he left the council chambers that night why he voted against the lease extension, he said he was uncomfortable with how he felt the Navajo Nation agreed to forfeit its claims to the Colorado River as part of the lease. He was the sole delegate to vote against the lease in its fifty-year history in the reservation.

For the next two months, members of the Navajo Nation Council and the Salt River Project negotiated the NGS extension. But Speaker Naize was losing his support in the Navajo Nation Council. A group of detractors in the council was formed. They did not like the way the lease was negotiated and did not support how the speaker was advancing it. On April 17, 2013, Speaker Naize told the council, "We are at the crossroads. We have to make a decision for the people. We have to keep our Nation's economy health and keep our dedication to the people by sustaining their jobs." However, Council Delegate Lorenzo Curley, my father, said, "I stand to support the

Nation to continue to have a business relationship with NGS in the form of a lease, but maybe not this particular lease. We need to address the concerns of the grassroots people."[10]

The particulars of this "particular lease" involved rights to water and the Navajo hiring preference. In this case, two delegates continued to amend the lease for these purposes—Dwight Witherspoon from Black Mesa and Russell Begaye from Shiprock. Begaye offered an amendment that simply asked the Salt River Project not to oppose the Navajo Nation's efforts to claim water from the fifty thousand acre-feet allocated to the State of Arizona in the 1922 Colorado River Compact. As before, the Navajo Nation Council debated the amendments for hours. But in this case, the Salt River Project told the Navajo Nation Council that any reference to water was a "deal killer" for the lease extension. Delegates opposed to the amendments mentioned this several times during the debate. As Naize put it in the memo he sent out to the council delegates encouraging them to support the lease:

> Within the legislation there are several amendments that differ from the approved Council legislation CAP-21–13. This would include SRP's disagreement with language that refers to the potential settlement of our water rights in the Upper Colorado Basin. SRP feels that without knowing the particulars of a proposed settlement, they could not blindly agree to support the Nation in this endeavor, however beneficial it may be to both parties.

For his part, supporter of the lease and current Navajo Nation speaker LoRenzo Bates, from Upper Fruitland (between Shiprock and Farmington, New Mexico), said that if the Navajo Generating Station shut down, it would jeopardize the Navajo Nation's claim to the water. In the lease, NGS uses thirty thousand acre-feet of the fifty thousand allocated to Arizona. His point is that when this shuts down, that thirty thousand acre-feet is suddenly up for grabs and political actors such as the City of Page, located near the power plant, will capitalize on it and snatch it up. These are all political uncertainties. But these were the larger concerns rattling around in the minds of the delegates. The immediate political debate was concerned about who presented the more likely scenario: opponents of the lease who believed the Navajo Nation was getting a bad deal, or proponents of the lease extension who felt this was the best arrangement the Navajo Nation could get under the current political circumstances.

THE TERMS OF THE LEASE

The legislation itself focused on two core issues. It provided "continued employment at the Peabody Kayenta Mine" and would deliver approximately $42 million a year to the tribal government in revenues.[11] Compared to water and labor ("deal killers" for SRP), when talking about revenues, the agreement was much more promising. It said that the Navajo Nation would receive $42 million a year starting in 2019 compared to $3 million annually it receives currently from the lease. In a memo to the Navajo Nation Council, President Ben Shelly wrote:

> We have been told by SRP there is little, if no room to renegotiate. They consider the major points of the agreement to be exhausted, such as jurisdiction and money. Because of the mitigating circumstances the water concerns are unlikely to be resolved before the timeframe needed to finalize the lease extension.

This is perhaps the most crucial and sobering passage in all the material on the renegotiations. It summarizes the Navajo Nation's weak bargaining position. The Navajo Nation could take the $42 million a year for an additional twenty-five years.[12] Or the tribe could say no to the deal and watch the mine and power plant close, drying up revenues and laying off hundreds of workers in the process. The points of Navajo hiring preference and rights to the Colorado River were not negotiable but would come up again during the debate to pass the legislation. "Jurisdiction" had to do with the Navajo Nation's right to enforce Navajo labor laws in the power plant. The language in the original 1969 lease said that the Salt River Project was exempt from local labor laws.

The other important detail of the memo was a reference to the rights to water in the area. Since 1922, when the seven states that stake claims to the Colorado River (California, Arizona, Nevada, Utah, Wyoming, Colorado, and New Mexico) and its tributaries signed a compact allocating the entirety of the river to non-Indian settlers, tribal claims to this water have been pushed aside or simply ignored (TG5). In 1968, to get Congress to agree to the Central Arizona Project, which allocated millions of dollars in federal spending over a thirty-year period to the State of Arizona for the construction of critical water infrastructure, Secretary of the Interior Stewart Udall needed the tribe to waive a significant portion of its rights to the Colorado River for fifty years in exchange for the coal-fired power plant royalties and jobs associated with mining. The end of the waiver came in 2013 as the Navajo Nation Council reconsidered the lease.

At this time, as the president of the Navajo Nation wrote, "Because of the mitigating circumstance the water concerns are unlikely to be resolved before the timeframe needed to finalize the lease extension."

When Navajo Nation Council delegates discussed the matter with the NGS renewal negotiating team and Harrison Tsosie, they said that bringing up water was a "deal killer." If the Navajo Nation claimed any of the fifty thousand acre-feet per year that the Colorado Compact provided to Arizona in the Upper Colorado River Basin, the Salt River Project would walk away from the deal. Water rights as a deal killer was confirmed in notes I have from private meetings between the NGS negotiating team and the Navajo Nation Council. My notes also include testimony I observed in the Navajo Nation Council chamber when the council eventually passed the lease in April 2013. Water proved to be a central concern for the Navajo Nation as it discussed the lease. And as mentioned previously, only one delegate voted against the renewal in April, when fifteen amendments pertaining to water and labor were included in the lease; the delegate felt the renewal was still a giveaway of Navajo water. He told me this as he left the Navajo Nation Council chamber in disgust moments after the April vote.

Another important provision to the lease was that it allowed the Navajo Nation or a related enterprise to buy the 21.2 percent in shares that the Los Angeles Department of Water and Power (LADWP) owned of the Navajo Generating Station. The tribe's negotiating team was able to open possibilities of ownership over the power plant in the lease, but not for the region's water resources.[13] SRP suggested that if LADWP withdrew from NGS (by that time, they had already said as much), they would buy LADWP's shares and sell them to the Navajo Nation. The possibility of the Navajo Nation buying shares of the Navajo Generating Station was something SRP and the negotiating team already knew about since they included it in the lease. In a 2012 study by the National Renewable Energy Laboratory (NREL), the authors wrote:

> While ownership positions in Navajo GS have not changed during the entire time the plant has been operating, LADWP's ownership interest will likely be affected soon by legislative action in the State of California. Senate Bill 1368 (2006 legislative session) precludes a utility from making investments to extend the life of a plant that exceeds the rate of emission of greenhouse gases for a combined-cycle natural gas power plant. (Hurlbut et al. 2012, 10)

In 2006 California changed how it regulates energy to encourage the state's utilities from divesting from coal-fired power plants. In the report, NREL simply assumed that LADWP would withdraw from the plant given this political reality. This report was distributed to council delegates at the time, and this is how I learned about it. Foreseeing California's utilities divesting from NGS, it is likely that the tribe's negotiating team included a possibility for Navajo ownership in the power plant. This has long been a goal of resource nationalism in the Navajo Nation. In the literature on dependency and development, for example, the economist Lorraine Ruffing made it clear that the tribe needs to own and control its resources, not just sell them. Others, such as Al Henderson, former director of the Navajo Nation Division of Economic Development, said much the same thing (R. Dunbar-Ortiz 1979; see also Aberle 1969; Reno 1981; Ruffing 1976; Weiss 1984). As the anthropologist Dana Powell wrote in her 2011 dissertation on coal in the Navajo Nation, members of the tribal government "work[ed] together to position the proposed power plant as the machinery for sovereignty through its economic power to generate $50 million annually in tribal revenue and its symbolic power to override the state of New Mexico" (271).

In 2015, two years after the lease passed the Navajo Nation Council, the Los Angeles Department of Water and Power publicly announced it was withdrawing from NGS when the fifty-year lease expired in 2019, and the Salt River Project immediately said it would acquire LADWP's shares of the power plant.[14] The Navajo Transitional Energy Company (NTEC) was also a potential buyer of LADWP's shares. Two prominent members of the tribe's negotiating team, Attorney General Harrison Tsosie and former energy advisor to the president Sam Woods, had by 2015 left their work in the tribal government and were working for NTEC. With an ideology that defines sovereignty as resource nationalism, owning both a mine and part of the power plant would be a huge advancement. Tsosie's and Woods's actions in 2013 signal this ideology in action. They worked hard for Navajo ownership over the power plant, which was understood as a boost in tribal sovereignty.

The choice for the Navajo Nation Council was simple: renew the Navajo Generating Station lease or shut it down. The tribe's negotiating team, along with the industry representatives, created this impression in the minds of elected officials. As mentioned previously, every subsequent attempt of Navajo Nation Council delegates to change this scenario was flatly denied. The term "deal killer" became common parlance in council floor debates. Water became a central concern for some delegates, including future Navajo Nation president Russell

Begaye. But another issue for tribal officials was the enforcement of Navajo labor laws in the Navajo Generating Station. There were several attempts to amend the lease. Most of these passed. The Navajo Nation had long wanted to extend its sovereignty over its entire territory. Council delegates offered amendments along these lines again and again as the lease renewal was considered. They were added to the lease and dropped again during secretive negotiations. For SRP, these were "deal killers." The amendments were finally stripped from the lease in the final version of the agreement that the Navajo Nation endorsed in July 2013.

The central conditioning factor of carbon sovereignty in this case was the fact that the Salt River Project could simply walk away if the Navajo Nation Council did not renew the lease. If the Navajo Nation said no, it would lose millions of dollars in revenue. This was not something the tribe was able to do. It could not make up this revenue or the jobs at the mine through any existing alternative. SRP understood this and played the tribe's limited options to its advantage. The federal government had no play in the negotiation. The BIA was a nonfactor. The two entities talking to each other were the Navajo Nation Council and the Salt River Project. In this case, the dependency theory literature proved largely correct. The tribe had become dependent on its relationship with the outside corporations and energy interests during its fifty-year history with the mineral. It was maybe even more dependent since the relationships were first critiqued in the late 1970s and early 1980s. If the lease was not renewed, the tribe would have lost millions of dollars in annual revenue and hundreds of jobs.

JULY 2013—CEMENTING THE NAVAJO NATION'S WATER AND ENERGY FUTURE

The Navajo Nation Council passed the lease extension in April, but it was certain to be rejected by SRP. SRP had told the Navajo Nation that any movement on renegotiating water rights or labor rights was a "deal killer." This meant that SRP would not renew it. There is a lot to observe about the power inequalities already. The actions of SRP to automatically reject any amendment to a fifty-year-old lease with outdated terms speaks to how the conditions of settler colonialism are perpetuated. It wasn't in a public forum but behind closed doors where SRP resumed its renegotiation with the tribe. It wanted to—needed to—convince the Navajo Nation Council that it had to return to the original lease that the so-called negotiating team had agreed to, a lease that virtually kept intact vague language about water rights and exempted the Navajo Nation from labor jurisdiction over the power plant. What was gained was a signing bonus and a promise of continued coal royalties, estimated at $10 million a year. The lease also allowed for a potential ownership stake—meaning the Navajo Nation could buy one of the units that was left abandoned by one of the two utilities leaving the project.

To deal with some of these technical aspects of the lease, the speaker organized a work session for the council. I was able to attend and took detailed notes. This work session was held on July 17, 2013. The council had until the end of the month to renew the lease to get a $1 million signing bonus that SRP offered. The meeting was held where the NTEC meeting was held months earlier, in the little conference space attached to the Quality Inn. A handful of delegates met. A projector was placed in the center of the room, projecting PowerPoint graphs, statistics, and monetary promises. The tribe's lead tax attorney, Marcelino Gomez, informed the Navajo Nation Council that the royalty payments were based on how much power NGS sold to utility companies. If the power plant sold less energy because of climate change legislation, it would dramatically affect the amount of money the tribe received as revenue. Delegate Witherspoon suggested that the royalty payments should be changed to an absolute number and not based on megawatts sold so that this money could help fund a transition out of coal. During the discussion, Council Delegate Nelson Begay said he wanted stronger water claims. Delegate Leonard Tsosie, who voted against the lease renewal, thought the language protecting the tribe was weak. After two hours of discussion, the meeting ended. Delegates drifted out of the room to get lunch and do other things.

That afternoon, I arrived at the council chamber as the discussion on the legislation began. Again, the room was full. There were workers, tribal members, opponents, and industry officials mixed in the audience. Every delegate except for Kenneth Maryboy from the Utah part of the reservation was there. I felt fatigued by the issue at this point, and I think many other people felt the same way. The vibrancy was dim. The mood in front of the Navajo Nation Council chamber from April, when delegates showed up to support the lease renewal, was gone.

Council Delegate Leonard Tsosie spoke against the lease renewal: "Unfortunately, comparing what we did with [the] resolution that we passed before [in April], I think the resolution CAP-21–13 to be the stronger resolution that we passed. This is the weaker resolution. And we are giving up. We are giving in. I can't subscribe to that." Tsosie was in the minority in his dissent against what looked like the inevitable passage of the NGS lease renewal that now had all the council's amendments from April removed. These amendments were meant to protect Navajo resources and rights. But SRP had rejected these.

Tsosie continued, "I submit that a fatigue factor has creeped in. People are just kind of tired and I'm tired of talking about it. So maybe that is the strategy. Everyone is tired of it, so let's just pass it. And I hope you don't do that," Tsosie said. "In the last resolution we were trying to hold the U.S. government responsible for its trust responsibility; that has been taken out." Tsosie concluded by asking "whether the cost of tribal sovereignty is worth $40 million—I say not."

The most critical part of the entire conversation—missed in the local press—was when Council Delegate Russell Begaye put forward an amendment to legally force SRP not to challenge Navajo water claims to the Colorado River. The delegates who opposed the amendments, including Speaker Naize and Lorenzo Bates, were opposed to it not out of principle but from fear. They feared that SRP would reject the lease and the Navajo Nation would lose all the revenues from the plant and the Kayenta Mine. Bates said power flows downward toward Phoenix and they would take all the tribe's water if the Navajo Nation did not approve the lease. Delegate Witherspoon said that in the future, water would be more valuable than gold and that the Navajo Nation should do everything in its power to protect its water rights.

The water rights amendment proved to be the crucial amendment. Two factions emerged. It became such a heated issue that Speaker Pro Tem Mel Begay brought in the Navajo Nation Department of Justice's lead water rights attorney, Stanley Pollack, to testify about the implications of the amendment on larger water claims to the Colorado River. Pollack provided vague and ultimately unhelpful answers. But bringing him in showed how uncertain tribal delegates were about the water issue. In the end, the vote to add the amendment to the lease was an 11–11 split. Council delegates who voted in favor of the amendment did so in defiance of SRP's threats to walk away. But in the case of a tie, the speaker (who normally abstains) is allowed to vote. Speaker Pro Tem Begay shifted in his seat and turned toward the legislative recorder, in the direction where I was standing in the audience area, and gave a downward thumb to show his disapproval of the amendment.

FIGURE 11. Navajo Nation Council considering legislation, July 18, 2013. Photograph by Andrew Curley.

As soon as the speaker did this, Council Delegate Katherine Benally yelled out from her seat and changed her vote. It shocked everyone. She said she wanted to vote yes, in favor of the amendment. It was an outburst rare for the Navajo Nation Council. This action suddenly nullified the speaker pro tem's vote because it changed the early vote from an 11–11 split to a 12–10 majority in favor of the amendment. Then one of the strangest things happened in the many years that I have followed the Navajo Nation Council. Rather than accept the amendment to the lease, the speaker pro tem called a five-minute recess for a supposed "malfunction" of one of his voting buttons. Suddenly everyone was out of their seats and walking around. There was loud chatter. I could see the speaker and the speaker's staff lobby council delegates Katherine Benally and Mel Begay on the council floor (see figure 12). I do not know what was said to them, but when the recess ended (after twenty minutes, not five), they both switched their votes to "no" (against the amendment) and it ultimately failed. After the amendment failed, the Navajo Nation Council went back to the "main motion," the lease renewal, and passed it 16–6. The delegates who ultimately opposed the lease extension were Nelson Begay, Russell Begaye, Jonathan Hale, Leonard Pete, Leonard Tsosie, and Dwight Witherspoon. Ten of the sixteen delegates who voted in favor of the lease are no longer on the Navajo Nation Council.

FIGURE 12. Unprecedented suspension of debate to negotiate votes on the NGS lease, July 18, 2013. Photograph by Andrew Curley.

On social media, someone who worked in the speaker's office (an older man) posted a public message that read:

> Nearly 3 years of negotiations and many days of Council debates and we finally got the Navajo Generating Station lease amendments approved! This preserves thousands of high paying Navajo jobs in a 65% unemployed area, creates billions of dollars in revenues to our regional market, millions of annual Dollars to the Navajo Nations budget and adds some of the most aggressive pollution controls systems in the Nation!

In response, a critic of the deal, a younger Diné woman with training in law and public policy who had ties to environmental organizations, responded:

> I truly wish our Nation would be receiving such a windfall. Sadly, the opposite is the case. The market for coal is not what it used to be. In less than 5 years, we'll be left standing with a worthless power plant that will cost us hundreds of thousands of dollars in upgrade costs. It is my generation that will have to clean up the mess.

Members of the Navajo Nation debated whether the lease extension was good for the Navajo Nation. The considerations were difficult and the political terrain hard to determine.

CONCLUSION

The significance of the Navajo Nation's 2013 coal renewal was to highlight the embedded moral economies (more on these in chapter 4) and structural limitations operating in and around the Navajo Nation. The Salt River Project was the power broker during the entire renewal process. It dictated the terms of the lease almost completely. This was almost the same scenario tribal lawmakers faced in the mid-1960s when the power plant was originally proposed. Why had the terms of the negotiations failed to change despite years of social, political, and ideological change among tribal lawmakers between then and now? The answer is related to colonial difference making and the lack of meaningful options for tribes. In other words, the lease renewal was an illusion of choice, a façade on par with the treaties from 150 years ago that cemented land dispossession.

While ethnography helps sheds light on the deliberation of the Navajo Nation Council lawmakers, there are limitations in this research approach. It is restricted to the data I do have, the observations I made during the lease renewal, and the private interviews I had with some of these lawmakers before and after the passage of the lease. That my father was a council delegate at the time might bias me in favor of his interpretation of events. He would regularly give me a matter-of-fact explanation of what was going on while it was happening, which influenced how I interpreted things. There is also much to be gained in having connections with and understandings of the people involved. Such connections create a more in-depth and richer understanding of the process, even if understood through the lens of one participant's perspectives. What we have in the colonial record from the 1960s is a complete absence of any of this. The larger point of this chapter is not to say who was right or wrong in the detailed questions about the passage of the lease. I had my opinions at the time, both as a member of the Navajo Nation and as someone with a sense of an invested future in the outcome of the decision. At the same time, I thought about the meaning and the significance of the renewal beyond the moment and the questions involved.

The renewal, as a political process, shone a light on some areas and hid other things in the shadows. To this day, we know little about what was discussed preceding the renewal between members of the Navajo Nation president's staff and the Salt River Project. This was where crucial decisions were made. When I asked some of the most consequential actors about what they discussed during this time, like then attorney general Harrison Tsosie, they were unforthcoming in their responses. As the public face of the administration, Tsosie didn't disclose anything that was confidential. It was for us, the public, to interpret the meaning behind the administration's silence on questions about the lease renewal. Why were some things restricted to "executive privilege" and others allowed to be part of the official public discourse? In this way, the attorney general was acting more like a corporate attorney than the lead attorney for the Navajo Nation government. Or, put differently, perhaps this reveals that in matters of extraction and mineral leasing, the Navajo Nation is more of a corporation than a government. What do "citizenship" and "sovereignty" or even "membership" mean for such an entity?

This speaks to the idea of carbon treaties, the flipside of carbon sovereignty. In principle, the treaty should be a fair agreement between actors, but for Indigenous nations it was a way of adding a legal face to what was otherwise violent dispossession. Treaties between Indigenous nations and the federal government centered around final land statuses. I posit carbon treaties to think about similar arrangements and political advantages and disadvantages involving issues beyond land and the status of reservation boundaries. Carbon treaties combine the political inequalities of treaties with the business practices of corporate agreements. The NGS lease serves here as an example of a carbon treaty—making the arrangements around the Navajo Nation's use of fossil fuels.

The theoretical basis of sovereignty speaks to the powers of modern states to control internal populations. It is a territorial claim but with extraterritorial implications. Sovereignty defines as much of the external as internal, and this is a legacy of statecraft and state making. The implications for carbon sovereignty are to think about how sovereign powers are territorially reconfigured in fossil fuel contracts. Also, what are terms of the configuration? Whereas traditional notions of sovereignty are for forever, contracts set time limits—even if the time limits are far into the future. A question is, what was the original purpose of a seventy-five-year lease for the land on which the NGS was built? It was clearly extending the life of the power plant beyond the natural lifetimes of the people who signed the lease. As Normal Little indicated when he asked the Navajo Tribal Council to support coal development, he acknowledged his inevitable death and the fact that the social processes decided today would have ramifications for future generations. The coal contract works in this liminal understanding of time. It is not forever; neither is it *un*-permanent. Seventy-five years into the future, from 1969, what did they imagine? At the time of this writing, we are still not at this threshold in time. We are still twenty-two years away from this arbitrary point in time, and we see so much has changed in the span of just a few years.

There are places in the world that have (had) liminal timeframes when thinking about sovereignty and territorial claims. Hong Kong was originally a ninety-nine-year lease between China and the UK in 1898. At the initial signing of the lease, China was weak and decentralized. European powers cut it to pieces during the Opium Wars. The lessons of imperial meddling are still fresh in the minds of Chinese officials. By 1997, with the end of the lease, China was a very different China. It was centralized under the authority, power, and dominance of the Chinese Communist Party. China's communist party was born in anti-imperial struggle and is largely defined internally to protect China from external threats. The retaking of Hong Kong was never in doubt when the lease expired. The status of Hong Kong as a place, culture, and site of politics is changing. Territorial configurations are redrawn in the column and authority of China.

The land on which NGS was built is not a Hong Kong. But it is a land that is part of the Navajo Nation and was subjected to similar territorial exceptions. The land was brought out of the jurisdiction of the Navajo Nation and into the control of the Salt River Project—a nominally public utility that operates like a private corporation. In this way, SRP's territorial claims included parts of the Navajo Nation. In the leased area, subject to the seventy-five-year lease, the rules of the utility, not the tribe, were paramount.

CHAPTER 4

WORKERS' PERSPECTIVES ON COAL

IN THE SUMMER of 2014, it was already a year since the Navajo Nation renewed its stake in coal. By this point, I was living in Sanders, Arizona, in the southeast corner of the reservation. I had moved from Kayenta, Arizona, where I had lived for a year and interviewed community members and coal workers on their thoughts on coal as a continued source of revenues, jobs, and "development." It was then that I was asked to moderate a forum between Navajo Nation presidential candidates as they campaigned ahead of the election that fall. The forum was called "Navajo Youth Forum" and its purpose was to hold the potential political leaders accountable to the perspective of young Navajo people.

Since the beginning of 2014, I had watched staff of the *Navajo Times* (my employer at the time) conduct presidential debates across the reservation. The moderators were good at being systematic and structured, but to a fault. I found that they failed to ask follow-up questions to a candidate's rehearsed answers. This is where I was asked to step in. Organizers felt I knew enough about the Diné political experience to ask quick follow-up questions of the candidates. In my case, I wanted to know what they thought about coal.

During the debate, I asked presidential candidate and former coal worker Edison "Chip" Begay how he felt about the future of the industry given its external pressures. I asked him if it was a viable industry for the future with climate change regulation increasing, power plants shutting down, and young Diné community members pursuing different kinds of work outside the reservation. His response was indicative of a generation of Diné workers who grew up with mining around them. He explained, "I was raised in a coal mine. I spent thirty-three years in a coal mine. As a single parent, I got two kids that I've raised. This is our national resource. Abundant natural resource." I said, "Talk to the young people out there who are getting degrees, other skills. Do they have a future in the Navajo coal industry? Do you see coal as a tenable form of employment in the future?" He replied, "Yes. To me, yes, it is. Because we [coal workers] supported the Navajo Nation, we supported the youth with scholarships, we supported the veterans, we support our elders with that money."

This was the sentiment of a working-class Diné man who found opportunity, security, and a sense of livelihood in coal work. This was the voice that is muted in the scholarship on coal and development in the Navajo Nation. Yet it is the coal worker who will bear the greatest costs if the industry suddenly dries up. This chapter is the story of the Navajo coal worker and the peculiar place he or she fills in Diné social, cultural, and political institutions. This chapter is about the Diné coal worker and how he or she feels about life and livelihood.[1]

TABLE 2. Kayenta resident and coal worker interviews

	DATE	AGE	GENDER	EDUCATION	OCCUPATION
CW1	5/22/13	61	M	High school	Welder
CW2	5/14/13	NA	M	High school	Electrician
CW3	5/13/13	66	M	NA	Administrator
CW4	7/18/13	64	M	High school	Truck driver
CW5	7/19/13	NA	M	College	Dragline operator
CW6	NA	60s*	M	College	Works for SRP
CW7	NA	NA	M	High school	Truck driver
CW8	6/22/13	NA	F	College	Truck driver
KR9	NA	30	F	College	Researcher
KR10	NA	23	F	College	Not-for-profit
KR11	NA	35	F	Graduate	Government
KR12	9/1/13	34	M	Graduate	Government
KR13	NA	30s	M	Graduate	Researcher
CW14	1/27/19	50s	M	NA	Welder
CW15	1/30/19	60s	M	NA	Loader
CW16	2/4/19	70s	M	NA	Machine Repair
CW17	2/8/19	60s	F	NA	—
CW18	2/8/19	60s	M	NA	Dragline operator

THE BEGINNING OF CRISIS

In the fall of 2005, crisis splashed across the *Navajo Times* in headlines such as "An Uncertain New Year: Black Mesa Workers Face Layoffs, Upheaval After Decades of Service," "Closure Causing Layoffs of Longtime Workers," and "Chapters Lament Lost Perks in Wake of Mine Closure," with one article explaining, "Measured in jobs, the cost will be 150 mine positions and another 31 on the slurry line."[2] As Hopi slurry worker Everett Cainimptewa said, although the work was hard, he did not regret it because it paid for his children's college tuition. "I'm really grateful for that. They deserved that."

The shutting down of the coal mine and power plant was a traumatic experience for the Navajo Nation. It was "the end of an era." It signaled the end of coal in the Navajo Nation. But although this was the beginning of the end, the end was far in the distance. The Navajo coal economy has experienced a long and painful death. At the time of this writing, one coal mine remains open, and all the rest have closed. With them, the jobs are gone and the monies dried up. The last remaining mine is Navajo Mine, ironically the first mine to open.

The closure of the Black Mesa Mine in 2006 was mentioned in several interviews with coal workers in 2013. In the lead-up to the NGS lease renewal, the specter of Black Mesa Mine's closure weighed heavily on the minds of Diné coal workers. Some of the workers I interviewed had worked at the Black Mesa Mine for decades. Suddenly, in 2005 their futures were uncertain. When the mine closed, they were out of work and unsure if they could find work again. More than one of the Kayenta Mine workers I interviewed had worked in the Black Mesa Mine before it closed and then moved over to the next mine. The fact that Peabody Coal operated both mines made the transition somewhat easier.

Although the Black Mesa Mine and Kayenta Mines were adjacent, the political context of the two mines was very different. The Black Mesa Mine opened in 1968 and provided the raw fuel for the Mohave Generating Station, a 1,500-megawatt power plant, based 273 miles away in Laughlin, Nevada. Southern Californian Edison, the utility that owned the Mohave Generating Station, convinced the Navajo Nation Council to slurry the coal to the power plant rather than use rail, which was the practice at the time. Many people don't know this, but Southern California Edison insisted on the slurry. It was a way for the utility to save on costs. But the Navajo Nation provided the water for the slurry. The water was from the N-Aquifer beneath Black Mesa and was considered by some to be pristine water capable of supplying household needs. For the power utility, the N-Aquifer, like the Colorado River, was abstract and made into a cost.

This was how the colonial ontology of resources entered into everyday practices in the Navajo Nation. The land and water became numbers in lease agreements and contracts. The conditions of the earth were established by colonial forces, and Diné leaders could agree to participate or not and likely see these lands converted into resources anyway.

The Mohave Generating Station operated for decades. The water was used once and contaminated in the movement of coal through a nearly three-hundred-mile pipeline. While the Navajo Nation received revenues and jobs, Arizona and California got permanent water infrastructure and decades of cheap energy. As the previous chapter showed, the coal industry expanded and consolidated in the Navajo Nation in the 1970s and 1980s. For residents on Black Mesa, the people directly impacted by the mine, N-Aquifer became something real, something that represented two fundamentally different ways of thinking about the environment: one that was based on exploited colonial capitalism, and the other about environmental health and sustainability.

In 1998 the Sierra Club and other environmental organizations sued Southern California Edison and the plant's owners for not adhering to provisions of the Clean Air Act. The provisions had to do with regional haze rules over national parks and monuments like the Grand Canyon. Southern California Edison, the owner and operator of the power plant, decided to settle the lawsuit. Cynically, the utility agreed to retrofit the power plant by 2006 or shut down. Southern California Edison did nothing. As SRP would do a decade later, the utility tricked the tribe and Diné coal workers into thinking the plant and mine would remain open. Instead, the utility managers found cheaper sources of energy elsewhere and planned for the shutdown and demolishment of the power plant.

Power plants and their feeder mines are complex systems, moving people, material, and energy into capital circulations. There are state and federal regulators, tribal governments, workers and contracts, unions, rate payers, transmission lines, water rights and water sources, industrial equipment, boilers, and toxic waste. Energy produces some of the most complicated logistical systems in the United States. These energy systems coordinate around temporal and material abstractions like acre-feet of water per year, tons of coal, and dollars per hour. Then there are the long-term contracts—fifty-year terms, seventy-five-year terms. Logistically, extraction requires temporal bending, the movement of time from hours per week to half centuries or more of land leases. The world dramatically changed between 1969 and 2019, but the coal contract doesn't care about this. It's all about access, property, and profit. In search of this ideal, for a time-cost calculation that is most advantageous, utilities and large energy producers are even abandoning the long-term contract that was a feature of coal production for decades. An underappreciated story about the death of coal and its replacement with natural gas is the way that the latter is made more flexible in capitalist temporal regimes—its production is less tied to permanent extractive infrastructure associated with coal and therefore can be conditioned as more responsive to flexible "market" purchases.

Southern California Edison did nothing for seven years. What it did, it turns out, was buy time to find new sources of power so that it could close the coal plant and save money. Although this bolstered the bottom line for the private utility, it was devastating for the Navajo Nation—the worst possible outcome, in fact. The implications of Southern California Edison's decision were lost jobs and revenues for the Navajo Nation—the collapse of a major part of the economy with little warning and no sense of responsibility. The agreement the utility made with environmental groups was little more than a stalling tactic. The utility decided to close the power plant on the deadline of the day of the agreement, January 1, 2006. With no one to sell coal to, Peabody Coal closed the Black Mesa Mine. Southern California Edison received offset credits for closing the plant and the Navajo coal workers lost their jobs. Many Diné workers blamed environmental organizations for the shutdown.

T'ÁÁ HWÓ' AJÍ T'ÉEGO

Although the circumstances leading up to the closures of both the Mohave Generating Station and the Navajo Generating Station looked similar, there remained important differences between both coal infrastructures. NGS was a unique configuration of private, public, and federal ownership. It was the only power plant that the Bureau of Reclamation owned. It was key to the power of the Central Arizona Project for decades, supplying 90 percent of its power. Without NGS, Phoenix and Tucson couldn't get water from the Colorado River, which was vital for both cities. As was discussed in the previous chapter, the NGS annually consumed thirty-four thousand acre-feet of water in Arizona's apportionment of the Upper Colorado River water. That water was set aside in the NGS lease so that Congress would initially fund CAP (Curley 2021a), but now it's free for any user in Arizona to claim.

NGS was different from the Mohave Generating Station in that most users were from Arizona, not California or elsewhere. SRP owned 21.7 percent of the power plant, Arizona Public Service (APS) 14 percent, and Tucson Electric Power 7.5 percent. Arizona utilities own 43.2 percent of the power plant. Additionally, the Bureau of Reclamation owned 24.3 percent of the NGS. The Bureau of Reclamation owned the power plant as part of its commitment to CAP—an Arizona project. This puts NGS's commitment to Arizona energy and water at 67.5 percent of the plant. The other owners were Nevada Power at 11.3 percent and Los Angeles Department of Water and Power at 21.2 percent.

David, like many of the mine workers I interviewed, presented a consistent understanding about his work with coal. He told me that the coal mines were a source of jobs and livelihood in a place with few opportunities. During our interview, almost as a passing thought, David described the importance of coal work for people like him through the expression *t'áá hwó' ají t'éego*, which means "do it yourself" or "it's up to you" to take care of yourself. Referring to lessons he learned from his parents and his grandparents about hard work, David said, "We are doing as we were told." Then he repeated the phrase *t'áá hwó' ají t'éego*. "We get up early in the morning and come back and we bought just a little bit of progress" (CW2).

Diné people historically have had a strong sense of independence and self-reliance. It is for this reason that dependency on the federal government feels like failure for many tribal members. I suggest that this attitude of "do it yourself" was easily adapted to a subsistence economy reliant on sheep. In those times, a family's well-being depended on how hard its members worked. Prior to colonization, Indigenous peoples did not exist in a primitive state as many anthropologists alluded to over the years. Indigenous peoples had different ideas of property, work, and value that were tied to ideas of personal character and production of useful labor. In other words, in Diné notions of social and community responsibility, expressed in idioms such as *t'áá hwó' ají t'éego*, the maintaining of a livelihood through hard work is key and it can be done in the form of sheep herding, small-scale agriculture, or mine work.

With the expansion of colonialism and capitalism across the region, Diné attitudes toward work did not suddenly disappear or become replaced by capitalist logic. As the labor historian Colleen O'Neill (2005) writes, early

Diné coal mines were small, family run, and reflected traditional ideas of land tenure, work, and reciprocity. Between the 1920s and 1940s, Diné men established small mines where coal was near the surface. This coal was unevenly extracted and became extra cash when it could be sold to trading posts or outposts for stoves. This was a small-scale version of mining that was responding to new regional pressures and opportunities. O'Neill shows that Diné people staked claims to mines much like they had for sheep pastures, sharing a mine site among a family unit, with different members of the family taking turns digging, hauling, and selling. These mines were not supported by notions of property rights but understood ideas of family unit territorialization (O'Neill 2004). This was similar to how Diné people grazed their sheep over areas that families informally claimed. It was this process of moving further and further onto the Colorado Plateau in search of better grazing lands that led the Navajo people westward from New Mexico into modern Arizona (Weisiger 2011).

Because subsistence ethics bleed into regimes of wage labor, one's sense of doing meaningful work is not changed. For instance, Diné weavers sell their rugs primarily to white buyers and make small imperfections in their craft so that their sense of personal investment does not become permanently tied to the objects they make (Bsumek 2008). It is a way to release their invested labor from the object. Consequently, certain things that are produced for trade carry as much importance as things that are produced on the land and for the family to consume. Not all work is viewed as hard work or worthy work, however, and the corresponding opposite of t'áá hwó' ají t'éego were accusations of cheating, corruption, or sometimes even witchcraft (Kluckhohn and Leighton [1946] 1956).

Wealth can be interpreted as the outcome of hard work and good character or corruption and bad character. From my experience, work that moves further and further away from physical labor is interpreted with less and less intrinsic value. Even though government work and elected political leadership are significant sources of income for many people, this work is easily chastised and understood as corrupt. It is not too different from popular attitudes among working classes generally against white-collar or desk jobs, but for the Diné people many of these attitudes are directly related to a regime of ethics in production that were learned in subsistence times.

The phrase *t'áá hwó' ají t'éego* is popular in Diné society today and is used regularly in conversations about self-reliance. For example, the popular summer footrace series Just Move It, held throughout the reservation to combat obesity and diabetes, uses the phrase *t'aa hwo' aji t'eego* as the slogan for the run. The organizers of the series translate the phrase as "It's up to you."[3] In consecutive State of the Nation addresses, Navajo Nation vice president Rex Lee Jim used the phase to reiterate the importance of Navajo people taking personal responsibility for their livelihoods, explaining: "I wanted to encourage Navajos to take responsibility for their own actions and their own future." In another example, the Navajo Nation Department for Self Reliance (the Tribal Temporary Assistance for Needy Families program) uses t'áá hwó ajítéego as a core value of its work.[4] Finally, the chief justice of the Navajo Nation Supreme Court used the concept to reduce child support obligations to a woman who divorced her husband. Chief Justice Herb Yazzie wrote:

> Our elders have always taught the concept of t'áá hwó' ají t'éego (self-reliance). The emphasis of this value is that one must prepare himself/herself for the difficulties in life—one needs to rise early to meet the dawn and be blessed with the desire, commitment and capabilities necessary for a strong positive mental attitude, physical strength and endurance and capabilities in dealing with life's challenges. . . . These values apply to all; particularly, to a woman who marries and becomes a parent. Should the marriage end, the mother remains responsible for maintaining the home and raising the children despite the difficulties she may encounter. "Traditionally, the responsibility for a family whose male spouse either has deserted or is deceased falls upon the family of the female." (Navajo Nation Supreme Court Opinion SC-CV-40–07, p. 18)

The expression is often described as something that comes from the past when Navajo people relied mainly on sheep for subsistence. In identifying the source of t'áá hwó' ají t'éego with "elders," in the Supreme Court opinion quoted here, Yazzie dates the origin of the phrase to the past when Diné people lived under much different circumstances. Or as David explained, "it is something our grandparents taught us." Although the notion was related to work and life common in a subsistence economy, it is something that has translated directly into regimes of wage labor and settler colonialism, or colonial capitalism.

For a generation of people in Kayenta, the first wage-labor opportunities came in the form of uranium mining, which left a terrible and tragic legacy across the Navajo Nation. The mines were crude and irresponsibly administered. Companies who leased land from the Navajo Nation to open these mines left many of the mine sites contaminated (Eichstaedt 1994). One of my interviewees who worked in the Kayenta Mine all his life learned the trade because his father worked as a uranium miner in the 1940s and 1950s (CW1).

By the time he started work at the Kayenta Mine in the 1970s, the negative health effects on his father, like many in the previous generation of uranium miners, had started to metastasize. Workers who had never smoked developed lung cancer years after they had ended their time in uranium mines. On investigation, federal officials and members of the Navajo Nation learned that the mines were poorly insulated, and the workers did not use protective masks or gear when digging in these radioactive sites. They were not informed of the danger, and spread the uranium dust to their family members when they shook off their clothes at home.

Despite these negative health effects, many young people graduating from high school in the 1970s applied for employment at the new coal mines. As one interviewee told me, "Uranium to coal mining, it has benefited our people" (CW1). With little education and even less opportunity, these workers took on coal mining as a way to provide for their families and fulfill their duties at home. There was a sense of masculinity tied to this work. This is how an industry like the coal industry, although clearly an environmental and health risk to miners and members of the community, could quickly embed itself in the reservation during the era of development. Although the work displaced families who lived on the mine site and contributed to environmental problems in the area, many who sought and gained employment in the industry weighed these consequences against the benefits of providing a good living for themselves and resources for their family.

The sociologist Rebecca R. Scott (2010) identified a similar tendency among coal workers in West Virginia. In one interview, she talked to a community member whose house and family land were destroyed through the controversial mining technique "mountaintop removal," in which entire mountains are destroyed to expose their coal. The interviewee acknowledged that coal displaced her family and obliterated generations of history with the land, but at least it provided the area's local men with jobs and sources of livelihood (Scott 2010). Environmentalists will decry the destruction of the land, but the interviewee in West Virginia focused on themes of work and livelihood, which brings us back to David. He lamented the work of environmentalists and the lackluster response of Navajo Nation Council delegates to defend the industry.

> To me, I did not go to the last [Navajo Nation Council session]. The only time we went there is when we met. Because I saw the exact same thing they were doing [when they were considering the renewal of the Black Mesa Mine in 2005]. They were giving more debates and everything to the environmentalists. They would not listen to the workers because I heard one of the council members say all they do is drive duallys [dual rear-wheel trucks that are usually more expensive than regular trucks] and four-door trucks.
>
> Already they are prejudiced because we are practicing what our great-grandmas and great-grandpas said: t'áá hwó' ají t'éego—"It's going to be up to you to be something." We are not practicing what those councilmen over there are doing, just sitting around and going to bars. No. We are doing what we were told, t'áá hwó' ají t'éego. Get up in the morning and make some money. Good things will come to you. We get up early in the morning and come back and we bought just a little bit of progress. (CW2)

Another interviewee, who grew up in Kayenta but not in a coal-mining family, told me that the children of coal workers were distinguishable in the local school because they always had new shoes and nice backpacks (KR14). Two other people I interviewed, who were children of coal workers, told me that the revenues from coal work were an important part of their household income when they were growing up (KR10, KR11). Although they themselves had questions about the industry, they understood and emphasized the importance of it for their parents and their parents' generation. For some Navajo people, dressing nicely in new clothes is a sign of a good work ethic (KR14). Therefore, new clothes and trucks are not negative or flashy things but the result of hard work.[5] Most of the children of mine workers whom I interviewed explained that even when they disagree with the coal economy because it is bad for the environment or a failed approach toward economic development, they respect their parents' work and the material security it had brought them. To have a job, regardless of the circumstances, meant that you were providing for yourself and your family. As one informant who worked in coal mining for more than thirty years told me:

> You will be swept away by how much the environment is sometimes hostile and discriminative, but for dear life, our livelihood lies within it, so the feelings that I have through my experience working, I think through our generation, my generation, we respect how the corporations come along, they use their guns, their

> money, the money and ability to maneuver. I do respect my job and I really did enjoy working because for me and my livelihood and my kids, I would say that it has given me a good life, but there are times when you just felt like walking away from it. That was the source of income. That's the only thing that I knew was to mine. I did [my share] in training people and I did my job well and I was praised for it. So it was good and bad.
>
> . . .
>
> I have lived in the mining environment all my life. It was the mineral source that helped me from childhood to high school. I'm accustomed to it. I do know the value to the family, my mom and dad when they were alive, and I was raised as a miner. And me again, I raised my family from coal mining. . . . It is very benefiting to be near or live on our own soil.

This idea of being close to one's ancestral land with the means of both physical and social reproduction weighed heavily on the minds of Diné coal workers. This was a central rationale that was given for the support of Peabody Coal and the jobs that exist at the mine. Although a majority of the workforce were men, some women worked at the mine. The gender division of labor was different from previous generations of work within the Navajo Nation. One interviewee joked with my research assistant Majerle Lister in 2019 that the men at the mine were lazy and the women had to push them to work (CW17).

Many of the interviewees talked about the work being close to home. White members of Peabody use this sense of belonging to serve their own interests. In one instance, at a public debate about coal and alternative energy during a local chapter house meeting, I observed a Peabody official prod a former mine worker to talk about the benefits of the mine and how working at the mine allowed him to stay close to his home to maintain a living.

He was a member of an organization called Black Mesa United. Members of the organization attended a meeting of the Navajo Nation Council's Resource and Development Committee to consider whether to allow the site of the Black Mesa Mine to become a solar field. Under U.S. law, the land had to remain untouched for ten years to allow it to recover. However, environmental organizers wanted to use the land as a place to develop solar energy, as a symbolic transition from extractive industries into sustainable ones. Members of Black Mesa United opposed this plan because they said this land was theirs before it was used for mining. Members of this group attended this meeting to express their concerns. They believed the land under discussion was their land and that they still maintained grazing rights to it, even if the land was toxic. This argument was legally weak but symbolically important.

As I discussed these things with a member of this group outside the chapter house, a white employee from Peabody Coal interrupted my interview and asked the man to discuss the benefits of the Kayenta Mine for his community and his family. The Peabody official asked the man to talk about how the mine allowed him to live and work in the reservation. This was certainly a line that employees used to justify the work at the mine. During our conversation, the white representative from Peabody asked me if I was with the members of the environmental group, and then he asked the man I was speaking with to talk about how working at Peabody allowed him to stay close to home. The man seemed to agree and repeated to me what the Peabody official had asked him to say.

Another person I interviewed, a coal worker, told me that the population of Kayenta declined after the Black Mesa Mine closed in 2005. He believed that the closure of the mine created a community crisis. To him the Kayenta Mine was the main source of livelihood for the Kayenta community (CW2). A different coal worker I spoke with in his home told me that his daughter's educational success was funded through the money he earned while working at the mine. "That is the reason why I brought you back over here to my house," he said. "Being closer to work and working on the reservation has produced those things for me" (CW4). He then pointed to his daughter's awards hung on the wall of his living room. "And then with the money that I made she went to college. With our help, but I had to stay right here [in Kayenta]. . . . I bring in money right here. It's just right there." In a 2019 interview, a former coal worker told Majerle Lister:

> I was traveling all these years and I was away from my family, you know, all the time. My wife was the only one, she couldn't get my kids through school; elementary, junior year, and then high school. But me, most of the time, I was out there working trying to provide for them. And then when I came back in 2005 I was at home with them. And I seen the younger ones go through elementary, junior high, and then high school. Still they didn't pay me enough money but you know my major reason is to be with my family. (CW14)

Another coal worker told me that being in the area helped him learn traditional ceremonial knowledge, knowledge he could not have acquired had he been out "chasing my dreams" (CW2). Because he stayed in the Kayenta area working at the mine, he could learn ceremonial knowledge from a medicine man and start practicing his own ceremonies. This would not have been possible if he had to live outside the reservation for work, he said. Yet another coal worker told me that coal mining was a good form of employment. He said it was hard to find work in the Kayenta area and that work at the mine was secure and provided benefits (CW5). He said that at the mine one had the opportunity for job advancement, paid leave, and so forth. For him and many others, it was the type of work and the job benefits at the mine that distinguished coal work from other jobs, such as a sales clerk, in the reservation. For these workers, coal work was a good source of income—on par with historic forms of livelihood.

This valorization of labor, one that is rooted in providing for one's family, comprises the moral economy of coal on display in Window Rock. This is the core feature of this collective sentiment, work, and livelihood in service of self-determination. There is a significant difference between the subsistence understanding of t'áá hwó' ají t'éego and how it has translated into modern wage labor. Historically, work and livelihood were rooted in a concern for one's family unit—providing for oneself from work on the land, through food sovereignty and security. Although this is still true in practice, rhetorically the concept has taken on meaning for larger groups of actors.

So how do we understand t'áá hwó' ají t'éego today? How did it gain a sense of collective application and rights vis-à-vis the Navajo tribal government for a *community* of workers? In my analysis, the role of labor in collectivizing the voice of Diné coal workers was critical in translating this subsistence ethic to one that represents the community. Labor is a new feature in Diné society. It is one that is rather uncommon today. Navajo labor laws protect tribal employees from wrongful termination, and the tribe maintains generous benefits and retirement packages. As a former employee at Diné College and the *Navajo Times*, I had full health coverage and even a retirement account. But for most Diné people who worked in the private sector, which includes gas stations, hotels, and other forms of services, they live precariously. They do not enjoy union representation, health benefits, or retirement. These trappings of the welfare state are both recent and unevenly distributed across the Navajo Nation. In the next section, I consider the role of labor in transforming t'áá hwó' ají t'éego from an expression rooted in subsistence work to one that is part of the wage-labor economy.

THE ROLE OF LABOR

Unions are not a common organization in reservation communities, and tribal governments continue to maintain ambivalent relationships with them. Many tribal leaders have historically viewed unions as a source of agitation and in some cases a threat to tribal sovereignty (O'Neill 2005; Robbins 1978). In 1958 the Navajo Nation Council passed a resolution banning unions from operating within the reservation. Then in 1960 the Navajo Nation challenged the AFL-CIO's right to organize under the National Labor Relations Act of 1935, claiming that treaty rights give tribes plenary power in their own lands. The U.S. District Court said otherwise and argued Congress had the authority over labor issues on Indian reservations. After losing the right to ban unions, tribal officials adopted a more pragmatic view toward labor. Today, tribal officials view them as a vehicle to gain more rights for Diné workers in off-reservation power plants as well as at reservation coal mines. As the anthropologist Lynn A. Robbins (1978, 23) wrote, "Although the economic impacts of energy developments are depressingly slight, and even harmful, the introduction of huge energy projects has strongly affected Navajo labor relations with unions and federal agencies." Robbins estimated that there were 6,650 union workers in the reservation in 1977. Out of these, the United Mine Workers constituted 950 members.

The United Mine Workers of America (UMWA) Local 1924 is one of two unions that currently operate in the reservation, the other being Union of Operating Engineers Local 953, which represents the workers at Navajo Mine. Other unions have existed in the region with Diné members, but they were based outside the reservation and abided by state laws. For example, the union that represented workers in the Navajo Generating Station, who were largely Diné, was the International Brotherhood of Electric Workers Local 266. This union, although representing workers in a power plant that operates on Navajo land, was based in the border town of Page, Arizona, and is registered with the state. The Navajo Nation also maintains strong labor rights within the Navajo Nation Code to ensure grievance procedures for most types of employment disputes. This authority is vested in the Office of Navajo Labor Relations, which is a branch of the Navajo Nation Council.

Although I could not find documentation on the history of UMWA in the Navajo Nation in particular, the union formed within the first five years of operation of the two mines. The Black Mesa Mine started operations in 1968 and the Kayenta Mine in 1973. According to several of the coal workers I interviewed, the mine had no union representation when it opened. As one of the workers told me:

> [The union] was introduced after the mine came into the area. I think [by] the late Lauren Williams. He was an Anglo guy from Farmington [New Mexico]. He is the one who proposed the Local 1916 to be established. The local 1916 is [now] closed. That was the union for the Black Mesa Mine. Now [when] Kayenta Mine opened [in 1973], we set up Local 1924. (CW1)

The UMWA originally had two chapters on Black Mesa, but Local 1620 closed when the Black Mesa Mine did in 2006. The workers I interviewed expressed mixed perspectives about Peabody Coal. On the one hand, they applauded the opportunity to work that the company provided and the capital and resources it has been able to mobilize in bringing industry to the reservation. On the other hand, the workers understood that the company exploited their labor. Peabody paid most of its Navajo employees hourly. They had to work forty hours per week and sometimes put in many more hours to make ends meet. One interviewee put it this way:

> I've been forced to live with a lot of overtime. Being away from my family. I work 24/7. It causes you to be away from home. Working fourteen to sixteen hours a day. That takes a lot. . . . One day I never realized it but I stayed home and my oldest daughter was five years old. I said, "Come here, baby." They didn't know me. They ran from me. All this time I was going to work when they were asleep, coming back when they were asleep. Spend three and four hours at home and then take off again. (CW1)

He continued to speak about how the demanding nature of the work can split families apart and lead to domestic disputes. The work at the mine was grueling and wages were hourly. During the time of mining, Peabody Coal often emphasized the number of Native workers employed at the mine, but very few of them were salaried employees. Most of the salaried employees were "company men" who were white and did not live within the reservation on a full-time basis. As another coal worker put it:

> What I hear at the community level is that Peabody has grown too much income and maybe they need to increase our wages. We make wages, not sala-

> ries. We call it the hourly wage employee and the salary employee. The company will make the salary and we make the wages. We have to work for every cent that we get. [Conversely] there's a base on a salary yearly.

Unions helped alleviate this difference and played an important role as mediator between the Navajo people and the company. Speaking from more than thirty years of work at the mine, one coal worker put it to me this way:

> I grew up with the idea that [a] union is bad. . . . My dad was against unions. But I am a true-blue union guy. With the different companies that I've worked for, there are a lot of grievances and the union will stand behind you. Just look at the teachers—if there was no union, then teachers would be fired left and right.

He told me that he felt that the union was a good thing and it had helped improve working conditions since he had begun working there in the mid-1970s. He said, "When we first joined the union, that was the only way to get a good wage scale, and the union helped us a lot." He continued, "They helped secure jobs through the bidding process," which ensures that workers with senior rank get the jobs and shifts they want. This process was won through union contracts and was not something Peabody Coal used prior to the union. As he explained, "We had that Indian [hiring] preference and monetary wise and also health wise. We are the only union that offers 100 percent health benefits." It was this sense of solidarity that developed in the union halls and that translated the sense of collective responsibility among Navajo coal workers from just family members to a community of workers with a collective sense of well-being. The appeal to "the community" in this case was not only to Kayenta as a place where people lived but to the town where people were socially and culturally connected. Coal workers recognized that this form of wage work was important for their livelihood and survival, but they also identified themselves as a class, distinct from tribal officials and salaried employees at the mine (who were mainly non-Native). In this way, t'áá hwó' ají t'éego took on new spatial and social dynamics. It was no longer rooted in the family unit but in "the community" and among workers.

I met with a former coal worker on the front porch of his home in Kayenta, in the Peabody trailer court. Maybe because he no longer worked at the mine, he was more candid in his critique of the industry and even the union. He told me he had ambivalent feelings toward the UMWA. He said that the organization was founded in 1890, when miners worked hard and needed protection. Today, he feels that it breeds laziness and corruption. As John Gaventa documented in his famous book *Power and Powerlessness* (1982), unions become a power unto themselves and this was the interviewee's point: "I've seen documents of overstaffing at the Union Hall. People are sleeping and drinking on the job" (CW3). His point was to say that the union, in its grievance process, protected bad employees. The early anthropological literature on ideas of wealth among Diné people is interesting on this point. In their famous 1946 book, Kluckhohn and Leighton write, "Industry is enormously valued. A family must arise and be about their tasks early." Kluckhohn and Leighton ([1946] 1956, 221) futher cite the white anthropologist John Adair's early work on Diné silversmithing to note that "display of wealth is not a personal matter as much as it is a family matter. It is not 'See how much money I have,' but 'See how much money we have in our family.'" Kluckhohn, Leighton, and Adair suggests that Diné people think about wealth accumulation as something that is measured at the family level and not at the individual level as in rational-choice theory or other assumptions found in the work of economists. This implies an ideal form of distribution in which the wealth one earns is normatively distributed among family and kin members. This is a form of collectivity that does not exist in the union. Adair (1946, 98) writes, "In a similar fashion, members of a Navajo family herd their sheep together, although every animal is owned by individual members of the family."

The union is formed through solidarity among workers who share the same occupation. It assumes a proletarianized worker who is supposed to subsume his or her identity and interest into his larger organization. For some Diné workers, this sense of collectivity exists, especially during contentious political circumstances, but at other times this solidarity is simply nonexistent, and each worker fends for himself in the interest of his extended family. This measure of wealth at the level of the family and not the individual is ironically a vulnerability for unions in the Navajo Nation. As the sociologist Rogers Brubaker notes, group identity is not a permanent category mobilized around events. For the Diné coal worker, group solidarity in the form of "the coal worker" manifests during consequential political decisions between workers and the tribal government, such as the Navajo Generating Station lease renewal, but may disappear in everyday reservation life that is centered more firmly around kinship networks (Brubaker 2004; Brubaker and Cooper 2000). The weakness of this kind of collectivization is that it requires the right kind of event to produce solidarity. In everyday coal work for those at the Kayenta Mine, it was difference and not solidarity that was noticed.

Unionization created a system of seniority among the Kayenta workforce that benefited more senior workers. In some cases, this protected troubled employees. It also limited the opportunities for younger workers to find employment at the mine. To one interviewee, the seniority system did not express the deeper meaning of t'áá hwó' ají t'éego. Instead, it created unnecessary forms of hierarchy and authority that corrupted workers and made them lazy. This is not a neoliberal critique of unions but one based on unique Diné cultural values. As noted in earlier anthropological ideas of how Diné people understood the idea of wealth, if you are too wealthy, one may suspect you of wrongdoing. In the case of my interviewee, he felt the union had corrupted people's work ethic. Another worker spoke about how his father, a public official, was against unions. Robbins (1978) showed that in the 1950s the Navajo Nation Council viewed unions as a threat to its political authority and initially opposed unions from operating in the reservation. Still, coal workers appreciated the power of a collective voice the union provided. Another coal worker, speaking to Majerle Lister in 2019, said:

> Well the union, they'll speak for me if I do something wrong. By being a company man they could let me go anytime when I make a mistake or something. . . . The union, they speak for you if you do something wrong and the grievance and everything. They'll speak for you and put you back on. (CW15)

When Lister asked if he had ever been a company man, he responded: "I've never been a company man. I've always been with the union. Well, up here I make thirty-eight, almost thirty-nine."

In 2013 the union hall in Kayenta that represented Kayenta Mine workers maintained six permanent employees. These people were paid through union dues. Their jobs were to assist the workers during their negotiations against Peabody Coal. Most of the mine workers I interviewed approved of the union and articulated real benefits it brought to the workforce. They spoke of higher wages, paid leave, and improved safety at the mine site. The United Mine Workers of America was once the most powerful labor union in the Navajo Nation, regularly involving itself in tribal politics and elections. It contributed funds to the winner of the Navajo Nation presidential election for three election cycles in a row. Its agenda was clear—to continue Navajo investment in its coal economy. For example, when Lynda Lovejoy won the most votes in a 2010 presidential primary and gained national attention as the first potential female president of the Navajo Nation, the UMWA donated $6,000 to her strongest opponent, Ben

Shelly. This was about half of his entire campaign budget during the general election. Shelly won the election later that fall. It is not hard to understand why members of the UMWA would support Shelly over Lovejoy. On the one hand, as a former council delegate and the Navajo Nation vice president for Joe Shirley Jr., Shelly had a track record of supporting coal projects. Lovejoy, on the other hand, gained a lot of support from environmental organizations. She ran with the Diné activist Earl Tulley, a board member of Diné Citizens Against Ruining our Environment (Diné C.A.R.E.).

The UMWA also supported the campaigns of individual Navajo Nation council delegates with the intent of influencing their votes on coal-related questions, especially those that might affect the Kayenta Mine. One delegate told me that the UMWA had donated several hundred dollars to his campaign (TGG6). He felt that the union's intent was to influence his stance on coal-related questions. He did not mind the money and ultimately was critical of the renewal of the lease. But he questioned whether candidates who received significant donations from the union could resist pressure to renew the lease. The delegate ultimately voted for the renewal, but after trying to amend a lot of the language of the proposed resolution as it pertained to labor and water rights. In 2013, when the Navajo Nation Council considered the passage of legislation to extend the lease of the Kayenta Mine for twenty-five years, UMWA Local 1924 chartered a bus to bring coal workers from Kayenta to Window Rock to demonstrate their support of the lease renewal (figure 13).

FIGURE 13. Kayenta Mine workers in front of the Navajo Nation Council chambers petitioning for the NGS lease renewal, April 11, 2013. Photograph by Andrew Curley.

Labor unions have changed the working conditions of mine work in the Navajo Nation. Their efforts substantially increased the rights and benefits of coal workers. Because of union activism, the company not only had to ensure fairer treatment of its workers, but it was also obligated to pay into health insurance and retirement funds. The company would likely not do this otherwise. In one of its recent renegotiations with the UMWA, Peabody suggested that it should drop its health coverage for mine workers because they could get free health service through the Indian Health Service (IHS), which many Native people believe is a lackluster fulfillment of treaty obligations and not an adequate replacement for health care. The UMWA rejected this proposal and secured continued health coverage for its workers. In these areas, the union improved the conditions for its workers. It was also an active political organization, involving its membership in questions that will affect the continuance of the mine.

In important ways, the union created a sense of solidarity and cohesion among mine workers and helped define the Navajo working class. For the Kayenta workers who were members of the United Mine Workers of America, it reinforced their sense of class conscience and the notion that working hard is its own virtue expressed in t'áá hwó' ají t'éego. The unique history of the mine, labor unions, and an inherent Diné sense of work and livelihood created a class consciousness among working-class Diné people whose livelihood depended on the continuance of coal mining in the reservation. The work was not only consistent with historic Diné values in labor; it has also merged with a sense of class-consciousness forged through the union over the past thirty years.

IN THE SHADOW OF A CLOSED MINE

During the debate about the renewal of the NGS lease, coal workers reminded me that they were campaigning for their jobs. They feared that if the Navajo Nation Council rejected the lease or pushed too hard on SRP to renegotiate the terms of the contract, the owners of the power plant would walk away and shut it down. I asked one of the organizers outside the council chambers what he knew about the lease. I asked him about the question of water rights that troubled council delegates and if he agreed with the Little Colorado River Settlement from the previous year, the settlement initially tied to the lease renewal. He looked at me like he never heard of this issue. In fact, he didn't seem to know the terms of the lease. That information wasn't shared with the Diné public. What they knew was that their jobs and livelihood were tied to the lease renewal. They believed the Navajo Tribal Council had agency to decide their fate. The performance of the lease renewal would suggest all things were in the hands of the Navajo Nation Council, but in truth SRP, CAP, and state planners had control over the fate of the mine and the power plant, as subsequent events would reveal.

In recent years, the idea of t'áá hwó' ají t'éego has become more visible within tribal institutions. It was used in Navajo Nation law, in the proclamations of tribal officials. Most famously, it was used as the slogan for a series of foot races throughout the Navajo Nation. The coal workers I interviewed understood t'áá hwó' ají t'éego through the way their grandparents taught them, as a value in getting up early and starting the day with hard work. This work ethic was something they identified with and incorporated into the day-to-day work in the coal field.

T'áá hwó' ají t'éego does not specify a mode of production. What is important is the notion of cultural sustainability, meaningful livelihood, and national self-determination. By 1940 Kluckhohn and Leighton ([1946] 1956, 59) estimated that a third of Diné income came in the form of wages earned outside the reservation. Thirty years later, Ruffing (1978) found that Diné men and women moved easily between wage labor and subsistence work: from rail and road construction to sheep herding and small-scale farming. The latest and already dated statistic on "unemployment" in the Navajo Nation was 48 percent of working adults throughout the reservation (Choudhary 2005). It did not include Diné people living outside the reservation; many live in faraway cities for school or work but return home frequently. Ruffing showed in 1978 that Diné laborers left the reservation in search of seasonal work and returned during planting months. O'Neill (2005) found the same pattern in her archival work focusing on labor in the 1930s. Diné men and women left the reservation for work on large farms outside the reservation and returned home when they needed to maintain their own fields and livestock. In other words, Diné people filled a labor niche that would later be filled by migrant labor, whose presence in the United States as "illegal" allowed for poorer work conditions and cheaper wages. They participated in large-scale agriculture during picking season and then returned home (Iverson 2002).

CONCLUSION

For Diné coal workers, their sense of collective and social responsibility brought them to Window Rock to petition for their jobs. Diné members of the UMWA turned t'áá hwó' ají t'éego into a political cause, mobilizing their membership for the preservation of their work and livelihood. They articulated an ideology of cultural sustainability and responsibility for the livelihood of their kin and family. Diné coal workers stood at the juncture of a rapidly changing energy economy. In the politics of climate change, coal was under new kinds of scrutiny and already in decline. Because of California's actions in 2006, the state's utilities like LADWP and Southern California Edison were actively divesting from coal. Even with the Navajo government's renewal of NGS in 2013, the power plant was already in decline. There was already talk that it would shut down one or two units in 2019 when the original lease ended. This scenario would likely lead to layoffs at the mine as production declined, regardless of what the tribal council did. In the end, things were much worse than this. In 2017 SRP reneged on the contract, although it would argue it never signed the renewal, and it made plans to shut down the plant at the end of the first fifty-year lease. SRP said it was looking toward the interest of rate payers (settler communities). The welfare of Diné people was not SRP's main concern. It was just something it would promote if Diné sovereignty happened to align with its cynical calculations. It was a structure of colonial resource relations long imposed on Diné lands. The failure of the lease to continue to prospect Navajo coal signals the clear limitations of a sovereignty imagined and understood through carbon.

CHAPTER 5

TOWARD ENERGY TRANSITION

IT WAS MID-JUNE 2013, only a couple of months after the Navajo Nation Council passed an extension of the NGS lease. The weather had warmed considerably since May. It was already a season of extreme weather. There had been deadly tornados in Oklahoma, drought in New Mexico, and a number of forest fires in Arizona, where several firefighters were killed. Some considered these violent expressions of weather a part of global climate change. It was in this context that the Navajo Nation experienced its most intense debate about the future of coal and energy as a source of jobs and revenues. This would be the year when the tribe doubled down on coal.

By 2013 the political momentum for sustainable energy projects had significantly changed course from only four years previously. Programs associated with the highly touted "Navajo Green Jobs," passed in 2009, were effectively moribund. The new Navajo Nation president, Ben Shelly, had twice vetoed funding for the commission designed to oversee the use of money associated with the fund. Environmental groups introduced the rhetoric of "transition" from "dirty" to "clean" energy technologies in 2006 when the Black Mesa Mine closed. In 2010 the Navajo Nation used similar language in its updated energy policy and creation of a new Navajo-owned coal company, the Navajo Transitional Energy Company (NTEC).

The notion of "transition" from coal to sustainable energy technology was an accepted approach in the mainstream of Diné discourse by 2013. When environmental organizers and activists first talked about transition in 2005, it was a radical departure from the extractive industries that shaped carbon sovereignty in the Navajo Nation. What environmental organizers proposed was a new kind of technology, one that was designed to produce exportable energy but would not release carbon emissions that contribute to global climate change. This was a different kind of understanding of carbon and a different understanding of tribal sovereignty.

In this way, the term *carbon sovereignty* still retains meaning, but with an opposite understanding about carbon and sovereignty from previous generations of Diné leaders. It is the way this changed comprehension of energy as something in need of transition that this chapter documents. In North America, energy transition challenges are connected to decades of colonial policy, land theft, and pressures to exploit resources on Indigenous lands: British Colombia (Sloan Morgan 2020), Alberta (McCreary and Milligan 2014), North Carolina (Emanuel 2019), and Arizona (Curley 2019b). These pressures and the need to develop combined to create a sense of carbon sovereignty among tribal nations. It is no surprise, therefore, that the idea of transition wasn't revolutionary itself but was made to fit existing governing practices.

President Shelly took the idea of "transition" and made it a major part of his agenda. He used it during a presidential speech in the fall of 2013. He incorporated it again in his new energy policy, amended in 2013, that focused on moving out of coal and into other kinds of resource technologies. This was the first time the Navajo Nation's energy policy was amended in more than thirty years and demonstrates how sustainable energy technology was made to fit the existing frameworks used by tribes. Although transition was still aspirational, Shelly's actions did signal politically where his administration was going on questions of energy and development. When the council proposed the formation of the Navajo Transitional Energy Company later that year, "transition" was in the company's name and already part of the tribe's governing agenda.

In its incorporating language, the Navajo Nation Council required NTEC to invest 10 percent of its profits into renewable and alternative energy research. Renewable and "alternative" were vague enough to include a wide range of possibilities. The chairman of the organization at the time, Steven Gunderson, told me during an interview for the *Navajo Times* that NTEC could serve as a vehicle by which the Navajo Nation might transition its economy from coal to sustainable and alternative energy technologies such as solar and wind. In 2013, notwithstanding the fact that the Navajo Nation renewed and revamped its stock in coal, it appears that this renewal was done in the political language of promoting alternatives and transition.

What is important to recognize here is that for the first time in Navajo Nation history, promoters of coal talked about the end of the industry even if it was simply rhetorical. Carbon sovereignty couldn't continue as it did. The conversation acknowledged that coal no longer enjoyed the luster of its initial promise when it came onto the reservation in the 1960s. In 2013 notions of modernization and progress in the framework of development were replaced with the language of "transition" and "sustainability" when tribal officials or environmentalists promoted alternative economies. The function and authority of the tribal government in energy development decisions remained intact. But the vehicle toward development and prosperity had changed. How did we get to this point where the language and understanding of "development" had changed from progress to sustainability? Part of the answer lies in the work and political advocacy of Diné environmental organizations over the years. This chapter intends to document part of that history and make the connection between environmentalism and development alternatives.

CONTINUING PARTITION, OPPOSING BLACK MESA MINE, AND NAVAJO-HOPI LAND DISPUTE

Before the ink dried on newly signed coal contracts in the late 1960s, Diné residents near the proposed sites of extraction challenged the legitimacy of these leases and the right of the Navajo Tribe to destroy their ancestral lands. Diné families living in remote areas on Black Mesa near prospective coal sites petitioned tribal leaders to reconsider these deals. In 1971 the *Navajo Times* published an article that quoted a seventy-three-year-old Diné man who said, "We the Navajos of the Black Mesa area never surrendered to Kit Carson and never even left our land to walk to Fort Sumner."[1] The man would have been born in 1898, only thirty years after the Navajo people returned from internment at Bosque Redondo.

In the article, the *Navajo Times* reporter Verna L. Harvey wrote that the man spoke out against Peabody Coal and the forced removal of Diné families from their ancestral lands to make way for coal mining. This was at a time of growing awareness about the dangers of industrialization and environmental pollution. It was on the verge of the Red Power movement and grassroots criticism of tribal governments. Already, before the mines opened, people on Black Mesa resisted them. Harvey wrote, "They felt that the contract between the Navajo Tribe and the Peabody Coal Company had been made without the true and full representation of the Navajo people, particularly those living in the mining area."[2]

The *Navajo Times* reported in 1971 that a resident of Black Mesa said:

> Peabody made all kinds of promises and even had a local Navajo who was at the time a councilman going around to convince people to consent to the coal mining. . . . We were told only the good side of the story but we were never warned about the bad side. We were told that there would be jobs and that we wouldn't have to go far to work. They said that the roads to every home would be improved for us and that water wells would be built. Are these promises fulfilled? No![3]

At the time of these disagreements with Peabody Coal, critics of coal development in reservation communities argued that modernization and capitalism created a situation of economic dependency. By the late 1970s, only ten years after the Navajo Tribal Council signed its coal leases, scholars and researchers started to examine the history of development in reservations more critically. In 1971 Vice Chairman Wilson Skeet said that the Navajo Tribe recently replaced its lawyer, and that the tribe was "reconsidering and renegotiating the contract with Peabody."[4]

While Peabody Coal opened mines across Black Mesa, the Hopi and Diné people experienced new colonial tensions. Preceding the signing of land leases and coal-mining contracts with the Navajo Nation, Peabody hired John Boyden, a Mormon lawyer, who litigated on behalf of the Hopi Tribe (while secretly still working for Peabody) (Wilkinson 1999). Boyden initially offered his services to the Navajo Tribe, but when he was refused, he went to the Hopi Council. Either way, Boyden was an agent provocateur. His larger agenda was to split the Diné and Hopi along colonial boundaries and open both reservations to coal mining. What was key for Peabody wasn't the dispossession of Diné people from their lands, although this was an assumed part of the mine-leasing process. What was more critical from a capitalist standpoint was the certainty of property rights. For the company, a boundary dispute meant uncertainty in contracts. If history played out differently and Hopi were dispossessed of land, coal mining would have resumed all the same. It was the mineral leasing that served as an important economic driver to what would become the Navajo–Hopi land dispute.

For BIA officials, the Hopi reservation was historically incorporated into the management of the Navajo Tribe and distinguishing between the two wasn't a major administrative concern. The reservation was created in 1882 through an executive order from Washington, D.C., and much of the land that was called "Hopi" was ancestral Diné homesteads. The Hopi people historically lived in villages on top of the high mesas near the southern edge of Black Mesa, whereas the Diné people lived in the vast wooded rangelands below the mesas, just north and east of these villages. The two peoples had cultural exchange for generations and lived off the land differently. It was the impetus to create boundaries, to make the land legible to coal companies, that drove a wedge between the political bodies nominally representing the two peoples. Following the tension initiated by the coal-leasing process, Congress met to divide the reservations in law. After testimony and opposition from Diné leaders and community members, Congress nevertheless passed the Navajo-Hopi Land Settlement Act in 1974. This was one of the worst injustices wrought on Indigenous peoples in the twentieth century. In simple terms, the legislation was a negotiated land swap between Navajo and Hopi tribes, regardless of who was living where.

For Peabody Coal, the settlement served its interest in solidifying boundaries between the two nations so that it could contract with the Navajo and Hopi tribal governments to mine coal. The act mandated that Diné people living "on" Hopi lands should relocate to new lands the federal government would provide that were the equivalent to the lands lost to Hopi. This was not acceptable for people living on the land that was swapped. The Diné people who suddenly found themselves on the Hopi Reservation had lived on their lands for generations. They had relatives buried nearby. Some were born to the land, with umbilical cords buried to keep them in place. None of this mattered to the colonial forces gathering in Phoenix and Washington, D.C. The land was turned from something with a relation to abstract lines on a map—with an 1882 date stamped on it. With a monopoly of violence on the side of the federal government, Diné families were asked to relocate. This action was the territorialization of colonists; from the partition in Palestine to Pakistan, the drawing of lines between centuries of cultural mapping engendered difference, opposition, and violence. With criminal indifference, then commissioner of Indian affairs Alfred Bennett simply declared that Diné people who refused to leave their family lands couldn't be forced off but they would also be denied basic infrastructure and couldn't improve upon their existing homes until the situation was resolved. Hopi police, funded by the BIA, enforced this freeze. They harassed Diné residences, impounded sheep, and let Diné homes fall into disrepair—broken windows had to remain broken.

Because of the new mines, obvious environmental destruction, and the forced removal of Diné families from their lands, Diné people on Black Mesa and elsewhere grew increasingly distrustful and oppositional of the actions of the tribal council. On the ground, attitudes during this time demonstrate a general distrust of coal companies and tribal officials. These attitudes are consistent with what the historian James Robert Allison III (2015) found in the history of coal mining on the reservations of the Crow and Northern Cheyenne nations.

Critics of development at the time, such as Roxanne Dunbar-Ortiz (1979), Vine Deloria (1985), and Richard White (1983), built critiques of coal mining and other extractive contracts based on the neo-Marxian idea of dependency theory. Whereas traditional Marxists focused on the commodity relationship of extractive industries as containing the seedbed of exploitation, the exploitation of the laborer in their production of "surplus value" (Weiss 1984), dependency theorists focused on the political economy of production within a regional and world-economic system designed to serve global capitalism (Snipp 1988). Although tribal lawmakers saw the money and jobs that coal and other extractive contracts brought in and tied it to emerging ideas of sovereignty, Diné community members organized in opposition to these development projects and identified them as colonial and a continuation of exploitation. Diné community members moved in the direction of an emerging environmentalism and anti-colonialism.

Carbon sovereignty, concretized in coal contracts, contained a flaw. Between new strip mines, dying uranium workers, and forced relocation, Diné community members started to question the wisdom and effectiveness of the tribal government. Sovereignty wasn't just a right to develop but a return to older values through self-determination. Not limited by the logic and terms of mining contracts, Diné people started imagining a life beyond and against the environmentally destructive industries tribal officials had invited onto the lands.

In 1988 the tribe's first environmental organization, Diné Citizens Against Ruining our Environment (Diné C.A.R.E.), was formed to contest a waste incinerator project in the western Diné community of Dilkon. From the beginning, Navajo environmentalists were chiefly concerned about ongoing and proposed development projects. In the case of the waste incinerator, organizers and activists believed that it would create pollution that was unhealthy for people.

On the other side of the reservation, Diné organizers and community members opposed the continuation of a sawmill at the base of the Chuska Mountains that was leading to deforestation. The mill was opened in the early 1960s and an entire town was founded around it—Navajo.[5] Activists and organizers worked to reduce the amount of logging on the mountain, but loggers took this as a threat to their jobs and in some cases threatened violence against the activists.

At the same time, community groups in Window Rock and Gallup worked to end the border town's predatory selling of alcohol to Diné people suffering from addiction. The city had an obscene number of liquor licenses, among the most concentrated in the state. Many places sold beer right through drive-thru windows. Diné community organizers marched from the Navajo Nation to Santa Fe to protest this injustice. They called on the State of New Mexico to reign in the practices of Gallup's alcohol vendors. This was during a time when the tribe was reworking its system of governance, following the allegations of theft against former chairman Peter MacDonald. He was removed from office for laundering money and the tribe adopted a three-branch government that mimicked the divisions of powers found in the U.S. constitutional system.

Peter MacDonald's main rival, Peterson Zah, was elected the tribe's first "president." He wanted to do things differently. He wanted to tap the voices of opposition groups and get them to work toward social and political reform that was desperately needed in the Navajo Nation. According to a recent interview with Earl Tulley, Zah gathered the leaders from these various movements and suggested that they work together. As with Diné C.A.R.E., these early environmental organizers started working as an oppositional voice to the development projects coming from outside the reservation, always promising modernization but often leaving pollution, destruction, and destitution. Zah and others in Window Rock wanted to decenter tribal governance and return it to traditional values. This was a renewal of cultural values along clear political lines. By the 1990s, the Navajo Nation passed its first environmental laws and Diné C.A.R.E. took on one of the first large and environmentally taxing development projects in the Navajo Nation—the Navajo Forestry Services, located in the small town of Navajo, New Mexico.

LOCAL EMPOWERMENT

In the late 1980s, the conversation about development in Indian Country shifted from Marxist critiques of underdevelopment to small-scale capitalist development initiatives. In 1992 the economist Joseph Kalt and the sociologist Stephen Cornell published a book on "what can tribes do," looking at ways tribal governments could use their existing power to advance economic development, measured initially in improvements in per capita income. In more than twenty years of publications, this school of thought (nation building) has been the most institutionalized and perhaps most successfully diffused economic framework operating throughout U.S. reservations.

Much of this work promotes the general idea of "cultural match," in that the institutions of governance ought to match the culture of the people they govern. The authors of this work found plenty of examples of tribal governments, imposed on tribes in 1934, that did not conform with "traditional" notions of Indigenous governance. For example, the Hopi had village elders who made decisions for the villages they belonged to and not on behalf of the entire Hopi nation. The Hopi government established in 1934 put a central and overriding government in charge of all Hopis and did not include traditional elders in its distribution of government power. This became a hotly contested issue in the 1960s when the traditional Hopi elders opposed coal mining on Black Mesa but the central government signed contracts with Peabody Coal.

The traditional Hopi government, composed of leadership that went back generations and not the elected leadership that was part of the IRA reforms, also wanted to live cooperatively with Diné neighbors, but the central Hopi government wanted to (and ultimately did) clear Navajos from their ancestral lands. This led in part to the disastrous Navajo–Hopi land dispute (Benally 2011).

The nation-building approach promotes constitutions not only because they might revive traditional and more culturally appropriate governing frameworks but also because constitutions institute "the rule of law" across reservation communities that are said to improve business conditions. They argue that rule of law creates the stability and institutional mechanisms, such as the ability to sue a contracting party, that Kalt and Cornell believe is necessary to attract businesses to reservations. Tribal governments that are mired with too much instability, such as the Navajo Nation in the 1980s, will discourage entrepreneurs from developing commerce in reservations. Although nation building promotes a general idea of "cultural match," much of the work is directed toward a capital match or creating the conditions for capitalism in reservations.

It was during this time that a new sense of Indigenous environmentalism emerged across reservation communities. Members of these organizations critiqued long-standing policies of their tribal governments that relied on extractive industries almost exclusively as a form of development (Churchill and LaDuke 1986; Gedicks 1993; LaDuke 1992, 1999, 2005, 2008; LaDuke and Cruz 2012). Although the scholarship on nation building and environmentalism was very different, it overlapped somewhat in the scale and approach to economic challenges in reservations. For the nation-building literature, tribes needed to focus on constitutional reform that would demonstrate political stability and would invite new kinds of industries into reservation communities and diversify tribal economies (Cornell and Kalt 1991, 1992; Grindle 1997; Henson 2008; Jorgensen 2007; Lemont 2006; Miller 2012; J. Taylor and Kalt 2005). Eventually environmental organizations would adopt parts of this economic argument and include them in proposed alternatives to coal and other extractive industries.

By the early 2000s, nation-building scholarship and Indigenous environmentalism were the dominant perspectives of development in reservation communities. Winona LaDuke, one of the central figures in this environmentalism, gained national recognition when she ran with Ralph Nader on the Green Party's 2000 presidential ticket. Diné environmentalists developed critiques that centered on rekindled notions of "tradition" among Indigenous spokespeople. Dana E. Powell and I argued that these groups interpreted the historical development of tribal governments as necessary conditions for exploitation of mineral resources (Powell and Curley 2009). I also show elsewhere that environmental organizers and activists articulate a decentered approach to development that challenges environmentally taxing extractive industries and rolls out neoliberal frameworks concurrently (Curley 2018). These recent works reflect critiques of development *discourse* that make normal its objectives as both natural and non-political (Escobar 1995).

TRANSITION

In 2005, when "transition" was introduced in the Navajo Nation for the first time, an entire generation of workers had learned how to maintain a livelihood at the coal mine. This was a sociological phenomenon underappreciated in scholarship on coal and climate change. The fact that miners mobilized around coal in preservation of the industry was hard to explain using dependency theory and resource curse frameworks.

It also highlighted the challenges of doing energy transition in places long accustomed to the production of carbon emissions. The mine played figuratively in narratives of moving people out of poverty. Environmental organizers and activists recognized the social importance of coal work for coal miners and their families. In interviews from 2012 to 2013, organizers and activists reflected on this need in how they did their work. One of my interviewees, a young woman who worked in a Diné environmental organization, said:

> Maybe that is why [coal] is such a big thing, it's part of our culture now, historically. . . . Natural resource development has been a huge piece of the revenue for Navajo. A lot of us are so attached to this new—new for us—economic scheme, maybe people are afraid that if coal is taken away that money and that revenue would go away too. (EJ2)

Theirs was not a complete recapitulation of the narrative of coal workers, however, and I sensed that much of the professed sentiment about jobs and livelihood was somewhat scripted. For environmental organizers, coal impeded on the lives of other Diné people. The organizers were quick to reaffirm that they are also "from" these same communities and have family members directly employed in coal work as well. Nevertheless, the entire premise in offering alternatives was to respond to the moral economy of coal workers and their need for jobs and a means to producing a livelihood (EJ3).

Between 2006 and 2013, the Just Transition Coalition worked through the slow and difficult process of petitioning the California Public Utilities Commission to recoup money Southern California Edison gained in pollution credit for closing the Mohave Generating Station. The coalition was assisted by attorneys working with large environmental organizations such as the Sierra Club. Ultimately, their effort was unsuccessful. California Public Utilities denied Just Transition's request, but that didn't stop the work. The organizers continued to lobby for solar and wind on Black Mesa. An opportunity came with the surprising win of Barack Obama in 2008 following the financial crisis and Great Recession. Obama campaigned on rebuilding the U.S. economy through an investment in green energy technologies. Diné environmental organizers always maintained strong connections with people in the national environmental movement who in turn had connections with people in the Democratic Party. With a Democratic majority in Congress and Obama in the White House, organizers felt the opportunity for change was suddenly available. The former members of the Just Transition Coalition shifted toward the Navajo Nation and the federal government.

Members from these groups formed Navajo Green Jobs, which pushed for the passage of two legislations in the Navajo Nation Council that were meant to create the legal and political infrastructure necessary to receive money from the federal government for alternative development projects. They promoted investment in green jobs in the Navajo Nation. They believed that if the Navajo Nation created a program to develop alternatives to fossil fuels, the tribe would be in an ideal position to receive federal funds through the American Recovery and Reinvestment Act of 2009. Navajo Green Jobs was impactful in the Navajo Nation. It partnered with the Office of the Speaker, and I was part of these early conversations. Organizers worked hard to lobby the council. I was peripheral to many of these conversations, but I could see the effort. In their campaign offices in Flagstaff, organizers made green shirts that said "green jobs," made signs, and planned a demonstration from the judicial building to the council chambers in Window Rock.

Navajo Green Jobs based its approach on the Human Rights Commission. That commission was created to put a focus on racial violence in border towns. Green Jobs was designed to undo decades of dependency on carbon-emitting fossil fuels. During early discussion of the enabling language, comparison was made to the work of the Human Rights Commission and its structure in the Navajo Nation. It would be "quasi-independent" and staffed with people who were knowledgeable in renewable energy technologies.[6] The plan was well designed and passed the council with little opposition. I got in an obscure argument with Council Delegate Leonard Tsosie about the role of government on the Navajo Nation and he voted against the legislation, saying that I was calling him an "anarchist." My father was on the Navajo Nation Council at the time and voted in favor of it. Still, members of Navajo Green Jobs were annoyed with me for starting a fight with Tsosie.

After the law was passed and President Shirley signed it, the commission was set up to start soliciting money from outside funders. Proponents of the commission imagined that it would recruit federal grants to the Navajo Nation. This was not such an unusual strategy. Enterprises in the Navajo Nation were created in the 1990s to capture federal spending. This was one way of thinking about development in the neoliberal era for tribal lawmakers. But because the commission was focused on green energy, some powerful people in the tribal government who have long thought through coal as the pathway toward development were immediately skeptical. Part of the problem was that the groups comprising Navajo Green Jobs were members of the same groups who sued the Mohave Generating Station. Mine workers and tribal officials were still upset about the way that the mine and power plant shut down. It was a bad lesson for tribal officials as the closure of Kayenta Mine and NGS would also meet the same fate and for similar reasons—because the utility no longer found it profitable to work in coal. Because of this distrust of Navajo Green Jobs, Ben Shelly suspended the work of the commission when he was elected president in 2010. He killed Navajo Green Jobs and its progress.

When I returned to the Navajo Nation in 2012, I observed that the failure of Shelly to fund Navajo Green Jobs left the tribe without a policy toward green energy transition. Shelly wanted transition to reinvest in the tribe's coal resources. As a reporter for the *Navajo Times* in 2014, I asked Commissioner Wahleah Johns about the status of Navajo Green Jobs; she admitted that it had experienced difficulties over the past couple of years but that the commissioners planned on revamping it soon. Today, hardly anyone remembers the coalition ever existed.

After 2010, members of Diné environmental groups changed tactics. Following early disappointment with the Shelly administration, Diné organizers concentrated more on work that wasn't directly tied to the everyday practices of the Navajo Nation. They didn't push for more legislation or a renewal of the commission. Some key organizers left the region and started to work on more national campaigns. In passing, they expressed disappointment with the tribal government. They worked hard to get Navajo Green Jobs legislation passed, only to see the tribe completely ignore it and double down on coal. Plans for solar fields to replace coal mines were challenged by community members who in some cases simply wanted access to their old grazing lands long since devoured by coal.

The main point of their work after Shelly killed the green jobs commission was to build on the discourse of transition and to expand its meaning. They focused on trainings, workshops, and presentations at public meetings—efforts that do not directly influence the thinking of tribal lawmakers but focus on educating future Diné leaders. These workshops and retreats were not a new kind of work but took on a new kind of focus following the end of the legislative process. The work of these organizations was marked by events such as the closure of the Black Mesa Mine and the passing of the Green Jobs Act. These events required a focus on the legislative and executive processes in the tribal government. But following the failure of the Navajo Green Jobs Coalition, this process appeared difficult to amend. In retrospect, we can say they ran against a sovereignty defined in a particular understanding of carbon that they were challenging. Consequently, the work of the tribal government was antagonistic and not sympathetic with their efforts.

DECOLONIZING DEVELOPMENT

Centralization and territorial integrity were central features of the federal government's consolidation of power for tribal nations in the United States at the time, particularly among the Diné. It is the recognition of this history, alongside the lived experiences of family members who worked in the industry, that led many environmental organizations to doubt the legitimacy and intent of the central tribal government as the best way to make decisions on behalf of the people.

As one of my interviewees suggested, if the Diné people had a different decision-making process in the 1960s when coal leases were signed, perhaps the history of coal and development would have played out much differently than it did. She wondered if there had been no outside pressures to develop and modernize the Navajo Nation, would coal have been considered at all (EJ2)? These counterfactuals are more than just thought experiments; they are premises for a competing ideology of development and governance for Navajo people that fundamentally differs from the resource nationalism in practice today.

"Decolonization" is an expression of a movement and ideology among Indigenous peoples. Broadly, it has come to mean a challenge to the discriminatory practices of Western epistemologies, but often this usage misses the political claims of Indigenous peoples (Tuck and Yang 2012; Yazzie and Baldy 2018). In Canada, the resurgence of Indigenous philosophies and governing practices is a pathway to decolonization (Alfred and Corntassel 2005; Corntassel 2012; Simpson 2016). In the United States, a Native "resurgence" was initially understood as an enhancement of the powers of tribal governments and a loose descriptor for the political solidarity that formed across Indigenous nations in response to colonization. These bonds were strengthened by the self-determination movement of the 1960s and 1970s. On the one hand, the Choctaw anthropologist Valerie Lambert (2007) describes insurgent nationalism, advocacy for land and water rights, and new forms and expressions of economic development within tribal lands and towns as "resurgence" (see also Cornell 1988; Nagel 1997). On the other hand, "liberation" is a synonymous call for decolonization that puts more emphasis on the colonial relationship. It is a politics rooted in leftist discourse that was part of the self-determination movement of the 1970s and also part of critical Indigenous scholarship in the 1990s (Churchill 1995). Today, Indigenous resistance movements in the Navajo Nation recirculate the language of liberation as a more Marxist approach toward decolonization (Estes 2019; Lister 2017).

In 2013 Diné environmental groups took a different approach toward decolonization, basing their definitions in part on the work of scholars such as

Michael Yellow Bird (Wilson and Yellow Bird 2005; Yellow Bird 2012). With an emphasis on practice over politics, opponents proposed alternative development projects that replicated the unequal relationship between the Navajo Nation and regional utilities in energy production. The use of "traditional" concepts in contemporary Diné political discourse is fraught with challenges. The Diné scholar Lloyd Lee (2013) highlights the contradictions of codification of traditional concepts, such as t'áá hwó' ají t'éego, in contemporary Indigenous nation building.

Within the Navajo Nation, resistance to extractive industries comes primarily from people and groups who opposed development projects that they felt contributed to processes of global climate change. Diné environmental organizers often emphasize the lack of legitimacy of the Navajo tribal government while promoting the idea of "the community" as the natural site of Navajo politics. In some narrations I've heard, the tribal government pillages Diné lands while "the community" preserves traditional relationships. The community is an alternative. It is natural, whereas the tribal government is a colonial imposition.

In this way, environmental activists and organizers are changing development discourse in the Navajo Nation, from one that prioritizes the exploitation of natural resources to one that highlights development alternatives as movements toward decolonization. They are reshaping the ideological premise of "development" that is based on ideas of modernization and progress to one that is built on sustainability and livelihood. All these activities are part of building a movement toward decolonization among Diné people—especially younger Navajo members living on the reservation who believe they can change how development is understood and practiced on the reservation. Their work is temporal bending. It is this new and nonlinear understanding of development in the rhetoric of decolonization that simultaneously talks about the past and the future.

Diné environmental organizers focus on the idea of "community" as the natural site of politics and development in the Navajo Nation. Under the notion of decolonization, the community contains the inherent traditions of Diné people, and the tribal government is an artificial creation of the federal government that is designed to help outside mineral corporations and white interests pillage their lands. Building on broader critiques of the colonial history of Indigenous peoples in the United States and their unique configuration within U.S. federalism, environmental organizers challenge the legitimacy of tribal government as a part of this configuration of Western colonialism. When I asked someone with professional experience in environmental activism about Navajo tribal governance, she said a core problem is how Diné people do not plan for their community anymore but expect the tribal government to do everything for them. She said, "Prior to westernization . . . prior to this IRA [Indian Reorganization Act] government for Navajo, how would they have approached coal? Let's say they understood its potential, and they understood a little bit of the economic systems" (EJ2). Here, she equates westernization with the existing tribal government, the "IRA government," reminding me that it was a government that was created from the framework of federal legislation in the 1930s. She went on to say that it was the logic of development that brought Diné people to destroy their own lands as a basis of economy. Development was teleological and moving in the direction of capitalist exploitation. It created the conditions for mineral extraction, coal leasing, and the wasting of water for coal slurry. The logic of the tribal government in a regime of carbon sovereignty was one ultimately bent on destruction of land, air, and water. The legitimacy of a government to make this possible is directly called into question.

In my experience, the critique about the legitimacy of the tribal government is a concern that is shared among most Diné people. Although no surveys exist on these questions, many Diné people remain deeply dissatisfied with and critical of the tribal government. In their rhetoric, elected officials regularly defer authority to "the people" on important questions facing the tribe, especially on questions of government reform. Because a broad portion of the Diné public and environmental organizations often question the legitimacy of the Navajo Nation, organizers understand their actions as operating outside the formal political process. Many express skepticism and distrust in the government. When asked what the tribal government should do about climate change, one organizer told me:

> We have no idea about what the impacts are of overconsumption. This leaves us in a very precarious situation where if we don't plan now and create a water budget that's sustainable . . . we're not going to be able to live here—screw jobs, we're not going to have water. That's the reality of climate change that no one is talking about. We are already past the tipping scale; we are in a particular vulnerable space. (EJ13)

In this statement was both a critique of the tribal government and a reiteration of the dangers of climate change for the Navajo Nation. Diné environmental organizers recognize that the Navajo Nation's annual source of revenues is highly dependent on monies coming from extractive industries. They know that this has been the reality for more than fifty years. They are also aware that before coal, the tribal government funded much of its operations through the extraction of other minerals such as oil and uranium (EJ3, EJ4, EJ8). They also realized that mineral development would not have occurred on the reservation if it were not for the persistence of outside companies and corporations wanting to initiate mining in the reservation. All these points were raised in personal interviews and focus group interviews I conducted with actors in Navajo environmental organizations (table 3). Many environmental organizers worked with members of the tribal government on issues of coal and development only to become frustrated by the process. They saw their language of transition co-opted into new energy projects while the small reforms they initiated, such as the Navajo Green Jobs Coalition, were ignored and underfunded.

TABLE 3. Diné environmental organizer interviews

	DATE	AGE	GENDER	EDUCATION	OCCUPATION
EJ1	5/3/12 and 11/27/12	mid-40s	M	Graduate	Not-for-profit
EJ2	11/20/12	early 30s	F	College	Student
EJ3	7/12/12	late 30s	F	College	Not-for-profit
EJ4	11/25/12	late 30s	F	High school	Not-for-profit
EJ5	11/29/12	mid-30s	F	College	Self-employed
EJ6	11/29/12	mid-40s	M	High school	Organizer
EJ7	12/6/12	mid-40s	M	College	Organizer
EJ8	12/6/12	mid-40s	M	Graduate	Not-for-profit
EJ9	Multiple	mid-30s	F	College	Not-for-profit
EJ10	Multiple	late 20s	F	College	Student
EJ11	Multiple	mid-30s	F	Graduate	Government
EJ12	Multiple	late 20s	F	College	Organizer
EJ13	Multiple	late 20s	F	College	Organizer
EJ14	Multiple	late 30s	M	Graduate	Government

Some of the interviewees were originally from areas of the reservation where there was a high degree of coal mining. They told me that the industry had split the attitudes of their family members. Diné community members who publicly challenged coal also had relatives who worked at the mine or NGS and who benefited from the coal industry (EJ3, EJ4). This difference of opinion caused tensions within families. I also interviewed direct beneficiaries of coal mining who had family members opposed to coal mining because mining activities impacted their land or livestock. These were the day-to-day tensions coal engendered in the reservation.

The grounded knowledge of Indigenous environmental organizers makes their work fundamentally distinct from mainstream U.S. environmentalism, even if they coordinate with these movements to a large degree. Diné organizers knew firsthand the social terrain of coal and understood the arguments used in support of it. Although they often disagreed with their relatives on whether the tribe should continue to support coal mining in the reservation, they could empathize with them. They knew how community members and the tribal government framed and justified the industry. It was for these reasons that they understood the Navajo Nation as a colonizing entity. They saw something of a false consciousness operating in the minds of Navajo supporters of coal.

Diné environmentalists recognized the degree to which carbon sovereignty was an entrenched practice in the reservation. Decolonization was a way to challenge this regime, governing practice, and understanding of time and progress. Decolonization meant returning to a status of life that existed before colonization. This was the ideology at hand and constantly under construction. As my interviewees explained, finding and using the form of governance that existed before the imposition of a tribal government was important in realizing what they considered real tribal sovereignty, a sovereignty beyond the carbon sovereignty that defines tribal state building today. This form of decolonization wasn't a distant memory but a renewal in kinship practices: introducing oneself by clan; relating to place and not government; and thinking about language, culture, and tradition in ways that were inherently political. Organizers talked about it in casual conversation. They used it as a justification for their activism.

The alternative development proposals environmental organizers brought forward emphasized "the community" as the natural site of development and political decision-making. The community was sometimes understood synonymously with chapter houses, but the overlap of popular notions of community and the hard boundaries of chapter houses was not exact. It was understood as something not in Window Rock, where the tribal capital is located and where the BIA created the only national capital for a tribal nation. Repeatedly, organizers defined their work as "community led" and for the benefit of "the community." Before any major decision was made, organizers would try to get insight and authorization from the people of "the community." For Diné organizers, in both action and intent, the community was legitimate, whereas the tribal government was colonial.

WORKSHOPPING WITH YOUTH

> We want to create an alternative economy in the Navajo Nation. There's nothing happening in Piñon, I spend a lot of time out there. It's been like that for years. We need a "green economy." How do we create opportunity for people to stay at home [in the reservation]? (EJ4)

One person who spoke to me about green economy had spent years working on these issues. She was my age and traveled frequently, promoting alternative development projects in the reservation. She was from Black Mesa and believed that it was in the community where development should occur. But this idea of community as the site and extent of sovereignty also implied that the centralization of power was wrong for the Diné people. Decades of colonialism that sought to change the language, culture, religion, politics, economics, and personal behavior of Diné people had directly informed the parameters of this sense of sovereignty among everyday Diné people and tribal officials. In this counterideology, it was understood that the tribal government was already subordinate to the interest of colonizers who wanted to exploit tribal resources.

Like coal workers, members of environmental groups emphasized self-sufficiency and traditional economies that are inherent in the idea of t'áá hwó' ají t'éego. This understanding of Diné values and social responsibility is related to notions of cultural renewal. Some interviewees said that without the work ethic inherent in t'áá hwó' ají t'éego, Diné people would continue to lose their culture, language, and independence (EJ13). For the environmentalists I interviewed, this was understood as returning to the land, growing food, and disengaging from modern capitalism. The ability of Diné people to be self-sufficient was part of the framework of decolonization and understood as restoring an original sense of sovereignty.

Acting on this notion, environmental organizers proposed several alternative development projects that were meant to work at the community level and not under the management of departments and offices of the tribal government. These organizers partnered with outside foundations or companies to bring money into projects that were small in scale and limited to a particular community. Some groups emphasized a need to "return" to subsistence-based livelihood that centered on livestock and agriculture. These activities were seen as strengthening both cultural life and the Diné economy. They were also understood as combating global climate change by reducing the amount of carbon Diné people generate. The types of activities that were described in alternative development proposals were a mix of both alternative energy technologies and traditional subsistent activities. This merging of the traditional and the modern appeal to younger Diné community members who grapple with a sense of cultural loss but depend on school and jobs outside the reservation.

Many of these workshops and meetings were geared toward Diné youth. There is considerable debate about what age constitutes youth, whether it is a quantifiable age or a relational one. I learned of one instance where an organizer accused another in a meeting out of the region of not being a youth because he was close to thirty years old. Two interviewees told me they think about it relationally compared to their parents, who are still the primary breadwinners in their household. Because the work of organizing is unstable and difficult, many organizers barely make a living and still rely on their parents for assistance. This relational dependency defines these organizers as "youth" according to this alternative definition. The geographer Mabel Gergan and I compared the way youth is understood and acted upon among environmental groups in Sikkim, India, and the Navajo Nation. We found similarities that reflected our shared colonial experience and greater aspirations toward decolonial futures (Gergan and Curley 2021).

Importantly, Diné environmentalists engaged in the active construction of a counterideology. They hosted meetings, workshops, camps, educational forums, summits, and so on that directly targeted the youth and talked to them about the importance of investing in alternative energy technologies to combat climate change. I had participated in a couple of these workshops. I remember one such event I attended, in 2007, when the Black Mesa Water Coalition (BMWC) hosted a youth summit in Window Rock during the annual Navajo Nation Fair. BMWC was a small but dedicated group of Diné organizers, many former students who challenged the coal slurry on Black Mesa. The organization was founded in 2004 to challenge the use of pristine water for coal. To me, these people were inspiring. I remember the first time I met some of the core organizers and how intimidated I was of them. They were traditional, listened to music I've never heard of, knew how to do ceremony, were artists or related to famous artists, and had politics that challenged the everyday practices of the tribal government.

The event featured thematic work sessions, a fashion show of used clothes, and a performance by the Diné punk rock band Black Fire. I brought three interns from Diné College to the first meeting, and we started by introducing ourselves by clan, work, and where we were from—the "traditional" way Navajo people introduce themselves in accordance with the kinship framework of k'é. This type of introduction is common in Navajo tribal politics but is increasingly uncommon with young Diné people. By opening the meeting with an introduction of one's clans, the coalition organizers acknowledged the tradition and included it in their ideal political practices. The organizers had us sit in a semicircle and introduce ourselves. This was different from the political practices in Window Rock. It included all of us in the conversation. It was a way to democratize the process that also built on historic ways of conducting meetings. Members of these groups partnered with the national Power Shift conferences in 2007 and 2008 to educate young Diné people throughout the reservation about the inherent dangers of climate change. I observed another such event held in Washington, D.C., in 2009 and I got to personally know two of the organizers who were part of this movement.

The larger point of these events was to educate younger community members about the structural inequality inherent in energy production, the health and environmental dangers of coal, and a need for development alternatives.

DEMONSTRATING AGAINST COAL AND CLIMATE CHANGE

There was one event during my fieldwork that articulated many of the characteristics of environmental organizations I describe in this chapter. This event, held in the summer after the Navajo Nation doubled down on coal, reflected the ideological disagreement environmental organizers and activists had with coal workers and tribal officials. In June 2013, I attended a series of workshops in Piñon, Arizona, in the center of the Navajo Nation, where I saw these dynamics play out both in planning and in action. These workshops were held at a "sheep camp."[7] It was an event that served a radical environmental organization in Oakland as well as Navajo environmentalists. This series of workshops was designed to teach participants how to engage in direct actions. Another point of the workshops was to talk about future strategies regarding the environment and climate change in the Navajo Nation. Groups in the western end of the reservation with a long history of opposing coal helped organize and sponsor the event. The land on which these workshops were held belonged to someone with a long history challenging the Navajo coal industry.

The workshops received outside sponsorship. Foundations and not-for-profits often support the work of organizers working on environmental issues on the reservation.[8] In the summer of 2013, the general feeling among Diné environmentalists was that despite the danger of climate change, the U.S. public was not reacting to it. President Obama had largely stalled on his alternative energy initiatives. At the time, it felt that people had become inured to uncomfortable heat in the summer and seeing their forests burn. In many ways, the tactics had not changed but interest had stalled. It felt like Diné environmentalists, like those at this sheep camp in Piñon, were still building public awareness about climate change but to declining public interest.

After the workshops concluded, coalition members who had attended the sheep camp traveled to Phoenix to put what they had learned into practice. Their goal, I learned later, was for some of the organizers to pump water out of one of the canals that comprise the Central Arizona Project near downtown Scottsdale. They used a truck and a solar generator to pump the water into a water tank. They then drove the water back to the reservation and used it to water some crops on the reservation. Their aim was to highlight the structural inequality both economically and politically between the Navajo Nation and the sprawling metropolis of Phoenix.

The organizers wanted to show how water from the Colorado River *should* be used. This demonstration was a symbolic action. The night before driving to Phoenix, workshop participants painted signs that they would use during the march. Nearly twenty workshop participants rallied outside an outdoor mall in Scottsdale. Meanwhile, one of the lead organizers with a couple of helpers drove a truck hauling a small water tank. They parked on a bridge that crossed the CAP. While we were marching around the Scottsdale fashion square, they pumped water from CAP into the back of the water tank. The organizers wore gray T-shirts printed with the words "Power without Pollution, Energy without Injustice."

The activists held banners and signs, chanted slogans, and employed a bullhorn while others took photos. Part of the coalition's goal was publicity. Participants chanted slogans that demanded SRP invest in solar and alternative energy technologies. Demonstrators made a general call for "solar." Activists shouted their support for "green" businesses and entrepreneurship. The activists and environmental organizers knew a lot about the finer details regarding this political economy of coal in the Navajo Nation, but in this instance, they omitted any consideration of how the Navajo Nation might benefit or suffer if SRP transitioned to solar. As it stands now, if SRP transitioned to 100 percent alternatives, it would cut off its ties with the Navajo Nation and all the revenues and jobs associated with coal would dry up. Revenues associated with coal alone provided a sizeable portion of the operating budget for the tribal government. Coal was especially important as a source of jobs and a stimulus to the local economy in the northern portion of the Navajo Nation. How would these changes affect Navajo peoples in these areas? It was this fear about losing resources and jobs that environmental activists did not address in their work, and this bred resentment among people who relied on the coal industry for their livelihoods.

I observed that environmental organizers and activists were disillusioned with tribal politics and focused most of their attention and actions on non-Navajo actors and interests who they viewed as having more influence within the Navajo "coal-industrial complex," as one organizer put it during the protest in Scottsdale. The use of the phrase was appropriate to describe how interest in coal had become institutionalized within Navajo communities, the Navajo Nation, and the State of Arizona. Despite this knowledge, the activists did not specify their actions, slogans, and rhetoric to reflect different interests within the coal-industrial complex. Rather, they treated it as a monolith. What Diné environmentalists called the coal-industrial complex was a network made up of different actors who shared the common interest of keeping the Navajo coal economy intact. Sometimes "Peabody" (St. Louis–based Peabody Energy, the mining company that operates Kayenta Mine) is seen as the leading company in this relationship. I observed many instances in which organizers and activists referred to "Peabody" as a blanket term when talking about the Navajo coal economy in a general sense. They were including not just Peabody Energy but the utility companies who owned the Navajo Generating Station that bought Navajo coal, especially the Salt River Project, and the workers near the mine site and the tribal officials who year after year approved leases for coal interests. Navajo environmentalists saw these disparate entities as one because they shared the common goal of continuing the coal industry within the Navajo Nation and in Arizona as a form of energy production.

But the coal-industrial complex is composed of actors with very different motivations for keeping coal going. It was in the interest of the Salt River Project to keep this coal-fired power plant in operation because it was consistent with its mandate to provide cheap electricity to the Phoenix area and because it was obligated to provide electricity to the Central Arizona Project from this power plant. The Navajo Nation wanted this plant to remain open because it was an important source of revenues and jobs within the reservation. Coal workers wanted coal to continue so that they maintained their employment there. Tribal officials wanted coal to continue so that the Navajo Nation would continue to receive millions of dollars a year in royalty payments that funded much of the government.

The environmentalists' call for "solar" on the streets of Scottsdale did not address these fundamental differences and even who was the target audience. Tribal officials, under intense lobbying and propagandizing from non-Navajo interests, came to believe that the interests of SRP, NGS, and the Navajo Nation were the same when they were not. For environmentalists, the point in lumping all these actors into the same category was to highlight the environmental impacts of the coal industry and the hegemony of coal. If SRP was isolated, the environmental groups would have to talk about energy for Phoenix. For the coal workers, they would have to talk about alternative jobs. For the tribal government, they would have to talk about economic development more broadly and provide alternative development proposals. Referring to all these actors as the coal-industrial complex had the benefit of highlighting the one thing they shared in common: their benefit from strip-mining the Navajo Nation of subterranean coal. Here, they could argue the point that motivated their work the most—the environmental damage that this industry caused to the land, water, air, and health of the Navajo people.

Another reason for why environmental activists and organizers collapsed the interests of different actors in the coal network into the coal-industrial complex had to do with the fact that they recognized something else was pushing coal mining in the reservation—there was a culture among powerful actors in the reservation that supported coal mining. It was not out of a purely economic rationale that the tribe had spent millions of dollars in keeping Navajo Mine open in the eastern end of the reservation. These actions fit within a cultural logic that said coal was good because it provided jobs and revenues—the moral economy of coal.

FIGURE 14. Tom Greyeyes, Inscription House mural depicting the hazards of NGS, July 2013. Photograph by Andrew Curley.

The work of environmental organizers and activists was to challenge this moral economy of coal on the reservation and among Diné people. They proposed a culture of alternatives in league with Michael Yellow Bird's approach to decolonization in his 2012 book, *For Indigenous Minds Only*. They were trying to change a general attitude on the reservation that saw coal as a source of jobs and livelihood. Environmental organizers and activists wanted to convince Navajo people, especially younger tribal members, that coal was a dangerous industry and should not continue as a form of development in the Navajo Nation (figure 14). This was something I recognized when I participated in the demonstrations in Scottsdale.

The demonstration was not meant to address something external to the community of environmental activists and organizers who challenged coal (ergo its lack of political utility), such as the Navajo Nation Council, coal workers, SRP, or even the broader community of Phoenix. Rather, it was directed inward to the people who participated in the demonstration. It was to give them a stake in the conversation through direct action in which they became committed to the greater cause of these groups. The photographs they took of one another were part of this—the photos were meant to reaffirm the event in the realm of social media, where new participants could be "tagged" and identified in a larger online community on Facebook, Twitter, or Tumblr. This was part of the "commitment" of being an activist in the Navajo Nation, where much of the public sphere of political discourse existed online. The speeches over the bullhorn were not only about conveying a message to the non-Native pedestrians walking around downtown Scottsdale; they were about reaffirming in a very public way the ideology of the organizers and activists. This is also true about the preparatory events that preceded the demonstration, such as the direct-action workshops, sign making, and sloganeering. The activities of environmental organizers and activists in these arenas were meant to build a culture of alternatives. This culture of alternatives was used to decenter the development discourse from resource extraction to prevailing ideas of sustainability.

MURAL MAKING

In the days surrounding the passage of the April 2013 NGS lease renewal, I experienced a very different side of the coal debate. At this time, I traveled back and forth between Window Rock and Phoenix for a total of 957 miles across Arizona in the span of three days. I did this to observe the dialogue between formal political actors in Window Rock and Navajo groups opposed to coal. There is a large Navajo population in Phoenix, the economic and political core of Arizona. Navajos there look for opportunities they cannot find in the economically depressed conditions of the Navajo Reservation. In the 2010 Census, it became a demographic fact for the first time that most Indigenous peoples in the United States live in cities and not in their reservation communities. But this population moves back and forth quite frequently between city and reservation. It is a pulsation more than a permanent displacement. My family, for example, lived in Albuquerque, New Mexico, while I was in high school. This is another large, urban space with a high Navajo population. But for holidays and family events, we would regularly return to my family's land on the reservation. This is a common circumstance for many Navajo people, especially the younger generations who look for work and education outside the reservation.[9]

The Sunday (April 28, 2013) before the Navajo Nation Council was scheduled to consider the NGS lease for a second time (the first time was in February 2013), a group of Native artists from Phoenix met downtown and painted a mural of an alternative landscape and energy economy for the region (figure 15). This was in direct protest to the impending actions of the Navajo Nation Council, and this mural centered on the importance of water for the Navajo people. It was called *tóh bi iina*, or *Water Is Life* (part of the series *Water Writes*). What the mural depicted was the destruction of the Navajo landscape and the theft of

FIGURE 15. Diné and Tohono O'odham artists painting the *Water Is Life* mural (part of the international series *Water Writes*) in downtown Phoenix on April 28, 2013. Artists included Jeff Slim, Angel Diaz, Kim Smith, Remy, Averian Chee, Xochitl Enrique, KEISR, Jules Badoni, Mario Alba, Sinek, Ivan Garcia, Edgar Fernandez, David Alvarez, Jeremy Fields, Ramon Aguirre, and Lalo Cota. Photograph by Andrew Curley.

Navajo water that is produced by the Navajo coal economy. At the center of the mural was a pregnant Indigenous woman who represented Mother Earth, or in Navajo cosmology, Changing Woman, who gave birth to the warrior twins who are said to have killed the monsters that had plagued the Navajo people. On the left side of Changing Woman was an interpretation of the contemporary situation—smog, pollution, and wasted water for Phoenix golf courses. On the right side was life—solar panels, wind turbines, blue skies, and harmony.

I traveled to Phoenix to see the completion of the mural and get a sense of its meaning to the young Navajo people there who put it together. I left Kayenta in the early morning and arrived at Phoenix at around 4:00 p.m., an hour after the event was scheduled to begin. The mural was in downtown Phoenix, across the street from a dorm for the sprawling Arizona State University. It was painted on the back wall of a theater studio. In the mural, a pregnant Mother Earth occupies the center; we can see the twin babies in her belly, each painted blue—made of water. This was the first reference to "water is life," a common refrain among environmental organizers in the Navajo Nation who challenge extractive industries and water settlements. The concept is a dichotomy or "duality," a notion that also figures prominently in Navajo ways of thinking (as well as among other Indigenous peoples in the area). To Mother Earth's right is negative space (what my former boss Robert Yazzie referred to as naayéé') and to her left is a positive area called hózhó. Conventionally and true to form, in the negative space was sketched the Navajo Generating Station and a silo that's used to store coal. On the right are sheep (representing the subsistence economy), solar panels, and wind turbines. At the base of the mural are natural fruits and vegetation. This was meant to convey optimism. The philosophy differed slightly from standard interpretations of duality; it emphasized a general direction toward hopefulness.

At first, it was hard to integrate into the crowd of young Native activists moving around the large mural. Nearly everyone there was younger than me—in their late twenties and early thirties. It was hot (around 100 degrees) and all the participants wore shorts and T-shirts. I saw others unbutton their shirts or wrap dampened scarves around their heads. I felt awkward just standing there while people painted. Only a few people were paid to design the mural; the rest were volunteers. I didn't want to be one of these anthropologist types who hang around taking notes while doing nothing. So, I decided to help.

As I helped paint and take pictures of the mural's progress, I walked around and talked with people I knew and did not yet know. Most of the participants in the mural project were young Natives who were part of an artistic community in Phoenix. Some of the artists were professional muralists. The caliber of their work showed in the quality of the mural's design. The timing of the mural was happenstance. It was not timed to occur when the Navajo Nation Council considered the lease extension. It just turned out that way. The funder, the not-for-profit organization Estria Foundation, was based in Oakland, California. This mural was something it paid for and was part of a series of murals throughout the world that focused on local challenges over water security and water rights. The organization worked with Diné environmental groups and identified this struggle over coal and water as a key topic of water politics.

In my conversations with people at the mural site, the artists and activists explained the message of the picture and its broader vision. The foreground focused on the natural life of the desert and traditional Indigenous economies like planting, hunting, and sheep herding. In the background was the relationship between the Navajo Nation, coal, and water in Arizona. Black Mesa rose from the landscape, as well as the silo in which mined coal is stored. The coal takes a path to the NGS and then connects to a water tunnel (depicting the Central Arizona Project), and this water travels to Phoenix to water golf courses. The scenario is represented as an environmental affront. On the hózhó side of the mural are traditional economies and sustainable energy technologies like windmills. The mural spoke in direct contrast to the politics at work in the Navajo Nation at the same time and was part of a larger project to create a "culture of alternatives" that I discuss in the conclusion of this book.

SHIFTING CARBON SOVEREIGNTY

Today, the Navajo Nation and Diné environmentalists have embraced a framework of development that does not reflect notions of modernization and progress inherent in classic development thinking. The change was subtle, but moving away from industries such as coal, oil, and natural gas in the language of "sustainability" and "alternatives" is still significant. There is a broad political effort among actors in the tribal government and at the community level to decenter development discourse and conform it to prevailing ideas of "sustainability." Sometimes these efforts are successful, in small ways.

During a focus group in 2008 and follow-up interviews in 2012–13 with key members of the Diné environmental organizations, they informed me that they first became aware of environmental issues facing the tribe during these trainings, workshops, and youth summits. Some learned about extractive industries in the reservation for the first time during these weeklong camps. Because group members wanted to bring youth into their ranks, they organized activities that reflected youth culture: mural painting, hip-hop shows, rock concerts, fashion shows, and spoken-word poetry. This is not to say that these genres of activities appealed only to young people, but they were included in the programing of events to attract them. This mix of culture and political education was part of the larger process of building a culture of alternatives. When the participants in these workshops, camps, trainings, and so on left these events, they left infused with a critique of conventional development projects in the Navajo Nation.

The counterideology challenged carbon sovereignty in the reservation. Diné organizers constructed a collective sense about alternative relationships with air, land, and water. In this sense, they were advocating for alternatives to development. They put forward strategies for solar energy plants and wind turbines. Members of these environmental organizations believed that the Navajo Nation had a strong potential for both forms of energy production. Their work critiqued conventional approaches to economic development in the Navajo Nation that had put a lot of emphasis on the coal development explored in earlier chapters.

The belief that coal was a strong contributor to processes of global climate change and that alternative energy and development technologies must be pursued was part of this ideology that the environmentalists put forward in workshops, meetings, and other events geared toward the youth and that instilled a culture of alternatives in the political sentiments. Of course, these beliefs had strong parallels with debates in U.S. politics. The ideology was to build a path toward development that did not replicate some of the worst features of modernization narratives (of which coal was a part), but they were also advocating for a return to "traditional" and historic ways of interacting with each other and the natural environment. The way the meetings were held, including the private nature of some and the purposeful use of traditional attire during public demonstrations, spoke to this deeper yearning to return to something that had been lost during the processes of colonization.

The environmentalists were not asking youth to give up their cell phones, computers, music, or dramatically change their lifestyles. They were calling on Diné people, tribal employees, and youth to build a community in which these technologies and cultural politics could exist sustainably. One interviewee critiqued this vision on traditional grounds, believing that it replicated capitalism in the Navajo Nation (EJ6). Another interviewee said that many of the leaders in the environmentalist movement did not live in the communities that they talked about and therefore their vision lacked necessary engagement with community members (EJ10). These were common critiques, often communicated privately, but still prominent.

There were, of course, many problems, inconsistencies, and outright contradictions in the counterideology. But the point was that this loose culture of alternatives was informed by the real threat of global climate change and other types of environmental destruction facing the Navajo Nation. It was also informed by older trends to preserve the Navajo culture, broaden Indigenous lifeways, and combat colonialism. It was an ideology that both recognized and incorporated the moral economy of coal in its attempt to identify work alternatives that could fulfill a broader sense of livelihood. Their work did not simply reject development as groups had done in the past. It advocated for returning to a life of herding, small-scale agriculture, weaving, and jewelry, which were staple activities for social and cultural reproduction generations before extractive industries. These activities were part of an ongoing political conflict about the future of coal. They were a competition for the resources of the state and, importantly, the support of the Diné people.

CONCLUSION

All That Is Solid Melts into Air

The Navajo Generating Station (NGS) was a government-owned coal-fired power plant on the western edge of the Navajo Nation. NGS began in the mid-1960s and ended in early 2021 when it was blown to bits—and with it, a generation of development, work and livelihood, and economic security. It also ended the use of pristine aquifer water for mining activities and indiscriminate strip-mining, a harrowing violence across much of the Diné landscape. What is telling about the NGS experience is who paid the cost of its closure; whether that was in the form of the environment or jobs, Diné people suffered the most. One of my last experiences on the NGS question was patiently waiting through an all-day hearing on the potential looming effects of the closure in Kayenta. This was during the summer of 2018, two years before the demolishment of the plant. It was a Saturday, a day when the benefactors of energy development and transition were enjoying the day off from work; they might even be lounging in a pool in Phoenix while we grappled with the costs of the closure. Some people talked about the mine's environmental impact on the land. For decades, shovels dug into the earth, blasted away at coal seams, and permanently changed the look of the land.

In October of that year, the United Nations' Intergovernmental Panel on Climate Change issued an alarming statement about the future of the planet. The world's leading body on climate research pleaded for policy makers to make "rapid, far-reaching, and unprecedented changes in all aspects of society" to prevent global temperatures from increasing beyond 1.5 degrees centigrade. Many climate scientists estimated that warming beyond this threshold would trigger catastrophic droughts and flooding.[1] If we were to take seriously the problem of climate change, we also had to talk about the social, political, and colonial arrangements that exacerbated these problems. These included centuries of murder and displacement of Indigenous peoples that formed the cornerstone of national projects in North and South America. Colonial relations begot carbon relations. Indigenous nations became victims of mineral extraction. However, many community members had built life and identities within these industries. The United States, the world's most polluting country per capita, occupies the lands of more than five hundred Indigenous nations. Although colonialism and climate change are rarely discussed together, this book asks, "What are the colonial implications of climate change on Indigenous nations under colonial occupation?"

This book was based on ethnographic research from 2012 to 2014 when the Navajo Nation rededicated itself to coal. But over the course of finishing my PhD and starting this book, the owners of NGS, the Salt River Project, decided that it was too expensive to continue. Although the Navajo Nation Council renewed the lease early, in 2013, SRP elected not to keep the power plant open for another twenty-five years. Despite all the trouble, protest, late nights, threats, and ultimatums, SRP decided to let the original lease expire in 2019 and close the plant. In a desperate attempt to keep the plant open for what turned out to be just six more years, the council worked out a deal to slowly decommission the NGS and leave some of its infrastructure behind, including the rail tracks that lead to the mine, a storage shed, and the water pump connected to Lake Mead. The deal reduced the demolition costs to SRP. But the power plant could not be salvaged.

There is scholarship on the impacts of climate change on Indigenous environments (Wildcat 2013). Many of these studies are concerned about climate change's impacts on Indigenous subsistence practices. Fewer consider life among tribal nations with their own political institutions and maybe somewhat their experiences with fossil fuels. It can be a way out of colonization and a greater entrapment into capitalist processes and limitations. The sociological questions about Indigenous peoples' economic and political entanglements within fossil fuel industries are rarely discussed. Indigenous nations are on the front lines of climate change as either victims or as a reservoir of resistance (Klein 2014). These narratives serve a politics different from those experienced in tribal communities. In my research, Diné people were as anxious about the future of the language, culture, and ability to live on the reservation as much as they were concerned about climate change, desertification, and water rights.

In the western half of North America, Indigenous territories are either on top of coveted resources or in the way of transmission lines, pipelines, and waterways that put these resources into capitalistic circulation. These realities of geography create the conditions through which tribal governments seek remedy for decades of colonialism and marginalization through their own participation in resource extraction and the energy industry. For Indigenous nations, these are anxious times.

Today, organizers and activists around climate change are calling for a green new deal to generate economic momentum and transition the United States toward sustainable energy technologies, but utilities control almost all U.S. energy sources. Even Donald Trump's declarative love in 2017 for "clean, beautiful coal" could not save the Navajo Generating Station from closing. The Salt River Project, the utility that had operated the plant for more than forty years, reneged on an agreement it had signed with the Navajo Nation in 2013 when it unilaterally decided to close the plant to save on costs. The tribal government's attempts to find a new utility owner for the power plant were unsuccessful and both the Navajo Generating Station power plant and the Kayenta Mine closed in the fall of 2019.

Most of the Diné workers at the mine lost their jobs, as did many from the power plant (some were reassigned to cleanup or transferred to different mines). The coal jobs were the sole source of income for many of these workers and their families. These families' tight budgets and upended lives are part of the larger story of climate change. What is more, the closure of the mine and power plant suggests that the transition away from fossil fuels, and especially coal, is already well underway. This transition is dictated not by social movements and forces of "progressive change" but by utilities like the Salt River Project that are responding to prices, regulation, or profit. Public utilities such as the Salt River Project add a different dynamic when thinking through the colonial questions of resources in the Southwest. They are regulated by an elected "corporate commission" that nominally works at the behest of the public. This rate-paying public is pitted against the interests of Indigenous nations, and it is the Indigenous interest that is ultimately sidelined. In this maturing neoliberal energy environment, energy buyers that had been reliant on Diné coal have now moved toward "market purchases" for new sources of power.[2] In this way, the energy market—as understood and practiced by public entities—rendered the Navajo Generation Station too expensive to maintain.

All these changes and transitions impact tribal sovereignty. Indigenous sovereignty in the United States cannot simply be understood in colonial terms. The capitalistic practices and processes that inform the actions of colonial actors—as well as those of Indigenous peoples—must also be accounted for. This book is an ethnography of the coal economy in the Navajo Nation, which includes the processes of energy transition, climate change, and new notions of carbon sovereignty. I follow different groups of Diné people, such as tribal officials, climate activists, and coal workers, who operated in and around the Navajo Nation during one of the most important debates in the nation's history. This study breaks apart a unitary account of Indigenous peoples that reduces complex social and political arrangements to a single idea (like Diné ideas of climate change) as if all Navajo people held one position on the issue of coal development. This project is anti-essentialist and challenges decades of ethnographic practices in the Navajo Nation.

This book examined how coal shapes attitudes and politics. For the Navajo Nation and Diné people, coal was tangible. It is a material substance unearthed from ancestral lands, or poison in lungs, or money in the bank. In this book, I argued for a deeper, more nuanced understanding of these phenomena through ethnography and in-depth interviews with the people who live in the impacted places. Similarly, colonialism is not a unitary social force, moving across space and time like a steamship. It is an oscillating, uneven, and inconsistent set of practices, produced and reproduced during events, that reshapes itself across different political, social, and cultural milieu. Colonialism is not a structure so much as it is an amoeba, a shape-shifter.

Coal was a social and political struggle within the Navajo Nation. The topic of coal first entered the political discourse of the Navajo Nation in the mid-twentieth century. Coal was a project of development that was meant to modernize the Navajo Nation. In this way, it was always a colonial project. Colonization, however, cannot be our *only* framework for understanding the social phenomenon of coal. Every year that coal existed in the reservation, it became more and more socially embedded. This intertwining of interests continues today as evidenced in the social disruption in the Navajo Nation and for coal-dependent families when the Navajo Generating Station leases expired at the end of 2019.

The eventual social consequence of coal was not considered or planned for when the original leases were signed in the mid-1960s. At that time, there was uncertainty about the future of coal. The original leases planned for seventy-five years of coal, whereas some tribal lawmakers thought it was an industry that might be overtaken by nuclear power in the near future. Coal was not anticipated to become a permanent feature of the landscape.

But by the 2000s, coal had become a regular source of jobs and revenues. The tribal government worked to preserve conditions favorable for coal production, even as the rest of the country moved away from the industry. While some Navajo actors anticipated the decline of the coal industry, many tribal lawmakers insisted on its rise. The Navajo Nation had one hundred years or more of coal extraction left (Clay 2014). Additionally, lawmakers believed that there were new energy technologies on the horizon that would salvage the coal market, such as coal liquification. There were new markets to be explored, such as China. For some tribal lawmakers, coal had to continue at all costs. Understanding this passion for coal on the part of Navajo actors was one of my motivations for this project. Why did the Navajo Nation continue to pursue coal despite decades of environmental damage, employee mistreatment, and bad-faith contracts with the tribe? It seemed as though there were unexplored forces at work.

On all sides of the debate over coal, anxiety about the prospects of the people and the future of the Navajo Nation was a major factor. Coal workers worried about their jobs, about the security of their families, and about the future of work for their coworkers, children, and communities. It was their perspective I worked hardest to understand. I felt their voices were lost in the debate on coal mining in the Navajo Nation. The elected members of the Navajo Nation Council, which included my father at the time, often pointed to the tribal programs and employees that coal revenues funded as the reason they supported coal. These monies were not small change to the tribe. Leases for land and coal mining paid the tribe hundreds of millions of dollars. These monies supported college scholarships, salaries for employees, and small infrastructure projects. The third group of actors, the Diné environmental organizers, understood coal as contributing not only to local environmental affronts but also to global climate change. And yet these were only the immediate, "modern" anxieties the Navajo coal industry produced in Diné people.

A historical reading of coal in the Navajo Nation shows that Diné attitudes and practices were shaped by a more sinister source of anxiety—anxiety of colonial violence. Since the 1830s, reservations were held "in trust" by the federal government. In the 1950s, U.S. lawmakers wanted to end this relationship, extinguish the reservation system, and assimilate the remaining Native peoples into

U.S. society. This policy was called "termination." Despite having the largest land base and serving as a stereotype for "Indian" in the minds of many in the U.S. public, the Navajo Tribe was not immune from these pressures. In the 1960s, the Navajo Tribal Council, as it was called before 1968, pursued coal leases as a way to maintain jurisdiction over lands and minerals at a time when the federal and state governments were terminating tribes.

The State of Arizona was jealous of the tribe's access to the Colorado River on the western end of the reservation and coveted the Navajo Nation's vast coal reserves. The state was desperate to move water from the Colorado River to the Salt River Valley, where the capital city of Phoenix was expanding. Diné tribal lawmakers knew the risks of thwarting Arizona's ambitions. The state had a well-earned reputation of being reactionary and reckless. Arizona lawmakers had brazenly walked away from the Colorado Compact of 1922 and sued the much larger and politically powerful State of California over access to Colorado River waters. And in 1963 Arizona won, bolstering an already large ego.

For the Navajo Nation in the 1960s, the State of Arizona threatened to develop energy infrastructure on tribal lands regardless of the Navajo government's opinion on the matter. It was a form of brazen racism often cast as "Western ruggedness." The Department of the Interior desired to incorporate the Navajo Nation into energy development to protect federal authority over the states (as reservations are considered federal lands). The anxiety between termination and state control over reservation lands and resources moved Navajo tribal delegates in the 1960s to make strategic decisions about what energy projects to endorse.

Diné tribal lawmakers had good reason to fear termination of the tribe. It informed how elected officials thought about competing resource development proposals from the State of Arizona and from the federal government. For elected council delegates in the 1960s, one colonial structure (the federal government) offered more security for the future of the people than the other (the State of Arizona). On the one hand, Arizona openly challenged Diné sovereignty and threatened to develop energy projects on Diné lands regardless of what Diné people had to say about it. On the other hand, the federal government offered to work with the tribes and offer monies in the form of jobs and revenues for the tribe. In exchange, the Navajo Nation was asked to forgo its claims to the Colorado River for fifty years. Between the two options, tribal lawmakers decided that the latter was better.

From the vantage point of tribal lawmakers at the time, regional energy development felt inevitable. Nuclear power was the technology of the future.

Hydropower smacked of colonial control. On Indian land, coal was the only kind of energy production that could materially benefit the tribe. It gave the tribe some leverage in an emerging energy-water nexus that was becoming increasingly important in the arid Southwest. But by 2017, the advantage of coal had dissipated. After fifty years, coal was more a source of political and economic dependency than control.

Looking at coal from the perspective of the twenty-first century, it is easy to see it as a debilitating industry designed to exploit tribes. It is easy to judge tribal lawmakers in the 1960s for agreeing to bad lease deals and for largely being unaware of what they were doing. There is truth in this critique. Some tribal officials paid little attention to the details of this important contract when it came before them. But appreciating the colonial conditions at the time and popular understandings and attitudes toward energy helps us better understand their actions.

The story of coal will inevitably continue beyond this closure date as cancers and other health impacts from long-term coal exposure are more widely known. Although these things are not measured in conventional health analysis, what might the decades of coal and environmental pollution have done to the health of the Diné people prior to COVID-19? The decades of strip-mining have changed the look of the land forever, and it will also take many more decades before vegetation fully recovers. The water used for coal's operations will never return, a burden passed onto future generations of Diné people who want to live on the land. However, as an active generator of revenues and jobs, the Navajo Generating Station has clear birth and death dates. It was conceived in postwar prosperity and shut down in an era of right-wing populism, declining U.S. global power, and after a tumultuous term of a "pro-coal" president. In its short life, coal mining forever transformed the Navajo Nation and landscape. It was a catalyst for a movement away from subsistence-based livelihood toward work in wage labor. For years, coal mining defined whole communities and the identities of workers who participated in the industry. Today, it is gone. The labor, the work, and the identity associated with coal will slowly disappear.

Colonial capitalism maintains a long history with a consistent logics of dispossession, racism, and what some characterize as racial capitalism (Pulido 2016; Robinson 1983). Colonial capitalism turned Indigenous homelands into peripheries and resource colonies (Dunbar-Ortiz 1979; Snipp 1988). It was the twin processes of colonialism and capitalism, each working together and sometimes in counterintuitive ways, that has reduced the oldest sites of sustainable living on the continent into places of abandonment (Voyles 2015), extraction (Powell 2017a), and exploitation (S. L. Smith and Frehner 2010). To the United States, Indigenous homelands are "reservations" valued for what they do for outside settler communities, spurring what the Diné scholar Melanie Yazzie (2018, 29) calls a "death drive of capitalism." Reservations supplied cheap labor, disposable land and waters, and raw commodities.

But capitalism and colonialism are not unchanging monolithic evils, selfishly devouring everything in their paths. They are contradictory, evolving, and ideologically diverse aggregates of events and actions, sometimes posing as benevolent and benign. Colonial capitalism does not unfold along a binary of the colonizing and the colonized but instead requires active participation—in many cases of those who ultimately suffer in the end, who are tricked, misled, and who sometimes undermine their own communities for lack of better options. This book has focused on the dying Navajo coal industry and the alternatives that Diné people are working to replace it with. It highlights how an economy and a livelihood tied to coal were maintained for decades with allusions of permanence, only to blow away with the winds of a changing energy market. This book is about the combined material, social, and cultural impacts of the coal industry on the Diné people.

For the Diné people, the landscape is not only a source of beauty; it is also a place of survival. It is not reducible to a picture in a frame but is all-consuming and omnipresent. It is where past, present, and future coexist. It is both a spiritual and a mundane plane. It is where people languish during droughts of employment, where they struggle paycheck to paycheck to survive, but where survival is made possible. Sometimes Diné people seek seasonal construction work, or they sell firewood and homemade burritos. Older women weave rugs and find temporary employment at local chapter houses. Men work at coal mines or build things around the house. Work was not always gendered in this way, but colonial intrusions have insisted on it.

At the same time, the Navajo Nation has fought for increased sovereignty and self-determination since the 1960s. It has gained political and economic power through the extraction and use of uranium, oil, coal, and natural gas—all at tremendous physical and environmental costs for the people. Fifty years ago, it was the high cost of natural gas that made coal attractive for regional developers. Utilities in the Southwest saw an opportunity to develop fast-growing cities with Navajo coal (Needham 2014). Today, the low cost of natural gas makes coal less appealing to those who care little about the impacts of a coal shutdown on

Indigenous communities. The coal market has collapsed and the U.S. energy landscape is moving like a massive tectonic plate. Like tectonic plates, those living closest to the fault line experience the greatest impact.

Coal takes the residues of ancient life, decaying for millions of years just below the earth's surface, and burns the stuff for energy, emitting noxious gases and carbon in the process. It is not just the ancestors of humans in the region but of all life that is implicated (Freese 2016). Our modern ways of viewing the world through ideas of modernization, capitalist expansion, and development convert subjective relationships with the earth and coal into objective ones. Coal becomes less of a thing, or a substance with a history and materiality. It becomes a resource to be exploited for abstract notions of energy that are in turn transported, stored, and used across vast amounts of space. Coal's promise was to bring development, jobs, modernization, and a better livelihood for Diné people. This was a promise made at a time when the tribal nations faced great political challenges. On these lands were vast deposits of oil, coal, natural gas, and uranium, and the development of "the West" required some degree of access to these resources. To get at Native resources, government officials, lawyers, private businesspeople, reporters, and others had to work in league with each other to create the legal-political-cultural environment for coal exploitation to occur in Diné Bikéyah and for Diné people to agree to it.

For the Navajo Nation and Diné people, living with a massive coal plant, coal mine, and power lines, the fault lines of national and global energy transitions are at their feet and extend to one's relatives between one's homes. The tremors shake the foundation of the economy. Stable jobs have disappeared. Industrial infrastructure was abandoned. Revenues to the tribal government have evaporated. Literally, all that was solid has melted into air—coal extracted, transported, burned, and converted into carbon. When coal finally ends, as it inevitably will for the Navajo Nation, what will the tribe have gained or lost? This is the existential dilemma. Was it worth it? Were there ever alternatives? Are there still alternatives? Both the future and the past of the Navajo Nation are bound up in the social and physical production of coal and its eventual demise.

NOTES

INTRODUCTION

1. Throughout the book, I use Navajo Nation to refer to the name of the tribal government after 1968. I use Navajo Tribe to refer to the official name of the government before 1968.
2. *High Country News* reporter Jonathan Thompson (2017) reported 935 permanent employees at the Navajo Generating Station and Kayenta Mine. However, this seems like a high calculation based on self-reported numbers from both Salt River Project and Peabody Coal.
3. During the winter session of the Navajo Nation Council meeting on January 27, 2020, Navajo Nation president Jonathan Nez told council delegates that the tribe would lose \$30 million to \$50 million in annual revenues with the closure of the power plant and mine (Associated Press 2020)

CHAPTER 1

1. The word now abbreviated once meant "where the snow doesn't melt." This was a description of the mountaintops, often covered with snow. In Diné geographic observations, captured in the name of the mountain, the temperature was cooler, and snow could be found on the mountain year-round.

CHAPTER 2

1. The "New Frontiersmen" was a phrase coined shortly after Kennedy's election in 1960 to refer to the academics and young policy advisors who surrounded him during his administration (Hill and Schnapper 1961).
2. "A History of Service," Salt River Project, accessed August 3, 2020, https://www.srpnet.com/about/history/timeline.aspx.
3. Navajo Tribal Council transcripts, May 22, 1961. The council passed the resolution "Urging Construction of Marble Canyon Dam by the Federal Government as a Bureau of Reclamation Project" (Appendix B).
4. Andrew Curley, letter to the editor, *Navajo Times*, September 24, 1970.
5. Navajo Tribal Council transcripts, August 3, 1966. The council passed the resolution "Opposing the Construction of Dams in Marble Gorge and Other Portions of the Grand Canyon" (Appendix C).
6. The BIA had established policing in reservations as part of its fulfillment of treaty rights and also to adhere to the 1885 Major Crimes Act—a unilateral Congressional decision to replace tribal institutions of justice, often restorative in nature, with adversarial forms. Public Law 93–638 allowed for the Navajo Nation to "contract" with the BIA to run its own police services. Navajo Nation police replaced BIA police. To this day, the Navajo Nation maintains its own police force, with limited authorities and resources. For members of the Navajo Nation living in remote places, a police response might take more than an hour. Today, tribes use "638 contracting" to take over BIA-funded institutions. This is a limited, constrained, conditioned form of sovereignty. But it does remove a layer of paternalistic oversight that plagued reservation governance prior to the passage of the Indian Self-Determination and Educational Assistance Act of 1975.
7. At first, Peabody Coal agreed to the terms of the lease that the Navajo Nation negotiated. But Peabody withdrew after Ronald Reagan's secretary of the interior encouraged the company to renegotiate it to a lower rate. When the Navajo Nation learned of this, the tribe sued the Department of the Interior for violating its "trust responsibility." The Navajo Nation ultimately lost this case in 2009 when the U.S. Supreme Court said the federal government was not obligated to act in the best interest of the tribe because of the authority that the Indian Mining and Leasing Act of 1938 granted tribes.

CHAPTER 3

1. My former landlord who worked at the McKinley Mine simply retired with the closure of the mine.
2. This information was presented to the Navajo Nation Council on March 29, 2013, when it considered spending $2.3 million to study the feasibility of buying Navajo Mine.

3. A March 30, 2011, memorandum titled "Appointment to Salt River Negotiating Team," from then president Shelly's chief of staff, Sherrick Roanhorse, to Sam Woods, then in the Policy Unit of the Shelly administration, stated that Woods was "assigned to sit on the Salt River Project Negotiating Team." Included on the NGS Negotiating Team were Harrison Tsosie, Dana Bobroff (deputy attorney general), Fred White (executive director of the Division of Natural Resources), Ahktar Zaman (director of the Department of Minerals), Marty Ashley (executive director of Tax Commission), and Stephen Etsitty (executive director of Navajo EPA).
4. I witnessed all these issues debated in the tribal council.
5. I wrote a letter to the editor to the *Navajo Times* in 2005 complaining about this practice when then speaker Lawrence T. Morgan, from a New Mexico community called Iyanbito, limited the debate on the tribe's first water settlement and allowed the Navajo Nation Council to vote for its passage with little debate on the issues. At least these were my impressions at the time and what I wrote in my letter.
6. Members of these organizations submitted comments attached to the legislation and provided to the council delegates. It is clear that they coordinated their responses, as each submission rearticulates, verbatim, the same central points. They asked for improved studies on the health and environmental impacts of NGS and public hearings from community members affected by the continued mining.
7. Ryan Randazzo, "APS Closes 3 Units at 4 Corners Power Plant," *Arizona Republic*, December 31, 2013.
8. The Colorado River Compact was signed in 1922.
9. "Navajo Nation Council Approves Navajo Generating Station Lease Extension," Navajo Nation Council, press release, May 1, 2013, http://www.navajo-nsn.gov/News%20Releases/NNCouncil/2013/may/NNC%20approves%20Navajo%20Generating%20Station%20lease%20extension.pdf.
10. "Navajo Nation Council Votes to Table NGS Lease Extension Legislation," Navajo Nation Council, press release, April 24, 2013, http://www.navajo-nsn.gov/News%20Releases/NNCouncil/2013/apr/NNC%20votes%20to%20table%20NGS%20lease%20extension%20legislation.pdf.
11. Legislative Summary Sheet, February 15, 2013, Tracking No. 0042–13.
12. The language of Resolution 0042–13 says that the Navajo Nation will receive "approximately" $42 million a year "annually adjusted" through 2044.
13. This provision is found in section XI of the lease agreement.
14. "SRP Seeks to Protect Future of Valuable Arizona Resource: Board Approves Purchase of LADWP Ownership Share of NGS," Salt River Project, press release, May 14, 2015, https://media.srpnet.com.

CHAPTER 4

1. All coal worker interviewees were men.

2. Marley Shebala, "An Uncertain New Year: Black Mesa Workers Face Layoffs, Upheaval After Decades of Service," *Navajo Times*, December 15, 2005, A1. See also Marley Shebala, "Closure Causing Layoffs of Longtime Workers," *Navajo Times*, December 15, 2005, A3; and Cindy Yurth, "Chapters Lament Lost Perks in Wake of Mine Closure," *Navajo Times*, December 22, 2005, A1.
3. "Shiprock JMI," accessed July 27, 2022, http://www.shiprockjmi.org/.
4. Cindy Yurth, "Shelly, Jim Promise Teaching Hospital if Elected," *Navajo Times*, May 22, 2014.
5. There is a lot of anthropological work on the Diné people about jealousy derived from an impression that someone has too much wealth, measured in the number of sheep a family has and that they get that wealth through duplicitous means like "witchcraft." There is a strong antigovernment attitude against elected tribal officials, particularly members of the Navajo Nation, because they are understood as financially benefiting from their position of influence. One former elected official told me he did not acquire new things because he did not want to give this impression. The way some of my informants interpreted the phrase *t'aa hwo aji t'eego* suggests the opposite, that obvious material wealth is a marker of hard work.

CHAPTER 5

1. Verna L. Harvey, "Resentment Is Expressed over Black Mesa Mining," *Navajo Times*, April 1, 1971, 12.
2. Harvey, "Resentment Is Expressed over Black Mesa Mining," 12. See also "Black Mesans Concerned About Relocation Program," *Navajo Times*, February 12, 1970, 11.
3. Harvey, "Resentment Is Expressed over Black Mesa Mining," 12.
4. Harvey, "Resentment Is Expressed over Black Mesa Mining," 12.
5. Since the 1960s, the Navajo Forest Products Industry (NFPI) had employed hundreds of Navajo loggers and supplied much of the income for the small town built around an industrial sawmill. As in the dynamics in Kayenta, workers in NFPI, a company owned by the Navajo Nation, believed logging was a source of livelihood. When environmentalists from Diné C.A.R.E. challenged their practices, they felt threatened. NFPI closed permanently in 1994 and the sawmill was demolished in 2013.
6. According to my notes from the Flagstaff meeting on July 7, 2008.
7. The term *sheep camp* was used historically to reference a place where families would move with their sheep during the summer months to let their sheep graze. These places are often more isolated than winter homes and have gained a reputation of being makeshift.
8. The demonstrations and trainings I witnessed were part of "Our Power Communities," a program of the Climate Justice Alliance. The workshop on Black Mesa was one of the first meetings of this new coalition of not-for-profits advocating for

"just transition." See "Our Power Commuties," Climate Justice Alliance, accessed July 27, 2022, https://climatejusticealliance.org/workgroup/our-power.

9. Consider the Diné Policy Institute's report "Career Dilemmas Among Diné (Navajo) College Graduates: An Exploration of the Dinétah (Navajo Nation) Brain Drain" (McKenzie et al. 2013).

CONCLUSION

1. Intergovernmental Panel on Climate Change, press release, October 8, 2018, https://www.ipcc.ch/site/assets/uploads/2018/11/pr_181008_P48_spm_en.pdf.
2. According to the Central Arizona Project, CAP plans on purchasing nearly 80 percent of its energy on "market forward" and "market daily short-term" purchases.

REFERENCES

Aberle, David Friend. 1969. "A Plan for Navajo Economic Development." In *Toward Economic Development for Native American Communities: A Compendium of Papers Submitted to the Subcommittee on Economy in Government of the Joint Economic Committee, Congress of the United States, 91st Congress, 1st Session, Joint Committee*, 223–76. Washington, D.C.: U.S. Government Printing Office.

Abrams, Philip. 1982. *Historical Sociology*. Ithaca, N.Y.: Cornell University Press.

Adair, John. 1946. *The Navajo and Pueblo Silversmiths*. Norman: University of Oklahoma Press.

Alfred, Taiaiake, and Jeff Corntassel. 2005. "Being Indigenous: Resurgences Against Contemporary Colonialism." *Government and Opposition* 40 (4): 597–614.

Allison, James Robert, III. 2015. *Sovereignty for Survival: American Energy Development and Indian Self-Determination*. New Haven, Conn.: Yale University Press.

Alonso, Ana, James C. Scott, Armando Bartra, Florencia E. Mallon, Marjorie Becker, Elsie Rockwell, Jan Rus, and Alan Knight. 1994. *Everyday Forms of State Formation: Revolution and the Negotiation of Rule in Modern Mexico*. Durham, N.C.: Duke University Press.

Ambler, Marjane. 1990. *Breaking the Iron Bonds: Indian Control of Energy Development*. Lawrence: University Press of Kansas.

Anderson, Kim, Maria Campbell, and Christi Belcourt. 2018. *Keetsahnak: Our Missing and Murdered Indigenous Sisters*. Edmonton: University of Alberta Press.

Åsbrink, Elisabeth. 2017. *1947: Where Now Begins*. New York: Other Press.

Associated Press. 2020. "Navajo Look to Arizona Utilities to Make Up for Coal Losses." AZ Central, January 28. https://www.azcentral.com/story/news/local/arizona/2020/01/28/navajo-look-arizona-utilities-make-up-coal-financial-environmental-losses/4602256002/.

Barker, Joanne. 2005. *Sovereignty Matters: Locations of Contestation and Possibility in Indigenous Struggles for Self-Determination*. Contemporary Indigenous Issues. Lincoln: University of Nebraska Press.

Benally, Malcolm D. 2011. *Bitter Water: Diné Oral Histories of the Navajo–Hopi Land Dispute*. Tucson: University of Arizona Press.

Biolsi, Thomas. 2005. "Imagined Geographies: Sovereignty, Indigenous Space, and American Indian Struggle." *American Ethnologist* 32 (2): 239–59.

Brubaker, Rogers. 2004. *Ethnicity Without Groups*. Cambridge, Mass.: Harvard University Press.

Brubaker, Rogers, and Frederick Cooper. 2000. "Beyond 'Identity.'" *Theory and Society* 29 (1): 1–47.

Brugge, Doug, Timothy Benally, and Esther Yazzie-Lewis. 2006. *The Navajo People and Uranium Mining*. Albuquerque: University of New Mexico Press.

Bsumek, Erika Marie. 2008. *Indian-Made: Navajo Culture in the Marketplace, 1868–1940*. Lawrence: University Press of Kansas.

Chamberlain, Kathleen. 2000. *Under Sacred Ground: A History of Navajo Oil, 1922–1982*. Albuquerque: University of New Mexico Press.

Chomsky, Noam. 1999. *Profit over People: Neoliberalism and Global Order*. New York: Seven Stories.

Choudhary, Trib. 2005. "2005–2006 Comprehensive Economic Development Strategy of the Navajo Nation." Navajo Nation Division of Economic Development. http://www.navajobusiness.com/pdf/CEDS/CEDS%202005%20-%2006%20Final.pdf.

Churchill, Ward. 1995. *Since Predator Came: Notes from the Struggle for American Indian Liberation*. Littleton, Colo.: Aigis Publications.

Churchill, Ward, and Winona LaDuke. 1986. "Native America: The Political Economy of Radioactive Colonialism." *Critical Sociology* 13 (3): 51–78.

Clay, Rebecca Fairfax. 2014. "Tribe at a Crossroads: The Navajo Nation Purchases a Coal Mine." *Environmental Health Perspectives* 122 (4): A104–7.

Cobb, Daniel M. 2008. *Native Activism in Cold War America: The Struggle for Sovereignty*. Lawrence: University Press of Kansas.

Cornell, Stephen E. 1988. *The Return of the Native: American Indian Political Resurgence*. New York: Oxford University Press.

Cornell, Stephen E., and Joseph P. Kalt. 1991. *Where's the Glue? Institutional Bases of American Indian Economic Development*. Cambridge, Mass.: Malcolm Wiener Center for Social Policy, John F. Kennedy School of Government, Harvard University.

Cornell, Stephen E., and Joseph P. Kalt. 1992. *What Can Tribes Do? Strategies and Institutions in American Indian Economic Development*. American Indian Manual and Handbook Series 4. Los Angeles: American Indian Studies Center, University of California, Los Angeles.

Corntassel, Jeff. 2012. "Re-envisioning Resurgence: Indigenous Pathways to Decolonization and Sustainable Self-Determination." *Decolonization: Indigeneity, Education & Society* 1 (1).

Curley, Andrew. 2008. "*Dóó nal yea dah*: Considering the Logic of the Diné Natural Resource Protection Act of 2005 and the Desert Rock Power Plant Project." Diné Policy Institute, February. https://www.dinecollege.edu/wp-content/uploads/2018/04/DNRPA-and-Desert-RockII.pdf.

Curley, Andrew. 2014. "The Origin of Legibility." In *Diné Perspectives: Revitalizing and Reclaiming Navajo Thought*, edited by Lloyd Lee, 129–50. Tucson: University of Arizona Press.

Curley, Andrew. 2018. "A Failed Green Future: Navajo Green Jobs and Energy 'Transition' in the Navajo Nation." *Geoforum* 88 (January): 57–65.

Curley, Andrew. 2019a. "'Our Winters' Rights': Challenging Colonial Water Laws." *Global Environmental Politics* 19 (3): 57–76.

Curley, Andrew. 2019b. "T'áá hwó ají t'éego and the Moral Economy of Navajo Coal Workers." *Annals of the American Association of Geographers* 109 (1): 71–86.

Curley, Andrew. 2021a. "Infrastructures as Colonial Beachheads: The Central Arizona Project and the Taking of Navajo Resources." *Environment and Planning D: Society and Space* 39 (3). https://doi.org/10.1177/0263775821991537.

Curley, Andrew. 2021b. "Unsettling Indian Water Settlements: The Little Colorado River, the San Juan River, and Colonial Enclosures." *Antipode* 53 (3): 705–23.

Davidson, Basil. 1992. *The Black Man's Burden: Africa and the Curse of the Nation-State.* London: James Currey.

Debo, Angie. 1973. *And Still the Waters Run: The Betrayal of the Five Civilized Tribes.* Princeton, N.J.: Princeton University Press.

Deloria, Vine. 1985. *American Indian Policy in the Twentieth Century.* Norman: University of Oklahoma Press.

Denetdale, Jennifer. 2006. "Chairmen, Presidents, and Princesses: The Navajo Nation, Gender, and the Politics of Tradition." *Wicazo Sa Review* 21 (1): 9–28.

Denetdale, Jennifer. 2007. *Reclaiming Diné History: The Legacies of Navajo Chief Manuelito and Juanita.* Tucson: University of Arizona Press.

Denetdale, Jennifer. 2009. *The Long Walk: The Forced Navajo Exile.* New York: Chelsea House.

Dennison, Jean. 2012. *Colonial Entanglement: Constituting a Twenty-First-Century Osage Nation.* Chapel Hill: University of North Carolina Press.

Dennison, Jean. 2017. "Entangled Sovereignties: The Osage Nation's Interconnections with Governmental and Corporate Authorities." *American Ethnologist* 44 (4): 684–96.

Dicken, Peter. 1998. *Global Shift: Transforming the World Economy.* 3rd ed. London: Paul Chapman.

Dorries, Heather, Robert Henry, David Hugill, Tyler McCreary, and Julie Tomiak. 2019. *Settler City Limits: Indigenous Resurgence and Colonial Violence in the Urban Prairie West.* Winnipeg: University of Manitoba Press.

Dunbar-Ortiz, Roxanne, ed. 1979. *Economic Development in American Indian Reservations.* Development Series 1. Albuquerque: Native American Studies, University of New Mexico.

Dunbar-Ortiz, Roxanne. 2014. *An Indigenous Peoples' History of the United States*. ReVisioning American History. Boston: Beacon.

Eichstaedt, Peter H. 1994. *If You Poison Us: Uranium and Native Americans*. Santa Fe, N.Mex.: Red Crane Books.

Einberger, Scott. 2018. *With Distance in His Eyes: The Environmental Life and Legacy of Stewart Udall*. Reno: University of Nevada Press.

Elden, Stuart. 2013. *The Birth of Territory*. Chicago: University of Chicago Press.

Ellinghaus, Katherine. 2017. *Blood Will Tell: Native Americans and Assimilation Policy*. Lincoln: University of Nebraska Press.

Emanuel, Ryan E. 2019. "Water in the Lumbee World: A River and Its People in a Time of Change." *Environmental History* 24 (1): 25–51.

Escobar, Arturo. 1995. *Encountering Development: The Making and Unmaking of Development*. Princeton, N.J.: Princeton University Press.

Estes, Nick. 2019. *Our History Is the Future: Standing Rock Versus the Dakota Access Pipeline, and the Long Tradition of Indigenous Resistance*. New York: Verso.

Fanon, Frantz. 1991. *Black Skin, White Masks*. New York: Grove Weidenfeld.

Ferguson, James. 2006. *Global Shadows: Africa in the Neoliberal World Order*. Durham, N.C.: Duke University Press.

Fixico, Donald L. 1986. *Termination and Relocation: Federal Indian Policy, 1945–1960*. Albuquerque: University of New Mexico Press.

Fixico, Donald Lee. 2012. *The Invasion of Indian Country in the Twentieth Century: American Capitalism and Tribal Natural Resources*. 2nd ed. Boulder: University Press of Colorado.

Frank, Andre Gunder. 1967. *Capitalism and Underdevelopment in Latin America*. Historical Studies of Chile and Brazil. New York: Monthly Review Press.

Freese, Barbara. 2016. *Coal: A Human History*. New York: Basic Books.

Gaventa, John. 1982. *Power and Powerlessness: Quiescence and Rebellion in an Appalachian Valley*. Champaign: University of Illinois Press.

Gedicks, Al. 1993. *The New Resource Wars: Native and Environmental Struggles Against Multinational Corporations*. Boston: South End Press.

Gergan, Mabel Denzin, and Andrew Curley. 2021. "Indigenous Youth and Decolonial Futures: Energy and Environmentalism Among the Diné in the Navajo Nation and the Lepchas of Sikkim, India." *Antipode*, July 26. https://doi.org/10.1111/anti.12763.

Glaser, Leah S. 2002. "Rural Electrification in Multiethnic Arizona: A Study of Power, Urbanization and Change." PhD diss., Arizona State University.

Goldstein, Alyosha. 2014. *Formations of United States Colonialism*. Durham, N.C.: Duke University Press.

Gottlieb, Robert. 2005. *Forcing the Spring: The Transformation of the American Environmental Movement*. Washington, D.C.: Island Press.

Grann, David. 2017. *Killers of the Flower Moon*. New York: Doubleday.

Grant, Soni. 2022. "Chess or Checkers? Fracking in Greater Chaco." In *The North American West in the Twenty-First Century*, edited by Brenden Rensink. Lincoln: University of Nebraska Press.

Greider, William. 1969. "A Tribal Water Fight." *Washington Post*, June 29.

Grindle, Merilee Serrill. 1997. *Getting Good Government: Capacity Building in the Public Sectors of Developing Countries*. Harvard Studies in International Development. Cambridge, Mass.: Harvard Institute for International Development.

Hansen, Brett. 2008. "Conquering the Arizona Desert: The Theodore Roosevelt Dam." *Civil Engineering* 78 (8): 44–45.

Harvey, David. 2001. "Globalization and the 'Spatial Fix.'" *Geographische Revue* 2:23–30.

Henson, Eric C. 2008. *The State of the Native Nations: Conditions Under U.S. Policies of Self-Determination*. The Harvard Project on American Indian Economic Development. New York: Oxford University Press.

Hilberg, Raul. 2003. *The Destruction of the European Jews*. Vol. 2. New Haven, Conn.: Yale University Press.

Hill, I. William, and M. B. Schnapper, eds. 1961. *The New Frontiersmen: Profiles of the Men Around Kennedy*. Washington, D.C.: Public Affairs Press.

Hosmer, Brian. 2010. *Native Americans and the Legacy of Harry S. Truman*. Vol. 4. Kirksville, Mo.: Truman State University Press.

Hosmer, Brian C., Colleen M. O'Neill, and Donald Lee Fixico. 2004. *Native Pathways: American Indian Culture and Economic Development in the Twentieth Century*. Boulder: University Press of Colorado.

Hurlbut, David J., et al. 2012. "Navajo Generating Station and Air Visibility Regulations: Alternatives and Impacts." National Renewable Energy Laboratory. https://permanent.fdlp.gov/gpo22540/53024.pdf.

Ignatiev, Noel. 2009. *How the Irish Became White*. New York: Routledge.

Isenberg, Nancy. 2017. *White Trash: The 400-Year Untold History of Class in America*. New York: Penguin Books.

Iverson, Peter. 2002. *Diné: A History of the Navajos*. Photographs by Monty Roessel. Albuquerque: University of New Mexico Press.

Jorgensen, Miriam. 2007. *Rebuilding Native Nations: Strategies for Governance and Development*. Tucson: University of Arizona Press.

Karuka, Manu. 2019. *Empire's Tracks: Indigenous Nations, Chinese Workers, and the Transcontinental Railroad*. American Crossroads 52. Oakland: University of California Press.

Kelley, Klara, and Harris Francis. 2019. *A Diné History of Navajoland*. Tucson: University of Arizona Press.

Kelly, Lawrence C. 1963. "The Navaho Indians: Land and Oil." *New Mexico Historical Review* 38 (1): 1–28.

Kelly, Lawrence C. 1968. *The Navajo Indians and Federal Indian Policy, 1900–1935*. Tucson: University of Arizona Press.

Kelly, Lawrence C. 1970. *Navajo Roundup: Selected Correspondence of Kit Carson's Expedition Against the Navajo, 1863–1865*. Boulder, Colo.: Pruett.

Kelman, Ari. 2013. *A Misplaced Massacre: Struggling over the Memory of Sand Creek*. Cambridge, Mass.: Harvard University Press.

King, Farina. 2016. "The Earth Memory Compass: Diné Educational Experiences in the Twentieth Century." PhD diss., Arizona State University, Tempe.

Klein, Naomi. 2000. *No Logo: Taking Aim at the Brand Bullies*. Toronto: Knopf Canada.

Klein, Naomi. 2014. *This Changes Everything: Capitalism vs. the Climate*. New York: Simon and Schuster.

Kluckhohn, Clyde, and Dorothea Leighton. (1946) 1956. *The Navaho*. Rev. ed. Cambridge, Mass.: Harvard University Press.

Kotlowski, Dean J. 2008. "From Backlash to Bingo: Ronald Reagan and Federal Indian Policy." *Pacific Historical Review* 77 (4): 617–52.

LaDuke, Winona. 1992. "Indigenous Environmental Perspectives: A North American Primer." *Akwe:kon Journal* 9 (2): 52–71.

LaDuke, Winona. 1999. *All Our Relations: Native Struggles for Land and Life*. Boston: South End Press.

LaDuke, Winona. 2005. *Voices from White Earth: Gaa-waabaabiganikaag*. Great Barrington, Mass.: E.F. Schumacher Society.

LaDuke, Winona. 2008. *Make a Beautiful Way: The Wisdom of Native American Women*. Lincoln: University of Nebraska Press.

LaDuke, Winona, and Deborah Cowen. 2020. "Beyond Wiindigo Infrastructure." *South Atlantic Quarterly* 119 (2): 243–68.

LaDuke, Winona, and Sean Aaron Cruz. 2012. *The Militarization of Indian Country*. The Makwa Enewed Series. East Lansing, Mich.: Makwa Enewed.

Lambert, Valerie. 2007. *Choctaw Nation: A Story of American Indian Resurgence*. Lincoln: University of Nebraska Press.

Lee, Lloyd Lance. 2013. "The Fundamental Laws: Codification for Decolonization?" *Decolonization: Indigeneity, Education & Society* 2 (2).

Lee, Tiffany S. 2007. "'If They Want Navajo to Be Learned, Then They Should Require It in All Schools': Navajo Teenagers' Experiences, Choices, and Demands Regarding Navajo Language." *Wicazo Sa Review* 22 (1): 7–33.

Leibowitz, Rachel. 2008. "Constructing the Navajo Capital: Landscape, Power, and Representation at Window Rock." PhD diss., University of Illinois at Urbana-Champaign.

Lemont, Eric D. 2006. *American Indian Constitutional Reform and the Rebuilding of Native Nations*. Austin: University of Texas Press.

Lightfoot, Sheryl. 2016. *Global Indigenous Politics: A Subtle Revolution*. New York: Routledge.

Lister, Majerle. 2017. "Considering a Navajo Name Change: Self-Identification, Land, and Liberation." *The Red Nation*, July 31. http://therednation.org/considering-a-navajo-name-change-self-identification-land-and-liberation/.

Lyons, Scott Richard. 2010. *X-marks: Native Signatures of Assent*. Minneapolis: University of Minnesota Press.

McCombe, Leonard, Evon Z. Vogt, and Clyde Kluckhohn. 1951. *Navaho Means People*. Nineteenth Century Collections Online 1343. Cambridge, Mass.: Harvard University Press.

McCreary, Tyler A., and Richard A Milligan. 2014. "Pipelines, Permits, and Protests: Carrier Sekani Encounters with the Enbridge Northern Gateway Project." *Cultural Geographies* 21 (1): 115–29.

McKenzie, James, Aaron P. Jackson, Robert Yazzie, Steven A. Smith, Amber K. Crotty, Donny Baum, Avery Denny, and Dana Bah'lgai Eldridge. "Career Dilemmas Among Diné (Navajo) College Graduates: An Exploration of the Dinétah (Navajo Nation) Brain Drain." *International Indigenous Policy Journal* 4, no. 4 (2013).

McLerran, Jennifer. 2012. *A New Deal for Native Art: Indian Arts and Federal Policy, 1933–1943*. Tucson: University of Arizona Press.

McMichael, Philip. 2011. *Development and Social Change: A Global Perspective*. 5th ed. Thousand Oaks, Calif.: SAGE.

McPherson, Robert S., and David A. Wolff. 1997. "Poverty, Politics, and Petroleum: The Utah Navajo and the Aneth Oil Field." *American Indian Quarterly* 21 (3): 451–70.

Miller, Robert J. 2012. *Reservation "Capitalism": Economic Development in Indian Country*. Santa Barbara: ABC-CLIO.

Mills, C. Wright. (1959) 2000. *The Sociological Imagination*. New York: Oxford University Press.

Mintz, Sidney Wilfred. 1986. *Sweetness and Power: The Place of Sugar in Modern History*. New York: Penguin Books.

Mitchell, Timothy. 2009. "Carbon Democracy." *Economy and Society* 38 (3): 399–432.

Montoya, Teresa. Forthcoming. "Permeable: Diné Politics of Extraction and Exposure." Unpublished manuscript in author's possession.

Murshed, Syed Mansoob. 2018. *The Resource Curse*. Newcastle upon Tyne: Agenda Publishing Limited.

Nadasdy, Paul. 2017. *Sovereignty's Entailments: First Nation State Formation in the Yukon*. Toronto: University of Toronto Press.

Nagel, Joane. 1997. *American Indian Ethnic Renewal: Red Power and the Resurgence of Identity and Culture*. New York: Oxford University Press.

Navajo Tribal Council. 1952. *Navajo Tribal Council Resolutions, 1922–1951*. Washington, D.C.: U.S. Government Printing Office.

Needham, Andrew. 2014. *Power Lines: Phoenix and the Making of the Modern Southwest*. Politics and Society in Twentieth-Century America. Princeton, N.J.: Princeton University Press.

Nelson, Megan Kate. 2020. *The Three-Cornered War: The Union, the Confederacy, and Native Peoples in the Fight for the West*. First Scribner hardcover edition. New York: Scribner.

Neumann, Franz Leopold. 2009. *Behemoth: The Structure and Practice of National Socialism, 1933–1944*. Chicago: Ivan R. Dee.

Nies, Judith. 2014. *Unreal City: Las Vegas, Black Mesa, and the Fate of the West*. New York: Nation Books.

Nkrumah, Kwame. 1965. *Neo-colonialism: The Last Stage of Imperialism*. London: Nelson.

Olson, Joel. 2004. *The Abolition of White Democracy*. Minneapolis: University of Minnesota Press.

Oman, Kerry R. 2002. "The Beginning of the End: The Indian Peace Commission of 1867–1868." *Great Plains Quarterly* 22 (1): 35–51.

O'Neill, Colleen. 2005. *Working the Navajo Way: Labor and Culture in the Twentieth Century*. Lawrence: University Press of Kansas.

Pasternak, Shiri. 2017. *Grounded Authority: The Algonquins of Barriere Lake Against the State*. Minneapolis: University of Minnesota Press.

Peck, Jamie, and Adam Tickell. 2002. "Neoliberalizing Space." *Antipode* 34 (3): 380–404.

Perdue, Theda. 2005. *"Mixed Blood" Indians: Racial Construction in the Early South*. Mercer University Lamar Memorial Lectures 45. Athens: University of Georgia Press.

Pevar, Stephen. 2012. *The Rights of Indians and Tribes*. New York: Oxford University Press.

Powell, Dana Elizabeth. 2011. "Landscapes of Power: An Ethnography of Energy Development on the Navajo Nation." PhD diss., University of North Carolina at Chapel Hill.

Powell, Dana E. 2017a. *Landscapes of Power: Politics of Energy in the Navajo Nation*. Durham, N.C.: Duke University Press.

Powell, Dana E. 2017b. "Toward Transition? Challenging Extractivism and the Politics of the Inevitable on the Navajo Nation." In *ExtrACTION: Impacts, Engagements, and Alternative Futures*, edited by Kirk Jalbert, Anna Willow, David Casagrande, and Stephanie Paladino, 211–26. New York: Routledge.

Powell, Dana E., and Andrew Curley. 2009. "*K'e*, *Hozhó*, and Non-governmental Politics on the Navajo Nation: Ontologies of Difference Manifest in Environmental Activism." *World Anthropologies Network E-Journal* 4:109–38. http://ram-wan.net/old/documents/05_e_Journal/journal-4/5-powell.pdf.

Prashad, Vijay. 2008. *The Darker Nations: A People's History of the Third World*. New York: New Press.

Prucha, Francis Paul. 1994. *American Indian Treaties: The History of a Political Anomaly*. Berkeley: University of California Press.

Pulido, Laura. 2017. "Geographies of Race and Ethnicity II: Environmental Racism, Racial Capitalism and State-Sanctioned Violence." *Progress in Human Geography* 41 (4): 524–33.

Reno, Philip. 1981. *Mother Earth, Father Sky, and Economic Development: Navajo Resources and Their Use*. Institute for Native American Development 3. Albuquerque: University of New Mexico Press.

Rist, Gilbert. 2002. *The History of Development: From Western Origins to Global Faith*. London: Zed Books.

Robbins, Lynn A. 1978. "Navajo Workers and Labor Unions." *Southwest Economy and Society* 3 (3): 4–23.

Robinson, Cedric J. 1983. *Black Marxism: The Making of the Black Radical Tradition*. Chapel Hill: University of North Carolina Press.

Rosser, Ezra. 2021. *A Nation Within: Navajo Land and Economic Development*. Cambridge: Cambridge University Press.

Rostow, W. W. (1960) 1991. *The Stages of Economic Growth: A Non-communist Manifesto*. 3rd ed. New York: Cambridge University Press.

Ruffing, Lorraine Turner. 1976. "Navajo Economic Development Subject to Cultural Constraints." *Economic Development and Cultural Change* 24 (3): 611–21.

Ruffing, Lorraine Turner. 1978. "Navajo Mineral Development." *American Indian Journal* 4 (9): 28–51.

Scott, Rebecca R. 2010. *Removing Mountains: Extracting Nature and Identity in the Appalachian Coalfields*. Minneapolis: University of Minnesota Press.

Seow, Victor. 2022. *Carbon Technocracy: Energy Regimes in Modern East Asia*. Chicago: University of Chicago Press.

Sewell, William H., Jr. 2005. *Logics of History: Social Theory and Social Transformation*. Chicago: University of Chicago Press.

Shoemaker, Nancy. 2006. *A Strange Likeness: Becoming Red and White in Eighteenth-Century North America*. New York: Oxford University Press.

Simpson, Leanne Betasamosake. 2016. "Indigenous Resurgence and Co-resistance." *Critical Ethnic Studies* 2 (2): 19–34.

Sloan Morgan, Vanessa. 2020. "'Why Would They Care?': Youth, Resource Extraction, and Climate Change in Northern British Columbia, Canada." *Canadian Geographer / Géographe canadien* 64 (3): 445–60.

Smith, Sara. 2020. *Intimate Geopolitics: Love, Territory, and the Future on India's Northern Threshold*. New Brunswick, N.J.: Rutgers University Press.

Smith, Sherry L., and Brian Frehner. 2010. *Indians & Energy: Exploitation and Opportunity in the American Southwest*. School for Advanced Research Advanced Seminar Series. Santa Fe, N.Mex.: School for Advanced Research Press.

Smith, Thomas G. 2017. *Stewart L. Udall: Steward of the Land*. Albuquerque: University of New Mexico Press.

Sneddon, Christopher. 2015. *Concrete Revolution: Large Dams, Cold War Geopolitics, and the US Bureau of Reclamation*. Chicago: University of Chicago Press.

Snipp, C. Matthew. 1986. "The Changing Political and Economic Status of the American Indians: From Captive Nations to Internal Colonies." *American Journal of Economics and Sociology* 45, no. 2: 145–57.

Snipp, C. Matthew, ed. 1988. *Public Policy Impacts on American Indian Economic Development*. Development Series 4. Albuquerque: Native American Studies, Institute for Native American Development, University of New Mexico.

Spruhan, Paul. 2006. "A Legal History of Blood Quantum in Federal Indian Law to 1935." *South Dakota Law Review* 51 (1): 1–50.

Spruhan, Paul. 2007. "The Origins, Current Status, and Future Prospects of Blood Quantum as the Definition of Membership in the Navajo Nation." *Tribal Law Journal* 8 (1): 1–17.

Strickland, Rennard. 1995. "Osage Oil: Mineral Law, Murder, Mayhem, and Manipulation." *Natural Resources & Environment* 10 (1): 39–43.

TallBear, Kim. 2013. *Native American DNA: Tribal Belonging and the False Promise of Genetic Science*. Minneapolis: University of Minnesota Press.

Taylor, Graham D. 1980. *The New Deal and American Indian Tribalism: The Administration of the Indian Reorganization Act, 1934–45*. Lincoln: University of Nebraska Press.

Taylor, Jonathan B., and Joseph P. Kalt. 2005. *American Indians on Reservations: A Databook of Socioeconomic Change Between the 1990 and 2000 Censuses*. Cambridge, Mass.:

Harvard Project on American Indian Economic Development, Malcolm Wiener Center for Social Policy, John F. Kennedy School of Government, Harvard University.

Thomas, Wesley. 1997. "Navajo Cultural Constructions of Gender and Sexuality." In *Two-Spirit People: Native American Gender Identity, Sexuality, and Spirituality*, edited by Sue-Ellen Jacobs, Wesley Thomas, and Sabine Lang, 156–73. Urbana: University of Illinois Press.

Thompson, Jonathan. 2017. "7 Things You Need to Know About Navajo Generating Station's 2019 Closure." *High Country News*, February 14.

Thornton, Russell. 1990. *American Indian Holocaust and Survival: A Population History Since 1492*. Civilization of the American Indian Series 186. Norman: University of Oklahoma Press.

Tsing, Anna Lowenhaupt. 2005a. *Friction: An Ethnography of Global Connection*. Princeton, N.J.: Princeton University Press.

Tuck, Eve, and K. Wayne Yang. 2012. "Decolonization Is Not a Metaphor." *Decolonization: Indigeneity, Education & Society* 1 (1): 1–40.

Voyles, Traci Brynne. 2015. *Wastelanding: Legacies of Uranium Mining in Navajo Country*. Minneapolis: University of Minnesota Press.

Wallerstein, Immanuel Maurice. 1974. *The Modern World-System*. Studies in Social Discontinuity. New York: Academic Press.

Weisiger, Marsha. 2011. *Dreaming of Sheep in Navajo Country*. Seattle: University of Washington Press.

Weiss, Lawrence David. 1984. *The Development of Capitalism in the Navajo Nation: A Political-Economic History*. Studies in Marxism 15. Minneapolis: MEP Publications.

White, Richard. 1983. *The Roots of Dependency: Subsistence, Environment, and Social Change Among the Choctaws, Pawnees, and Navajos*. Lincoln: University of Nebraska Press.

Wildcat, Daniel R. 2013. "Introduction: Climate Change and Indigenous Peoples of the USA." In *Climate Change and Indigenous Peoples in the United States*, edited by Julie Koppel Maldonado, Benedict Colombi, and Rajul Pandya, 1–7. New York: Springer.

Wilkins, David E. 1993. "Modernization, Colonialism, Dependency: How Appropriate Are These Models for Providing an Explanation of North American Indian 'Underdevelopment'?" *Ethnic and Racial Studies* 16 (3): 390–419.

Wilkins, David E. 2013. *The Navajo Political Experience*. Lanham, Md.: Rowman & Littlefield.

Wilkinson, Charles F. 1999. *Fire on the Plateau: Conflict and Endurance in the American Southwest*. Washington, D.C.: Island Press.

Wilkinson, Charles F. 2005. *Blood Struggle: The Rise of Modern Indian Nations*. New York: W. W. Norton.

Williams, Robert A., Jr. 2005. *Like a Loaded Weapon: The Rehnquist Court, Indian Rights, and the Legal History of Racism in America*. Minneapolis: University of Minnesota Press.

Wilson, Angela Cavender, and Michael Yellow Bird. 2005. *For Indigenous Eyes Only: A Decolonization Handbook*. Santa Fe, N.Mex.: School of American Research.

Wolfe, Patrick. 2006. "Settler Colonialism and the Elimination of the Native." *Journal of Genocide Research* 8, no. 4: 387–409.

Woolford, Andrew. 2015. *This Benevolent Experiment: Indigenous Boarding Schools, Genocide, and Redress in Canada and the United States.* Lincoln: University of Nebraska Press.

Worster, Donald. 1985. *Rivers of Empire: Water, Aridity, and the Growth of the American West.* New York: Pantheon.

Yazzie, Melanie K. 2018. "Decolonizing Development in Diné Bikeyah: Resource Extraction, Anti-capitalism, and Relational Futures." *Environment and Society* 9 (1): 25–39.

Yazzie, Melanie K., and Cutcha Risling Baldy. 2018. "Introduction: Indigenous Peoples and the Politics of Water." *Decolonization: Indigeneity, Education & Society* 7 (1): 1–18.

Yellow Bird, Michael. 2012. *For Indigenous Minds Only: A Decolonization Handbook.* Santa Fe, N.Mex.: School of American Research Press.

INDEX

ABOUT THE AUTHOR

Andrew Curley is a member of the Navajo Nation and an assistant professor in the School of Geography, Development & Environment at the University of Arizona. He has studied the social, cultural, and political implications of coal mining on the Navajo Nation. His current research is on the environmental history of water diversions on the Colorado River and the impact of colonial infrastructures on tribal nations.